3D Modeling Using Autodesk 3ds Max With Rendering View

Debabrata Samanta
CHRIST University, India

A volume in the Advances in Web
Technologies and Engineering
(AWTE) Book Series

Published in the United States of America by
>	IGI Global
>	Engineering Science Reference (an imprint of IGI Global)
>	701 E. Chocolate Avenue
>	Hershey PA, USA 17033
>	Tel: 717-533-8845
>	Fax: 717-533-8661
>	E-mail: cust@igi-global.com
>	Web site: http://www.igi-global.com

Library of Congress Cataloging-in-Publication Data

Names: Samanta, Debabrata, 1987- editor.
Title: 3D modeling using Autodesk 3ds max with rendering view / Debabrata
   Samanta, editor.
Description: Hershey PA : Engineering Science Reference, [2022] | Includes
   bibliographical references and index. | Summary: "This book guides you
   through the difficulty of mastering one of the most sophisticated
   computer programs ever created by concentrating on the aspects of the
   program that you need to know in order to create outstanding
   architectural visualisations"-- Provided by publisher.
Identifiers: LCCN 2021052925 (print) | LCCN 2021052926 (ebook) | ISBN
   9781668441398 (hardcover) | ISBN 9781668441404 (paperback) | ISBN
   9781668441411 (ebook)
Subjects: LCSH: 3ds max (Computer file) | Architectural rendering--Computer
   programs. | Computer-aided design. | Three-dimensional imaging in
   architecture.
Classification: LCC TR897.7 .A118 2022 (print) | LCC TR897.7 (ebook) |
   DDC 006.6/93--dc23/eng/20211122
LC record available at https://lccn.loc.gov/2021052925
LC ebook record available at https://lccn.loc.gov/2021052926

This book is published in the IGI Global book series Advances in Web Technologies and Engineering (AWTE) (ISSN: 2328-2762; eISSN: 2328-2754)

Advances in Web Technologies and Engineering (AWTE) Book Series

ISSN:2328-2762
EISSN:2328-2754

Editor-in-Chief: Ghazi I. Alkhatib The Hashemite University, Jordan David C. Rine George Mason University, USA

MISSION

The **Advances in Web Technologies and Engineering (AWTE) Book Series** aims to provide a platform for research in the area of Information Technology (IT) concepts, tools, methodologies, and ethnography, in the contexts of global communication systems and Web engineered applications. Organizations are continuously overwhelmed by a variety of new information technologies, many are Web based. These new technologies are capitalizing on the widespread use of network and communication technologies for seamless integration of various issues in information and knowledge sharing within and among organizations. This emphasis on integrated approaches is unique to this book series and dictates cross platform and multidisciplinary strategy to research and practice.

The **Advances in Web Technologies and Engineering (AWTE) Book Series** seeks to create a stage where comprehensive publications are distributed for the objective of bettering and expanding the field of web systems, knowledge capture, and communication technologies. The series will provide researchers and practitioners with solutions for improving how technology is utilized for the purpose of a growing awareness of the importance of web applications and engineering.

COVERAGE

- Web user interfaces design, development, and usability engineering studies
- Competitive/intelligent information systems
- IT readiness and technology transfer studies
- Quality of service and service level agreement issues among integrated systems
- Web Systems Architectures, Including Distributed, Grid Computer, and Communication Systems Processing
- Web systems performance engineering studies
- Ontology and semantic Web studies
- Integrated Heterogeneous and Homogeneous Workflows and Databases within and Across Organizations and with Suppliers and Customers
- Radio Frequency Identification (RFID) research and applications in Web engineered systems
- IT education and training

IGI Global is currently accepting manuscripts for publication within this series. To submit a proposal for a volume in this series, please contact our Acquisition Editors at Acquisitions@igi-global.com or visit: http://www.igi-global.com/publish/.

Titles in this Series

For a list of additional titles in this series, please visit:
www.igi-global.com/book-series/advances-web-technologies-engineering/37158

Advanced Practical Approaches to Web Mining Techniques and Application
Ahmed J. Obaid (University of Kufa, Iraq) Zdzislaw Polkowski (Wroclaw University of Economics, Poland) and Bharat Bhushan (Sharda University, India)
Engineering Science Reference • © 2022 • 357pp • H/C (ISBN: 9781799894261) • US $245.00

Handbook of Research on Opinion Mining and Text Analytics on Literary Works and Social Media
Pantea Keikhosrokiani (School of Computer Sciences, Universiti Sains Malaysia, Malaysia) and Moussa Pourya Asl (School of Humanities, Universiti Sains Malaysia, Malaysia)
Engineering Science Reference • © 2022 • 462pp • H/C (ISBN: 9781799895947) • US $345.00

Security, Data Analytics, and Energy-Aware Solutions in the IoT
Xiali Hei (University of Louisiana at Lafayette, USA)
Engineering Science Reference • © 2022 • 218pp • H/C (ISBN: 9781799873235) • US $225.00

Emerging Trends in IoT and Integration with Data Science, Cloud Computing, and Big Data Analytics
Pelin Yildirim Taser (Izmir Bakircay University, Turkey)
Information Science Reference • © 2022 • 334pp • H/C (ISBN: 9781799841869) • US $225.00

App and Website Accessibility Developments and Compliance Strategies
Yakup Akgül (Alanya Alaaddin Keykubat University, Turkey)
Engineering Science Reference • © 2022 • 322pp • H/C (ISBN: 9781799878483) • US $225.00

IoT Protocols and Applications for Improving Industry, Environment, and Society
Cristian González García (University of Oviedo, Spain) and Vicente García-Díaz (University of Oviedo, Spain)
Engineering Science Reference • © 2021 • 321pp • H/C (ISBN: 9781799864639) • US $245.00

701 East Chocolate Avenue, Hershey, PA 17033, USA
Tel: 717-533-8845 x100 • Fax: 717-533-8661
E-Mail: cust@igi-global.com • www.igi-global.com

To my parents, Mr. Dulal Chandra Samanta, Mrs. Ambujini Samanta; my elder sister, Mrs. Tanusree Samanta; brother-in-law, Mr. Soumendra Jana; and daughter, Ms. Aditri Samanta.

Editorial Advisory Board

Table of Contents

Detailed Table of Contents

Chapter 1
Critical Compound Objects Modelling Using Autodesk 1
> *Ritwika Das Gupta, CHRIST University, India*
> *Daksh Agarwal, University of Pennsylvania, USA*

Autodesk 3ds Max is a graphics program for making 3D models, animations, games, and images. Autodesk Media and Entertainment produced it. It has the capabilities to model in 3D and has a flexible plug-in architecture. It is majorly used by video game developers and TV commercial studios. It can also give movie effects to animations. It contains various tools and modifiers to modify a single standard object to different realistic models. It helps in creating natural textures for models and mapping them correctly to the objects. It helps in providing proper light and shadow effects to the models. It has different rendering options for making the models flexible to render. It has new icons, a customizable user interface, and its scripting language. 3ds Max is crucial to game asset artists and architectural designers the most. For animation and rigging, 3ds Max has everything mandatory for professional work.

Chapter 2
Constructive Outlook of Cafeteria Using Autodesk 3ds Max 3D Modelling
and Rendering 31
> *Dinesh Sharma, DXC Technology, Bangalore, India*

In this modern world, we intend to modernize everything and try to get everything at the tip of our fingers. It has been changed with technology based on individual creativity. In this chapter, we see a cafeteria that has been rendered to a new version with the help of Autodesk 3ds max. Autodesk 3ds Max is a professional 3D computer graphics program for making 3D animations, models, games, and images. As we all know, eye-catching visuals, ambiance attracts all kinds of crowds. The structure of the architecture, menu format, lighting effects, seating arrangement, serving ideas have been rendered here. Keeping the world crisis in mind, an approach to the same issue is shown. This chapter aims at designing a cafeteria with enhanced models with material effects. The process of rendering the cafeteria is shown in detail.

Chapter 3

Ritwika Das Gupta, CHRIST University, India
Daksh Agarwal, University of Pennsylvania, USA

Setting up the sources, working with editable poly, information in the inside of the kitchen design, and applying turbo-smooth and symmetry modifiers are all detailed in the process for generating a 3D model. In addition to lighting the scene and setting up the renderer, the method materials are introduced to the model. Methods and techniques for rendering are also defined. The final rendering was created by combining several pictures. The research aims to create a design that incorporates materials to enhance models. The shapes used were cylinder, sphere, box, plane, and spline. Modifiers include editable poly, editable spline, and UVW map. Finally, the authors used a material editor and target lighting to improve the model. The method of using meshes to create model is also used in this research. A mesh is a type of three-dimensional geometric model.

Chapter 4

Muskaan Jain, CHRIST University, India

The goal of this research work is to investigate the process of producing standard lighting for a bookshelf, as well as the process of rendering that scene. Lights in reality enable you to see things, and lights in 3ds Max do the same job. Furthermore, you may give characteristics to 3ds Max's lighting tools, allowing them to cast shadows and even control atmospheric lighting effects. If you haven't defined any lights, 3ds Max will use the default lighting. This allows you to observe any object you make without using any lights in the scene. The default lights vanish as soon as another light is added to the scene, and they mysteriously reappearance if all other lights in the area are removed. The 3D scene has comprised the boxes of varied parameters and a compound object named ProBoolean. Boxes of lesser length, width, and height are placed over the box of greater parameters, and smaller boxes are cut using ProCutter also named as ProBoolean compound object.

With the quick improvement of modem innovation, representing objects and scenes virtually is one of those major considerations made in technological sectors. A virtual three-dimensional representation of objects is not just to have a glimpse of the structure, but also to have a realistic view of the scene. This chapter mainly describes the usage and applications of 3ds Max related to which creating a 3D model of a kitchen is briefed. The chapter also includes the methodologies of designing and implementing various features of 3ds Max like editors and materials. The manner in which patterns are applied to objects, lighting effects, usage of modifiers like edit poly, edit mesh, turbo-smooth, mesh smooth bend, etc. are briefly described. This chapter can guarantee a variety of usage on texture maps with the help of rendering material editors which improves the quality of the rendering image and the structure.

Chapter 6

3ds Max is used in the video game industry for creating 3D character models, game assets, and animation. With an efficient workflow and powerful modeling tools, 3ds Max can save game artists a significant amount of time. 3ds Max fits into the animation pipeline at nearly every stage. From modeling and rigging to lighting and rendering, this program makes it easy to create professional-quality animations easier and simpler. Many industries use 3ds Max for generating graphics that are mechanical or even organic in nature. The engineering, manufacturing, educational, and medical industries all make use of 3ds Max for visualization needs as well. The real estate and architectural industries use 3ds Max to generate photorealistic images of buildings in the design phase. This way clients can visualize their living spaces accurately and offer critiques based on real models. 3ds Max uses polygon modeling which is a common technique in game design.

Rapid demands for the representation of various scenes and objects have bought in an evolution that ought to bring in the applications, usage, and development of various 3D modeling software. One would have the interest to have a glimpse of a sample (i.e., a 3D model of any structure to be created in the future). This chapter describes the usage and applications of 3ds Max with lights and camera view rendering related to which creating a 3D virtual scene of a living room is briefed. The chapter also includes the methodologies of designing and implementing various features of 3ds Max like editors, materials, lights, modifiers, and camera rendering. Usage of modifiers like edit poly, edit mesh, turbo-smooth, mesh smooth bend, etc. are briefly described. This chapter can assure a variety of map usages like texture maps with various camera angles to have a clear perspective of every object and scene in detail.

In the rapid developing of modern technology, the digital information management and the virtual reality simulation technology have become the research center. Virtual living room 3D model can not only express the real-world objects of natural, real, and vivid, and can expand the living room of the reality of time space dimensions, the combinations of living room environment and information. This chapter uses 3ds Max technology to create three-dimensional model of wall, floor, and television, etc. This research focuses on 3D objects effect with photometric lighting and living room scene modeling technology and the scene design process in a variety of real-time processing technology optimization strategy. Finally, the result of virtual living room scene with the help of photometric lights is summarized.

Most fluorescent lights have been designed for commercial purposes to light up streets, houses, buildings, etc., and as such, these lights possess a light tube wherein light is generated via a thin filament like source. Most 3ds Max lights are point-source based, and therefore require us to transform the light objects available in the 3ds Max software, in order to prevent any unnecessary delays in rendering a scene or produce non-similar light effects. Though less energy efficient than fluorescent lights, incandescent lights still are manufactured in a variety of shapes and sizes; however, these lights are slowly but surely being replaced by better energy-efficient lights sources. Some other natural sources of incandescent lights are burning fireplace, bonfires, lava, burners on a stove, etc. As noted from the examples, most natural incandescent light sources don't require electricity to illuminate the surroundings but still produce light through chemical reaction or burning.

Chapter 10
Raghav Sham Kamat, CHRIST University, India
Ritwika Das Gupta, CHRIST University, India

3D modelling software has its importance and requirement priority in various fields, mostly in design sectors. Visualization, creating 3D models, representing scenes, and adding animation to objects can have their complications, but with 3ds Max software results can be expected with the large availability of modifiers, cameras, and lights made available for the modelers to create something with their creative perspective. By going through this chapter, readers can have an insight into topics like lights, camera paths, modifiers, Boolean, pro-Boolean, viewport, mesh, AEC extend by which modelers can have their desired output as a result. It also gives a glimpse of how material editors can be useful in giving a realistic look to any object or scene being created. Usage of various lights is also included with the importance of cloning objects. Cloning objects is an important aspect when modeling is considered. Casting shadows to clone objects can be interesting and complex. This chapter makes it easy by giving a clear perspective of its usage and importance.

Preface

Welcome to the world of 3D architecture visualizations using 3ds Max, the world's most powerful and adaptable 3D software suite. The visualization sector has undoubtedly become the fastest-growing 3D industry in recent years, and it may soon eclipse all others in terms of an overall number of users. In the same way that practically all architectural, engineering, and construction businesses adopted the computer-aided design in the 1990s, 3D renderings have become commonplace today. Through easy-to-follow lessons and training, this book guides you through the difficulty of mastering one of the most sophisticated computer programs ever created. It concentrates on the aspects of the program that you need to know to create outstanding architectural visualizations. The goal isn't to show you every imaginable way to complete a work; instead, it's to show you some of the quickest and most efficient options. A marketing guide and 20 top ideas are included at the end of the book, which took the author almost ten years to learn in a manufacturing environment—sometimes the hard way. Although 3ds Max is a vast and complex program, understanding just the aspects that pertain to visualizations will teach you everything you need to know to advance in the profession in the least amount of time. Learning Autodesk 3ds Max 2010 Design Essentials is an excellent end-to-end reference that gives users comprehensive information on all of the features and options available in the current edition of 3ds Max Design, allowing them to use the software in a production setting confidently. Each chapter begins with a series of lessons that introduce Max Design's functional regions and go over all associated features (with examples), followed by a lab (which demonstrates a practical application of the lesson). All of the classes work together to provide a comprehensive overview of the functions, features, and principles of 3ds Max 2010 Design.

Chapter 1 focuses 3Ds Max is a graphics tool that allows you to create 3D models, animations, games, and photographs. Autodesk Media and Entertainment produced it. It offers 3D modeling capabilities and a plug-in architecture that is adaptable. Video game creators and TV commercial studios are the most common users. It can also give animated movie effects. It comes with several tools and modifications that may transform a single conventional object into a variety of realistic models. It aids in creating natural textures for models and the proper mapping of such surfaces to the objects. It aids in creating appropriate light and shadow effects for the models. It has a variety of rendering options that allow the models to be generated in various ways. It contains new icons, a user interface that can be customized, and a scripting language. The most important users of 3ds Max are gaming asset artists and architectural designers. 3ds Max contains everything you need for excellent animation and rigging. As a result, animators working on big-budget films or even tiny commercial pieces that require 3D motion frequently employ it. Artists may animate figures utilizing skeletons, kinematics, and bone restrictions in a simple method that anyone can pick up with experience. In 3ds Max, the animation is all about keyframing bone attributes, making creating complicated and organic motion a breeze. When it comes to modeling, 3ds Max is known as the "Supreme" software because of its powerful toolset that anyone can acquire with practice. 3ds Max teaches 3D art to beginners since it is easier to understand than other 3D graphic packages. This software is used in various secondary and tertiary classrooms for 3D graphics and animation. Setting up the scenes, dealing with editable poly, information on the inside of the food court design, and adding turbo-smooth and symmetry modifiers are all covered in detail in this tutorial. This research article covers all of the fundamental modeling ideas needed for crucial object modeling. It also thoroughly examines the principles and descriptions of all possibilities within that topic before offering examples of the provided topic. It also includes photos of the models and their renderings and a detailed description of how the models are created. It also contains information about 3Ds Max, its applications, and existing and future demands.

Chapter 2 deep dives plan to modernize everything in our modern world and get everything at the tip of our fingers as the world evolves. As the world becomes, cafes of all sorts, shops, apartments, colleges, and many other things have been transformed with technology based on human innovation. As we progress through this paper, we come across a cafeteria that has been rendered in a new version using Autodesk 3D Max. Autodesk 3Ds Max is a 3D computer graphics tool used to create 3D animations, models, games, and photographs. As we all know, eye-catching sights and ambiance draw in a wide range of people. The architectural structure, menu format, lighting effects, seating arrangement, and serving ideas have all been illustrated. A solution to the same problem is demonstrated with the global crisis in mind. This article aims to create a cafeteria with upgraded models and material effects. This chapter walks you through the process of rendering the cafeteria.

Chapter 3 intends this technique for creating a 3D model includes setting up the sources, working with editable poly, information from the inside of the kitchen design, and adding turbo-smooth and symmetry modifiers. The technique materials are introduced to the model is established in addition to lighting the scene and setting up the renderer. Rendering methods and procedures are also defined. Several images were combined to create the final depiction. Our study aims to develop a design that incorporates materials to improve models. Cylinder, sphere, box, plane, and spline were the shapes employed. Editable poly, Editable spline, and UVW map are some of the modifiers available. Finally, we improved the model using a Material editor and target lighting. The approach of creating models with meshes is also used in this study. A mesh is a three-dimensional geometric model of some sort. The mesh's basic shape is made up of vertices and edges. Faces or polygons make up the renderable surface. The sphere, teapot, and other basic primitive meshes are examples of basic standard primitive meshes. Each mesh may be changed using various modifiers and tools to create a new realistic model. A mesh's faces, vertices, edges, and polygons can all be adjusted individually.

In Chapter 4, the purpose of this study is to look into the process of creating standard lighting for a bookshelf, as well as rendering that scenario. Lights in reality help you see things, and lights in 3ds Max help you see things as well. Additionally, you may give 3ds Max's lighting tools features, allowing them to throw shadows and even manage atmospheric lighting effects. If no lights have been defined, 3ds Max will utilize the default lighting. This allows you to observe any object you create in the scene without utilizing any lighting. When another light is introduced to the scene, the default lights vanish, and when all other lights in the vicinity are removed, they magically reappeared. The 3D scene consists of boxes with various properties as well as a composite object called ProBoolean. Smaller boxes are trimmed using ProCutter, also known as ProBoolean compound object, which is placed over boxes with higher length, width, and height. As a result, there are no unique lighting effects on the bookcase. Omni lights are utilized to provide more intensity to the scene. The Bookshelf was photographed in high-quality, nearly uniform images as a result of this research. Additional adjustments to the bookshelf wall and other items, such as books, would have improved the scene even more, and rendering optimization would have resulted in faster rendering.

With the rapid advancement of modern innovation, one of the primary concerns in technological sectors is the virtual representation of items and settings. A virtual 3-Dimensional model of things, in any field, is not only for getting a peek of the structure but also for getting a realistic perspective of the scene. This article primarily discusses the use and uses of 3ds Max concerning producing a 3d model of a kitchen, interior design, and its objects, among other things. The methodology for designing and implementing key aspects of 3ds Max, such as Editors and Materials, is also covered in the article. The application of patterns to objects, lighting effects, and modifiers such as edit poly, edit mesh, turbo-smooth, mesh smooth bend, and others are briefly discussed. With the help of rendering material editors, this article can ensure a range of texture map usage, which improves the quality of the rendering picture and structure in this Chapter 5.

In the video game industry, 3ds Max creates 3D character models, game components, and animation. 3ds Max may save game artists time thanks to its quick workflow and robust modeling tools. 3ds Max is used in almost every stage of the animation process. This application makes it simple to create professional-quality animations, from modeling and rigging to lighting and rendering. 3ds Max is used in various sectors to produce mechanical or organic images. 3ds Max is also used for visualization in engineering, manufacturing, educational, and medical industries. 3ds Max is used in the real estate and architecture industries to create photorealistic renderings of structures throughout the design phase. Clients can more realistically picture their living areas and provide feedback based on actual models this way. Polygon modeling, a common technique in game creation, is used in 3ds Max. Artists can have a lot of control over individual polygons in polygonal modeling, allowing them to work with more detail and precision in Chapter 6.

In Chapter 7, Rapid demand for the representation of various sceneries and objects has ushered in an evolution that will inevitably lead to the invention, use, and use of numerous 3D modeling software. In any field, having a peek at a sample, i.e., a 3d Model of any construction to be built in the future would pique one's interest. This article focuses on the use and applications of 3ds Max with lights and camera view rendering, including creating a 3d virtual scene of a living room, interior design, and objects, among other things. The methodology for developing and implementing many aspects of 3ds Max, such as Editors, materials, lights, modifiers, and camera rendering, is also covered in the paper. They applied bitmaps to objects and other scene materials to provide a realistic appearance. Edit poly, edit mesh, turbo-smooth, mesh smooth bend, and other modifications are briefly described. This paper can guarantee a variety of map uses, such as texture maps with different camera angles for a clear perspective of every object and scene in detail.

Chapter 8 takes Digital information management and virtual reality simulation technologies have become the research focus in the rapid development of modern technology. The virtual living room 3D model may not only represent natural, accurate, and vivid real-world things, but it can also expand the living room of the reality of time and space dimensions, as well as the combinations of living room environment and information. The 3ds Max technology is mainly used in this article to construct three-dimensional models of the wall, floor, and television, among other things. The scene design process in a variety of real-time processing technology optimization strategies is the focus of this research, which focuses on 3D objects Effect with Photometric Lighting and living room scene modeling technology, as well as the scene design process in a variety of real-time processing technology optimization strategies. Finally, the outcome of the virtual living room set created using photometric lights is summed together.

Chapter 9 throws most fluorescent lights were created for commercial use to illuminate streets, residences, and buildings. As a result, they include a light tube with a thin filament-like source that generates light. Because most 3DS Max lights are point source-based, we must alter the light objects available in the 3DS Max software to avoid needless rendering delays or make non-similar light effects. Incandescent lights are still manufactured in various shapes and sizes, despite being less energy efficient than fluorescent lights; nevertheless, these lights are slowly but steadily being replaced by more energy-efficient lighting sources. Incandescent lights can also be found in burning fireplaces, bonfires, lava, stove burners, and other natural sources. The examples show that most natural incandescent light sources do not require electricity to enlighten the surroundings but produce light through chemical reactions or burning.

In Chapter 10, 3D modeling software is essential and required in various fields, most notably in the design industry. Visualization, making 3d models, depicting sceneries, and adding motion to things can all be challenging. Still, with 3ds Max software, enamoring results can be expected thanks to the enormous number of modifiers, cameras, and lights available for modelers to use. By reading this chapter, readers will understand subjects such as lights, camera routes, modifiers, Boolean, Pro-Boolean, Viewport, Mesh, and AEC Extend, all of which can help modelers achieve their desired outcome. It also shows how material editors can effectively give any object or scene being made a realistic look. The necessity of cloning objects is also involved in using varied lights. When it comes to modeling, cloning objects is a crucial consideration. Casting shadows to clone objects can be exciting and challenging; however, this chapter simplifies the process by clearly understanding its application and significance.

Debabrata Samanta
CHRIST University, India

Acknowledgment

We express our great pleasure, sincere thanks, and gratitude to the people who significantly helped, contributed and supported to the completion of this book entitled with *3D Modeling Using Autodesk 3ds Max With Rendering View*. Our sincere thanks to Fr. Benny Thomas, Professor, Department of Computer Science and Engineering, CHRIST (Deemed to be University), Bengaluru, Karnataka India, and Siddhartha Bhattacharyya, Principal, Rajnagar Mahavidyalaya, Rajnagar, Birbhum, India for their continuous support, advice and cordial guidance from the beginning to the completion of this book.

We would also like to express our honest appreciation to our colleagues at CHRIST (Deemed to be University), Bengaluru, Karnataka India, for their guidance and support.

We also thank all the authors who have contributed some chapters to this book. This book would not have been possible without their contribution.

We are also very thankful to the reviewers for reviewing the book chapters. This book would not have been possible without their continuous support and commitment towards completing the chapters' review on time.

To complete this book, all the publishing team members at IGI Global extended their king cooperation, timely response, expert comments, guidance, and we are very thankful to them.

Finally, we sincerely express our special and heartfelt respect, gratitude, and gratefulness to our family members and parents for their endless support and blessings.

Introduction

INTRODUCTION

3DS Max is software professionally used for video games, animation and movies. Modelling is the primary concept of 3DS Max. 3DS Max provides knowledge about 3d visualization of objects. Autodesk 3DS Max is used explicitly for the 3D entertainment industries. Autodesk Media and Entertainment produced it. Modelling capabilities inflexible architecture is used in this software. It is used for video games, pre-visualization, commercial TV shows, movies, architectural visualization, etc. IT contains various shaders, illuminators, glow options and lighting for modelling purposes (U. Castellani., et al. 2005) (Y. Arayici et al. 2005). Autodesk Media and Entertainment produced it. It can model in 3D and has a flexible plug-in architecture. It is majorly used by video game developers and TV commercial studios. It can also give movie effects to animations (V Kureethara et al. 2012). It contains various tools and modifiers to modify a single standard object to different realistic models. It helps create natural textures for models and map them correctly to the objects. It helps in providing proper light and shadow effects to the models. It has different rendering options for making the models flexible to render. It has new icons, a customizable user interface, and a scripting language (V. Murino. et al. 2005).

3ds Max is crucial to game asset artists and architectural designers the most. For animation and rigging, 3ds Max contains most of the things necessary for professional work. It is often required by the animators working on various films to use 3D motion (Anil Kumar et al. 2021). Through bone constraints, kinematics, and other options artists can easily animate motions. Animation contains key framing, bone properties and creating complex motions simply and organically. 3ds Max contains huge tools set which allows people to learn and practice easily. 3dd Max is easy to understand and thus it is mostly used to learn 3d Graphics (Anil Kumar et al. 2021).

3DS MAX TOOLS AND USES

For modelling purposes in 3ds Max, various tools and modifiers are used. Some of the valuable modifiers and their functions are listed below:

Turbo Smooth: The turbo smooth modifier smoothens any object to perfect smooth Shape. It has an iteration operation; upon increasing the value of this iteration, the amount of smoothness can be improved. (Livio De Luca et al. 2006)

Smooth: The smooth modifier also helps in smoothening any object. Unlike turbo smooth modifier, smooth modifier makes sure that the object's geometry is kept intact while smoothening it. The auto soft option smoothens the thing automatically to the threshold amount required, and the other numbers options smooth the objects up to a certain level given by the number. (Debabrata Samanta et al. 2011)

Edit Poly: The edit poly modifier helps edit the objects and form the model. It has assorted options for editing edges, vertices, faces and polygon of an object. This modifier has options like chamfer, extrude, bevel cut, which was used in designing this model (Anil Kumar et al. 2021). The chamfer option was used to create smoothness in corners of the refrigerator and sharp corner areas of any objects (Anil Kumar et al. 2021).

Shell Modifier: Shell modifier is used to give thickness to any object. It has two primary options: the inner and outer thickness options. These options help increase an object's inner and outer thickness, respectively (Binod Kumar et al. 2021).

Bend Modifier: This modifier is used to bend objects wrong direction. There are direction, angle, axis and limit options used for setting an object's bend limit and turning it in a particular direction, angle and axis (Binod Kumar et al. 2021).

UVW Map: This modifier is used for modifying the textures mapped to an object. It has a box, cylinder, sphere and other options, which helps map the thing in a specific Shape. And increasing or decreasing the size of that Shape mapped textures are also possible. It also allows enabling real-world mapping. (C.H. Esteban et al. 2003)

Lathe modifier- this modifier converts 2d shapes to 3d models.

Various splines are used to design a model in 3ds max; Splines are used to create 2-dimensional shapes in 3ds Max. These two-dimensional shapes can be used to create three-dimensional objects by extruding them. It is challenging to develop some complex models by editing a single standard 3D object in some cases. In such instances, splines are very useful. The splines option is found under Create panel -> (Shapes) -> Splines. The basic splines found in 3DS Max are: (C.H. Esteban et al. 2003).

- Line: line is used to create different 2D diagrams. A line consists of two vertices and a single edge. A combination of many line segments can form a

2D graph. The bar has an option off smoothening. Smooth lines can also be created to form a soft cornered 2D diagram (Manu M K et al. 2018).

- Rectangle: A rectangle is used to create a 2D rectangle or a square. A rectangle or a square consists of four vertices connected by four edges.
- Circle: A circle is used to create a circular or an elliptical 2D shape. Ellipse: An ellipse is used to create an elliptical or a circular 2D shape.
- Arc: an arc is used to create open or closed partial circular shapes made of four vertices.
- Doughnut: A donut is used to create two concentric circles placed in the form of a doughnut. Each circled in the donut is made up of four vertices.
- On: A on is used to create a circular spline with any number (N) of sides and vertices.
- Star: a star is used to create a star-like shape with each pointed corner of the star as vertices, and each vertex is are connected by edges.
- Text: the text is used to create shapes in the form of text. For example, if the 2D Shape of any text such as "Welcome" is required, the text option is used to create such shapes.
- Egg: it is used to create an egg-like shape.
- Section: Section is a particular type of spline that generates shapes based on a cross-sectional slice through geometry objects.
- Freehand: Freehand is used to make freehand drawings into the viewport.

As mentioned above, 2D diagrams can be created in the 3ds Max viewport using splines. To convert these 2D objects into 3D models, it is necessary to extrude them. Once the 2D diagram is completed in the viewport. (Abhijit Guha et al. 2021) Various modifiers are available in 3ds Max to convert these diagrams into 3D models. Before converting a 2D object to a 3D model, it is necessary to edit the 2D model properly so that the 3D object gets a perfect shape. To edit the 2D model, the edit spline modifier is used in 3ds Max. Edit spline modifier is used to edit this spline by editing its edges, vertices, and different spline parts separately. The edit spline is found under Select spline -> Modify panel -> Modifier list -> Object space modifier -> Edit Spline. After editing the spline, to extrude the spline into a 3D object extrude modifier is used. The extrude modifier is found under Select spline -> Modify panel -> Modifier list -> Object space modifier -> Extrude. The extrude modifier has the following necessary options to know:

- Amount: amount option is used to set the depth of extrusion of the 2D object.
- Segments: it is used to specify the number of segments created in the extruded object.
- Grid: arranges that the cap traces in the square grid at the shape boundaries.

- Mesh specifies that the 2D object created is an editable mesh, and it can be combined with two other meshes or 3D models. (Qin Lian et al. 2006)

The most straightforward way of creating 3D models in 3ds Max is using meshes. A mesh is a 3D object that can be editable and used to form different 3D models. There are various types of meshes found in 3ds Max. The basic standard meshes are under standard primitive, found under Create panel -> Geometry -> Standard Primitives. (M. Maheswari et al. 2021) These meshes are box, cone, sphere, geosphere, cylinder, tube, Torus, pyramid, teapot, plane, text plus. The other complex meshes are found under Extended primitives under Create panel -> Geometry -> Extended Primitives. These meshes are hydra, Taurus knot, Chamfer Box, Chamfer Cyl, oil tank, capsule, spindle, L-Ext, GenCon, C-Ext, ring wave, hose, prism. For convenience in modeling, 3ds Max also has predefined modelled meshes such as doors and windows. It also has trees (Foliage), railings, and walls under AEC extended, which is under Create panel -> Geometry -> AEC Extended. All these measures can be edited two form different realistic models by using the Edit Poly modifier. The edit Poly modifier helps edit the meshes by editing vertices, edges, faces, and polygons to form a proper 3D model. the edit Poly modifier is found under Select mesh ->Modify panel -> Modifier list -> Object space modifier -> Edit Poly. The other modifier used to edit meshes is the edit mesh modifier, which is similar to the Edit Poly modifier (Soon-Yong Park et al. 2005). The edit Poly modifier also consists of various options which can help in creating a realistic 3D model. Some of these effective options are:

- It allows the selection of vertices, edges, faces, borders, and polygons and edits them using different tools separately.
- It has ring and loop options. The ring is used to select all the edges in a round of the selected edge. Loop is used to select all the edges in a loop of the selected edge.
- The cut is used to cut from one edge to another or from one vertex to another. It creates an edge at the point where the cut is applied.
- Extrude is used to extrude the edges and faces of a mesh.
- The chamfer is used to smoothen the edges of a mesh.
- The bridge is used two create a face between two or more edges or vertices.
- Connect is used to create edges between two or more edges or vertices.
- Bevel is used to create a bevel or a hole kind of structure.
- Attach is used to attach vertices, faces, or models, and detach does the opposite job.
- Set ID is used to set the ID of a particular face of the model for proper material mapping of that face.

- View aligns and grid aligns are used to align a face or the model to the view of the scene or the grid of the scene, respectively. (M. Sainz et al. 2004)

Boolean objects are used to perform subtract, union, intersect and merge operations on models.

- Subtract: the subtract option helps in removing one model from the other. For this, the object from which a model is to be deducted is selected first; then, the Boolean operation is used by clicking on subtracting option and adding the object that is to be removed by add operand option. (Debabrata Samanta et al. 2012).
- Union: the union option helps in combining one model with other. For this, the object to be combined is selected first; then, the Boolean operation is used by clicking on the union option and adding the object to be combined by adding the operand option.
- Intersect: It helps keep the common model of two models by removing the rest of the model. For this, a model is to be selected, and by Boolean and intersect option, another model is to be added by add operand, and the common part is obtained as a result.
- Merge: It performs intersecting and combining two models without removing any of the original polygons.

Smoothing meshes is another essential part of 3D modelling. While making a model, meshes that are developed might have sharp corners and edges. Most of the realistic models existing in any environment do not have completely sharp corners and edges. Thus, to make a 3D model which is realistic, it is essential to smoothen them (W. Sun et al. 2005). In 3ds Max, there are three smooth modifiers available-turbosmooth, meshsmooth and smooth. Turbosmooth and meshsmooth perform a similar task. Applying these modifiers to a model, the corner edges and the vertices are completely smoothened by increasing the iteration off turbo smooth or mesh smooth the number of smoothness increases. Both the turbosmooth and meshsmooth modifiers are available under Select model -> Modify panel -> Modifier list -> Object space modifier -> Turbosmooth/ Meshsmooth. Another smoothing modifier in 3dsmax is smooth. Through the smooth modifier, the designer gets more control one smoothing the objects according to their need. The threshold option is available under smooth modifier, which sets the threshold of smoothing the model. Predefines smoothing groups are also available. The smooth modifier is found under Select model -> Modify panel -> Modifier list -> Object space modifier -> Smooth.

Lofting an object is important and a quick method of converting 2D diagrams to 3D models. Aloft is a compound object in 3ds Max, which helps convert 2D objects to 3D using various 2D spline objects (Debabrata Samanta et al. 2012).

- Creating a shape to be the loft path.
- Creating other shapes to be loft cross-sections.
- Now, this 3d model can be edited using edit poly modifier.

Ritwika Das Gupta
CHRIST University, India

REFERENCES

Arayici, Y., & Hamilton, A. (2005). Modeling 3D scanned data to visualize the built environment. *International Conference on Information Visualisation (IV'05),* 509-514.

Biswal, A. K., Singh, D., Pattanayak, B. K., Samanta, D., & Yang, M.-H. (2021). IoT-Based Smart Alert System for Drowsy Driver Detection. Wireless Communications and Mobile Computing. doi:10.1155/2021/6627217

Castellani, U., Fusiello, A., Murino, V., Papaleo, L., Puppo, E., & Pittore, M. (2005, October). A complete system for on-line 3D modelling from acoustic images. *Signal Processing Image Communication*, *20*(9-10), 832–852. doi:10.1016/j.image.2005.02.003

De Luca, L., Veron, P., & Florenzano, M. (2006, April). Reverse engineering of architectural buildings based on a hybrid modeling approach. *Computers & Graphics*, *30*(2), 160–176. doi:10.1016/j.cag.2006.01.020

Esteban, C. H., & Schmitt, F. (2003). Silhouette and stereo fusion for 3D object modeling. *Fourth International Conference on 3-D Digital Imaging and Modeling, 2003. 3DIM 2003. Proceedings,* 46-53.

Guha, A., Samanta, D., Banerjee, A., & Agarwal, D. (2021). A Deep Learning Model for Information Loss Prevention From Multi-Page Digital Documents. *IEEE Access: Practical Innovations, Open Solutions*, *9*, 80451–80465. doi:10.1109/ACCESS.2021.3084841

Kureethara, V., Biswas, J., & Debabrata Samanta, N. G. (n.d.). Balanced Constrained Partitioning of Distinct Objects. *International Journal of Innovative Technology and Exploring Engineering*. doi:10.35940/ijitee.K1023.09811S19

Lian, Q., Li, D.-C., Tang, Y.-P., & Zhang, Y.-R. (2006, May). Computer modeling approach for a novel internal architecture of artificial bone. *Computer Aided Design*, *38*(5), 507–514. doi:10.1016/j.cad.2005.12.001

Maheswari, M., Geetha, S., & Selva Kumar, S. (2021). PEVRM: Probabilistic Evolution Based Version Recommendation Model for Mobile Applications. *IEEE Access: Practical Innovations, Open Solutions*, *9*, 20819–20827. doi:10.1109/ACCESS.2021.3053583

Manu, Roy, & Samanta. (2018). Effects of Liver Cancer Drugs on Cellular Energy Metabolism in Hepatocellular Carcinoma Cells. *International Journal of Pharmaceutical Research, 10*(3). . doi:10.31838/ijpr/2018.10.03.079

Park & Subbarao. (2005). A multiview 3D modeling system based on stereo vision techniques. *Machine Vision and Applications, 16*(3), 148-156.

Sainz, Pajarola, Mercade, & Susin. (2004). A simple approach for point-based object capturing and rendering. *IEEE Computer Graphics and Applications, 24*(4), 24-33.

Samanta & Sanyal. (2012a). Segmentation technique of sar imagery based on fuzzy c-means clustering. Academic Press.

Samanta & Sanyal. (2012b). A novel approach of sar image classification using color space clustering and watersheds. Academic Press.

Sanyal & Samanta. (2011). Segmentation technique of sar imagery using entropy. *International Journal of Computer Technology and Applications*, *2*, 1548–1551.

Sun, W., Starly, B., Nam, J., & Darling, A. (2005, September). Bio-CAD modeling and its applications in computer-aided tissue engineering. *Computer Aided Design*, *37*(11), 1097–1114. doi:10.1016/j.cad.2005.02.002

Chapter 1
Critical Compound Objects Modelling Using Autodesk

Ritwika Das Gupta
CHRIST University, India

Daksh Agarwal
University of Pennsylvania, USA

ABSTRACT

Autodesk 3ds Max is a graphics program for making 3D models, animations, games, and images. Autodesk Media and Entertainment produced it. It has the capabilities to model in 3D and has a flexible plug-in architecture. It is majorly used by video game developers and TV commercial studios. It can also give movie effects to animations. It contains various tools and modifiers to modify a single standard object to different realistic models. It helps in creating natural textures for models and mapping them correctly to the objects. It helps in providing proper light and shadow effects to the models. It has different rendering options for making the models flexible to render. It has new icons, a customizable user interface, and its scripting language. 3ds Max is crucial to game asset artists and architectural designers the most. For animation and rigging, 3ds Max has everything mandatory for professional work.

INTRODUCTION

This research consists of all the requirements to model any critical object. Most of the major modelling and material concepts are explained in this research. This research contains the description of tools and modifiers and all techniques used in modelling in 3ds Max. Smoothing of models, using splines to create 3d models, and

DOI: 10.4018/978-1-6684-4139-8.ch001

model editing concepts are clearly defined and described using the design in this research (Samanta, Debabrata, & Paul, M. (2011)). Cloning and mirror concepts are also explained, along with material mapping concepts. The way materials are introduced to the model is defined, lighting the environment, and setting up the renderer (Anselmo Antunes Montenegro et al. 2004) (Tavares, J. et al. 2021). Rendering methods and procedures are also defined. Multiple images were drawn to create the final rendering. The goal of our research is to produce a food court design that uses materials to enhance models. Cylinder, Sphere, Box, Plane, and Splines, along with standard primitives, were the shapes employed. Editable poly, Editable spline, and UVW map are the modifiers. Finally, we enhanced the model using a Material editor (Slate and compact) and target lighting. Editing a material and several types of material and material editors are explained using an example (Carlos Hernández Esteban et al. 2014). The proper glow effect of materials and the making of materials were also presented. Editing the model using edit ply and different options within the edit poly modifier was broadly classified and discussed. This research thus contains all crucial points for critical compound object modelling (Samanta, Debabrata, Paul, M., & Sanyal, G. (2011)).

CRITICAL OBJECT MODELLING USING SPLINES

Splines are used to create 2-dimensional shapes in 3ds Max. These two-dimensional shapes can be used to create three-dimensional objects by extruding them. It is challenging to develop some complex models by editing a single standard 3D object in some cases. In such instances, splines are very useful (Livio De Luca et al. 2006). The splines option is found under Create panel -> (Shapes) -> Splines. The basic splines found in 3DS Max are:

- Line: line is used to create different 2D diagrams. A line consists of two vertices and a single edge. A combination of many line segments can form a 2D diagram. The line has an option off smoothening. Smooth lines can also be created to form a soft cornered 2D diagram.
- Rectangle: A rectangle is used to create a 2D rectangle or a square. A rectangle or a square consists of four vertices connected by four edges.
- Circle: A circle is used to create a circular or an elliptical 2D shape. Ellipse: An ellipse is used to create an elliptical or a circular 2D shape.
- Arc: an arc is used to create open or closed partial circular shapes made of four vertices.
- Donut: A donut is used to create two concentric circles placed in the form of a donut. Each circled in the donut is made up of four vertices.

- NGon: A NGon is used to create a circular spline with any number (N) of sides and vertices.
- Star: a star is used to create a star-like shape with each pointed corner of the star as vertices, and each vertex is are connected by edges.
- Text: the text is used to create shapes in the form of text. For example, if the 2D shape of any text such as "Welcome" is required, the text option is used to create such shapes.
- Egg: it is used to create an egg-like shape.
- Section: Section is a particular type of spline that generates shapes based on a cross-sectional slice through geometry objects.
- Freehand: Freehand is used to make freehand drawings into the viewport.

CRITICAL OBJECT MODELLING BY EXTRUDING SPLINES

As mentioned above, 2D diagrams can be created in the 3ds Max viewport using splines. To convert these 2D objects into 3D models, it is necessary to extrude them. Once the 2D diagram is completed in the viewport (Halim SETAN et al. 2004) (Kajiya et al. 1986). Various modifiers are available in 3ds Max to convert these diagrams into 3D models. Before converting a 2D object to a 3D model, it is necessary to edit the 2D model properly so that the 3D object gets a perfect shape. To edit the 2D model, the edit spline modifier is used in 3ds Max. Edit spline modifier is used to edit this spline by editing its edges, vertices, and different spline parts separately (Kelly L. Murdock 2014). The edit spline is found under Select spline -> Modify panel -> Modifier list -> Object space modifier -> Edit Spline. After editing the spline, to extrude the spline into a 3D object extrude modifier is used. The extrude modifier is found under Select spline -> Modify panel -> Modifier list -> Object space modifier -> Extrude. The extrude modifier has the following necessary options to know:

- Amount: amount option is used to set the depth of extrusion of the 2D object.
- Segments: it is used to specify the number of segments created in the extruded object.
- Cap start: it generates a flat surface over the start of the extruded object.
- Cap end: it generates a flat surface over the end of the extruded object.
- Morph: arranges the cap faces in a predictable and repeatable pattern.
- Grid: arranges that the cap traces in the square grid at the shape boundaries.
- Mesh specifies that the 2D object created is an editable mesh, and it can be combined with two other meshes or 3D models (Matthew Brand et al. 2004).

CRITICAL OBJECT MODELLING BY EDITING MESHES

The most straightforward way of creating 3D models in 3ds Max is using meshes. A mesh is a 3D object that can be editable and used to form different 3D models. There are various types of meshes found in 3ds Max (Miguel Sainz et al. 2004) (M Paul et al. 2011). The basic standard meshes are under standard primitive, found under Create panel -> Geometry -> Standard Primitives. These meshes are box, cone, sphere, geosphere, cylinder, tube, Torus, pyramid, teapot, plane, text plus (Dhenain M et al. 2001). The other complex meshes are found under Extended primitives under Create panel -> Geometry -> Extended Primitives. These meshes are hydra, Taurus knot, Chamfer Box, Chamfer Cyl, oil tank, capsule, spindle, L-Ext, Gengon, C-Ext, ring wave, hose, prism. For convenience in modeling, 3ds Max also has predefined modeled meshes such as doors and windows (Eyetronics, 2004). It also has trees (Foliage), railings, and walls under AEC extended, which is under Create panel -> Geometry -> AEC Extended (Hu, Jia Ying. 2013). All these measures can be edited two form different realistic models by using the Edit Poly modifier. The edit Poly modifier helps edit the meshes by editing vertices, edges, faces, and polygons to form a proper 3D model. the edit Poly modifier is found under Select mesh -> Modify panel -> Modifier list -> Object space modifier -> Edit Poly. The other modifier used to edit meshes is the edit mesh modifier, which is similar to the Edit Poly modifier (Kriete A. et al. 2001). The edit Poly modifier also consists of various options which can help in creating a realistic 3D model (Lin, T. H. et al. 2014). Some of these effective options are:

- It allows the selection of vertices, edges, faces, borders, and polygons and edits them using different tools separately.
- It has ring and loop options. The ring is used to select all the edges in a round of the selected edge. Loop is used to select all the edges in a loop of the selected edge.
- The cut is used to cut from one edge to other or from one vertex to other. It creates an edge at the point where the cut is applied.
- Extrude is used to extrude the edges and faces of a mesh.
- The chamfer is used to smooth the edges of a mesh.
- The bridge is used two create a face between two or more edges or vertices.
- Connect is used to create edges between two or more edges or vertices.
- Bevel is used to creating a bevel or a whole kind of structure.
- Attach is used to attach vertices, faces, or models, and detach does the opposite job.
- Set ID is used to set the ID of a particular face of the model for proper material mapping of that face (Liu Gang et al. 2004).

- View aligns, and grid aligns are used to align a face or the model to the view of the scene or the grid of the scene, respectively.

CRITICAL OBJECT MODELLING USING BOOLEAN OBJECTS

Boolean objects are used to perform subtract, union, intersect and merge operations on models (M. Levoy et al. 2000). The Boolean is found under Select an object. -> Create panel -> (Geometry)- > Compound Objects -> Object Type rollout- > Boolean The primary options available in Boolean are:

- Subtract: the subtract option helps in removing one model from the other. For this, the object from which a model is to be deducted is select first; then, the Boolean operation is used by clicking on subtracting option and adding the object that is to be removed by add operand option (Paul, M., Samanta, D., & Sanyal, G. (2011)).
- Union: the union option helps in combining one model with other. For this, the object to be combined is selected first; then, the Boolean operation is used by clicking on the union option and adding the object to be combined by adding the operand option (P. Mueller et al. 2005).
- Intersect: It helps keep the common model of two models by removing the rest of the model. For this, a model is to be selected, and by Boolean and intersect option, another model is to be added by add operand, and the common part is obtained as a result (Qin Lian et al. 2006).
- Merge: It performs intersect and combining two models without removing any of the original polygons (Sarti et al. 2002).

CRITICAL OBJECT MODELLING BY SMOOTHING MESHES

Smoothing meshes is another essential part of 3D modelling. While making a model, meshes that are developed might have sharp corners and edges. Most of the realistic models existing in any environment do not have completely sharp corners and edges. Thus, to make a 3D model which is realistic, it is essential to smooth them (Samanta, Debabrata, & Sanyal, G. (2011c)). In 3ds Max, there are three smooth modifiers available- turbosmooth, meshsmooth and smooth. Turbosmooth and meshsmooth perform a similar task. Applying these modifiers to a model, the corner edges and the vertices are completely smoothened by increasing the iteration off turbosmooth or meshsmooth the amount of smoothness increases. Both the turbosmooth and meshsmooth modifiers are available under Select model -> Modify panel -> Modifier list -> Object space modifier -> Turbosmooth/ Meshsmooth. Another smoothing modifier in 3dsmax is smooth (Samanta, Debabrata, & Sanyal, G. (2011d)). Through the smooth modifier, the designer gets more control one smoothing the objects according to their need. The threshold option is available under smooth modifier, which sets the threshold of smoothing the model (Samanta, Debabrata, & Sanyal, G. (2012b)). Predefines smoothing groups are also available. The smooth modifier is found under Select model -> Modify panel -> Modifier list -> Object space modifier -> Smooth.

CRITICAL OBJECT MODELLING BY LOFTING AN OBJECT

Lofting an object is important and a quick method of converting 2D diagrams to 3D models. A loft is a compound object in 3ds Max, which helps convert 2D objects to 3D using various 2D spline objects (Samanta, Debabrata, & Sanyal, G. (2011a)). It is found under Select a path or shape. -> Create panel -> (Geometry) -> Compound Objects -> Object Type rollout -> Loft. The process of using loft is:

- Creating a shape to be the loft path.
- Creating other shapes to be loft cross-sections.
- Then to convert 2d object to 3d either, select the path shape and use Get Shape to add the cross-sections to the loft or select a shape and use Get Path to assign a path to the loft. Use Get Shape to add additional shapes (Samanta, Debabrata. (2011)).
- Now, this 3d model can be edited using edit poly modifier.

RESULT AND OUTPUT

A food court model is designed and discussed to show various critical object modelling using different techniques mentioned above. The food court model consists of a food stall, variety of food items and utensils for making food (Samanta, Debabrata, & Sanyal, G. (2012a)) (Soon-Yong Park et al. 2005). It also consists of chairs and tables, part of the sitting area off the food court. Trees are also planted and decorated to enhance the beauty of the food court (Toshihiro ASAI et al. 2005). The detailed discussion of the food court design is done below.

FOOD STALL

The food stall design consists of chips, samosas, cake, sweets, etc. It also includes instruments like a gas oven, microwave oven, refrigerator coffeemaker as food making and storing devices. It also consists of the sink for washing hands and keeping the area clean. It consists of shelves to store necessary items. Start from the basic structure of the stall. The shop walls were made of a box on three sides (back and two sides) (U. Castellani et al. 2005). The top wall was made using a box which and each side of the box was divided and sub-divided into segments using connect option of edit poly modifier. Each segment was extruded and rotated at an angle to form a design. The lowermost face of the box is deleted, and a shell modifier was used to give the thickness. The name of the stall was written using text shape and converted into 3d using extrude modifier and style of text is changed (Samanta, Debabrata, & Sanyal, G.,2013). The door was made using the door option under meshes. Fig 1 shows Complete Food Stall Design.

COFFEE MAKER

The coffee maker was made using a box which is a standard primitive. The boxes are divided into segments and extruded inward from the centre. Then the top division of the box was further divided into segments. Then the top face of the segmented area was extruded inward and outward as per requirement. A box was used to make the coffee pouring area, again segmented and extruded inward and outward as per requirement. Then the holes were made for pouring the coffee using the Boolean operator (Ulaş Yılmaz et al. 2002) (Samanta, Debabrata, & Sanyal, G. (2012d)). The glasses were made using a teapot whose top lid was removed, and the material was added to form a glass-like structure. Shell modifier was used to give the thickness to the glass (Samanta, Debabrata, & Sanyal, G. (2012e)). A cylinder was used to make the coffee into the glass. The cylinder was extruded and rescaled to form the inside of the glass. The top face of the cylinder was excluded inward and outward and rescaled to form the waves of the pour. The cylindrical button was made using a cylinder whose faces were extruded and rescaled to form a button (Samanta, Debabrata, & Sanyal, G. (2012h)). Turbo smooth modifier was used to make the button smooth. The square switches were made using square, which was again extruded and rescaled to form a switch-like structure. The top face of the switch was rotated to give an on/off effect. The two small switches were made using a sphere. The text on each switch was made using the text option, a spline, and was extruded using an extrude modifier (Samanta, Debabrata, & Sanyal, G. (2012f)). The machine handles who's made using a cylinder extruded and rescaled and moved using a move tool to form a handle-like structure. At last turbo smooth was used to smooth the entire model. The coffee pour was made using a cone. At last, chamfer was used to smooth the corners, and turbo smooth was used wherever required. Fig 2 expresses The final mesh of the Coffee Maker.

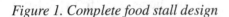

Figure 1. Complete food stall design

MIXER GRINDER

The mixer grinder was made using a cylinder whose top face was extruded and re-scaled to form the base of the mixer grinder. Turbo smooth modifier was used to smooth the base of the mixer grinder (Samanta, Debabrata, & Ghosh, A. (2012)). The top utensil off the mixer grinder was also made using a cylinder. The top face of the cylinder was extruded and re-scaled to form the utensil. The alternate edges of the utensil were extruded inward to create the design of the utensil. The utensil lid was made with a cylinder end that was extruded and re-scaled to form the lid (Samanta, Debabrata, & Sanyal, G. (2012g)). Turbo smooth modifier was used to the entire model to make it smooth. The regulator of the mixer grinder was made using a cylinder that was extruded and re-scaled. The top face of the cylinder was divided into segments using the connect option of the Edit Poly modifier. The

Figure 2. The final mesh of the coffee maker.

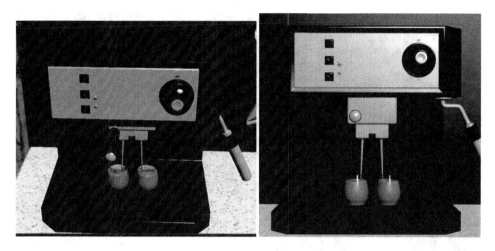

topmost segment is extruded to form a regulator-like structure. Turbo smooth modifier is used to smooth the regulator. The text on the regulator was made using the text option, a spline, and it was converted into 3d using an extrude modifier. The wire of the mixer grinder was made using line spline, which was extruded using extrude modifier (Samanta, Deababrata, & Sanyal, G. (2012)). The plug of the wire was made using a cylinder that is extruded and re-scale, and segmented to form a plug-like structure. Turbo smooth modifier was used to smooth the plug. The pins of the plug were made using an oil tank which is an extended primitive. Each pin was aligned properly to the holes of the switchboard. The switchboard behind was made using a box divided into segments, and the topmost square faces of each segment were extruded and re-scaled (Samanta, Debabrata, & Sanyal, G. (2011b)). Then the top faces were again divided and extruded. This extruded face was rotated to create an on-the-switch-like structure. The three pinholes were made using a sphere and Boolean operator (Samanta, Debabrata, & Sanyal, G. (2012c)). All the parts of the models were combined properly and arranged. Fig 3 shows The final mesh of the Mixer Grinder.

JUICER

The juicer was made using a cylinder that was extruded and re-scaled to form a juicer. The button was made using an extruded cylinder, and the re-scaled, and the Boolean operator was used to create a button with a sphere. The text was made using the text option, which was then extruded using extrude modifier. The inner

Figure 3. The final mesh of the mixer grinder

blade was made using a cylinder s base and a box extruded, moved, and re-scaled to make a blade. Both the cylinder and box were grouped and placed inside the juicer. Turbo smooth modifier was used to smooth the entire model. Fig 4 shows the final mesh of the Juicer (W. Sun et al. 2005).

GAS STOVE

The gas stove was made using a box whose top face was extruded and rescaled. Three cylinders were placed over the gas stove to form the cooking area. As shown in the figure, these cylinders were of varied sizes, and they were placed one on top of the other. The top face of the topmost cylinder was extruded and rescaled down. Turbo smooth modifier was used to smooth the cylinders. Boxes were used to form holders around the cooking area. Bend modifier was used to bed these boxes to a certain amount at a certain angle. A single box was made, and others were cloned and mirrored in a proper position. The entire cooking area was then grouped and cloned to form two cooking areas over the stove base (Wei Sunet al. 2002). The buttons were made using a cylinder and cloned to create six buttons. Turbo smooth modifier was used to smooth the buttons. The corners of the gas stove base were smoothened by selecting the corner edges and using the chamfer option under edit poly modifier. Fig 5 projected the final mesh of the Gas Stove.

REFRIGERATOR

The refrigerator was made using a box whose front face was divided into two segments. Each segmented square was extruded and rescaled. The corners of the fridge were chamfered. The refrigerator's handle was made using a box whose side faces were removed, and a turbo smooth modifier was used to smooth the box (Woop, Sven et al. 2005). The box did not have more than one segment; thus, it became oval and looked like a turbo smooth modifier handle. The iteration of turbo smooth modifier was kept three. This handle was then cloned as a copy and rescaled to increase its z-axis and make it longer. Then the handles were set into their places. The lock of the refrigerator was made using a cylinder whose top face was extruded and rescaled down. Then the topmost face was extruded inward, and all the side edges were extruded outward to form a design. Turbo smooth modifier was used to make the lock smooth. The refrigerator legs were made using a cylinder which was extruded and rescaled to form the leg. A single leg was cloned to form four legs. All the parts of the refrigerator were correctly arranged and grouped to form the entire refrigerator. Fig 6 shows the final mesh of the Refrigerator.

Figure 4. The final mesh of the juicer

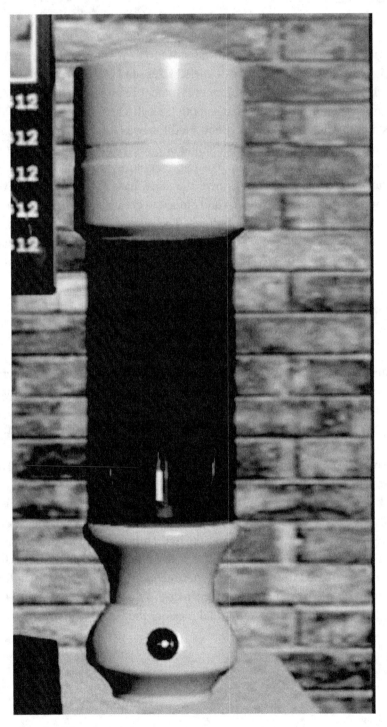

Figure 5. The final mesh of the gas stove

MICROWAVE OVEN

The microwave oven was made by extruding a segmented part of the shelf inward. They were then rescaling it and extruding outward. The top face was then segmented into two rectangles, one for the button and the microwave opening. Both segmented faces were extruded inward, rescaled, and extruded outward. The face was again segmented into a rectangle, extruded inward, and rescaled on the opening area (Yoo-Kil Yang et al. 2005). The buttons were made using a cylinder and cloned. These buttons were smoothened using a turbo smooth modifier. The handle was made using a box whose top and bottom faces were removed, and the corners were chamfered to smooth them. All these objects were appropriately arranged to form the microwave model. Fig 7 shows the final mesh of the Micro wave Oven.

BOTTLE RACK

The bottle rack was made using a box whose top face was segmented into a rectangle. This rectangular segmented face was extruded outwards. The corners of the box were chamfered to make it smooth. The racks of the box were created using boxes whose corners were chamfered to make them smooth. A single rack was cloned to form three more racks. The bottle was made using a cylinder that was extruded and rescaled the performer bottle. The cap of the bottle is an oil tank. The bottle was cloned without its cap and rescaled to make it smaller and moved inside the outer covering of the bottle (Yusuf Arayici et al. 2005). This forms the juice of the bottle. Each bottle was given different material and colour and cloned separately to form several bottles. The bottle was smoothened using a turbo smooth modifier. The handle of the bottle is a sphere that is rescaled for a handle. Fig 8 shows the final mesh of the Bottle Rack.

Figure 6. The final mesh of the refrigerator

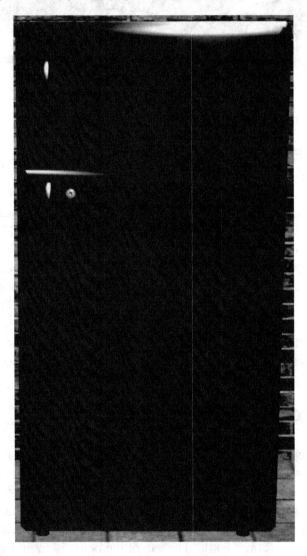

Figure 7. The final mesh of the microwave oven

SAMOSA RACK

The samosa rack was made using a box that was segmented, and each segmented rectangular face was extruded inward. The top, bottom, and corner faces were extruded outward. The samosas were made using a plane cut into a triangle using the cut option of edit Poly modifier and cutting the vertices from the diagonal. Then all the faces on one of the sides of the diagonal were removed to form a triangle. Then cloth modifier was used with a pressure intensity, and simulate button was pressed under the cloth modifier to make the triangle look fluffy. This triangular samosa was cloned into several samosas, mirrored, and moved to arrange them inside the rack. The corners of the rack were chamfered to make them smooth. Fig 9 shows the final mesh of the Samosa Rack.

CHIPS PACKETS

The chips packets were made using a plane which was made fluffy using cloth modifier by increasing the amount of pressure and simulating to a certain extent. The plane upon which cloth modifier was used was segmented in 100 length and

Figure 8. The final mesh of the bottle rack.

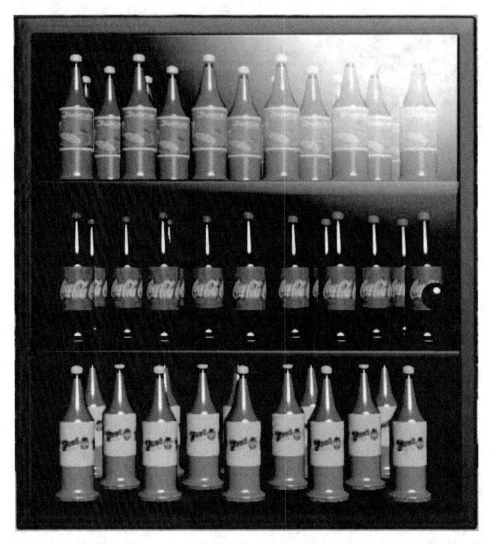

width segments. The top and the bottom edges were selected using the ring option, and they were extruded to a certain amount to form the packing area of the packet. Turbo smooth modifier was used to make the packet smooth. A single packet was cloned into several packets and arranged one below another. Different packets were given various materials. Fig 10 shows the final mesh of the Chips Packets.

Figure 9. The final mesh of the samosa rack.

CAKES AND SWEETS RACK

The cake is made of an extruded cylinder, and its side edges were selected with a loop option in the edit poly modifier and extruded. Turbo smooth modifier was used to smoothen the cake base. Icing spray on the cake was made using a cone whose side edges were selected using ring option of edit poly modifier and extruded, and turbo smooth modifier was used to smooth it. This cone was cloned and placed roundly on top of the cake. This cone was then scaled to be larger, and its topmost vertex was moved down to make it flat so that it looked like flat icing on the top base of the cake. Different materials were added to other cake bases, and icing and this cake were grouped and cloned into three more cakes. The sweets were made using a sphere that was arranged on top of the plate. The plate was made using a cylinder which was extruded and rescaled to form a plate. A single sweet sphere was cloned to form other sweet spheres. This sweet plate was grouped and cloned to form other sweet dishes. The sweet rack was made using a box segmented into several segments, and its top edges were selected using a loop and moved downward to form a slanting area of the rack. The corner faces of the rack were extruded outward to form corners of the rack. The rack frames were made using a box whose corner edges were chamfered using an edit poly to smooth it. The corner edges of the entire rack were chamfered to make it smooth, and a turbo smooth modifier was used to make the entire rack smooth. Then the cake and sweet items were aligned in their position and grouped. Fig 11 shows the final mesh of the Cakes and Sweets Rack.

Figure 10. The final mesh of the chips packets

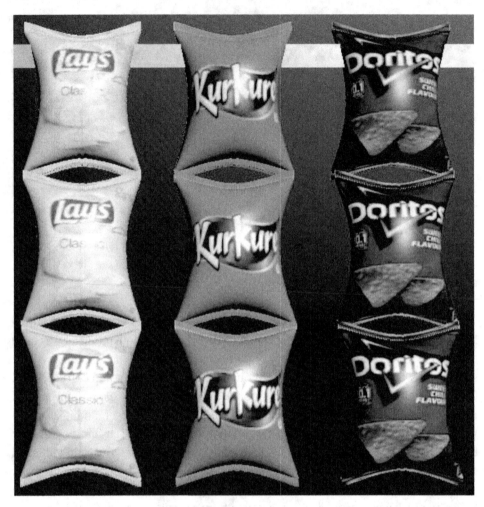

Figure 11. The final mesh of the cakes and sweets rack.

Figure 12. The final mesh of the menu board

MENU BOARD

The menu board is made up of a box, and material is used on the front face of the box as a menu. Fig 12 shows the final mesh of the Menu Board.

WASH BASIN

The top of the shelf is segmented for making the washbasin, and the segmented topmost face is extruded inward and rescaled down. The washbasin tap was made using a cylinder that was extruded and bent using a bend modifier. The top of the tap was made by a sphere rescaled to form a top structure and combined with a cylinder to form a perfect taps' top. The holder of that tap was made by extruding a cylinder and rescaling it as well as combining it with an oil tank, which is a compound primitive. All these objects were placed in a proper position and grouped as a tap. Fig 13 shows the final mesh of the Wash Basin.

Figure 13. The final mesh of the wash basin

THE SITTING AREA

The sitting area contains many plants, tables, and chairs. There is a cemented area from the food stall, which is kept for walking to the sitting area. The walls and floor of the sitting area were made using different boxes. The box was segmented into two on the floor, and the top face of one segment was extruded upward to give it a height. A plane was placed on the other lower segment where a hair and fur modifier was used to create the grass. The number of grasses was increased. Varied materials were used at different faces of the floor and different walls, respectively. Fig 14 shows the final mesh of the Sitting Area.

Figure 14. The final mesh of the sitting area.

TABLES AND STOOLS

The table bottom was firstly created by a box and edited by edit mesh and extruded to create a design. Cylinders were used for the legs of the table. Then it was smoothened by turbo smooth. The centre design is created by extruding edges and faces of cylinder and sphere and at the end using turbo smooth to smooth them. Then on top, two cylinders are used and smooth using turbo smooth. The table cloth was made using a plane on which shell modifier was used to give it thickness, and turbo smooth modifier was used to smoothen it. A cloth modifier was used, which was made a cotton cloth, and the table was added as a collision object. Then simulation was used to create the table cloth. The stool was made using a box that was extruded and rescaled to form a stool. In the lower area, the box was segmented, and alternative segmented faces were deleted. Then shell modifier was used to give thickness to the box, and the corners were chamfered to make it smooth. Turbo smooth modifiers were used to make the overall stool smooth. Then this table and stool were cloned and arranged to form the sitting area. The food items and plates on the table were just grouped and cloned from the food items of the food stall and placed on tables. Fig 15 shows the final Mesh of the Tables and Stools.

FLOWER VASE LIGHTS

The flower vase was made using a cylinder which was extruded and rescaled to form a flower vase structure. The edges around the flower were selected using the ring option of edit poly and extruded to get a design. Turbo smooth modifier was used to make the vase smooth. The top face of the flower vase was removed, and a shell modifier was used to give it thickness. The light inside the flower vase was made using a cylinder smoothened by turbo smooth modifier, and its top face was removed, and a shell modifier was used to give a thickness. The flowers were made using flowering plants, which are found as foliage under AEC extended. Different colour material was given to different flowers. Flowers were cloned and mirrored, and placed in proper position over the vase. This flower vase light was grouped and cloned to form several flower vase lights. Fig 16 shows the final mesh of Flower vase lights.

TREES AND PLANTS

Tree and plants were made, which were a part of AEC extended. And the stand of these plants was made using a box whose top face was segmented and was extruded

Figure 15. The final mesh of the tables and stools

inwards, rescaled down a bit, and extruded outward. This formed the tree stand and mud. Different materials were added to different areas. These trees and plants were grouped with their respective stand and cloned. The bulbs on the tree were made using a sphere on which glow effect was used on its material and cloned into several bulbs which were placed properly. Fig 17 shows the final mesh of Trees and Plants.

DISCOUNT BOARD

The discount board was created using a box upon which material was used to create a discount board structure. Fig 18 shows the final mesh of Discount Board.

Figure 16. The final mesh of flower vase lights

MATERIAL MAPPING

Materials were made using various images and colors. The slate material editor was used, and each material was recaster material to give it appropriate shine. The

Figure 17. The final mesh of Trees and Plants

Figure 18. The final mesh of Discount Board

glossiness and specular level were increased and brought to a proper amount to give all the materials a shine. For creating glass material, a recaster material was used, which was given black color. Glossiness and specular level were increased appropriately, and transparency was increased along with the Self-Illum level. Under maps, reflect was given fall off the map. The fall-off map was edited by adding a point to its Mix curve at the center of the curve and moving it downwards. This creates a dense feel to the glass material and gives proper glass reflection. After creating all the materials, Multi/ Sub Object material was used to map all the materials to their respective id. Then these materials were assigned to faces of different models by mapping their id with the id of the faces using set id option in edit poly. The glow effect was created by giving material to a model using the compact material editor and setting id to that material. Under the rendering option, by clicking effects, the lens effect can be added. Under lens effects, parameters glow was selected. Under glow elements and options, material id is to be set, and under the parameters, the color of glow was changed, and the intensity and size of the glow were set. This is how to glow material was added to the models. The materials were appropriately edited, using a UVW map modifier to fit the models well.

CONCLUSION

The food court design is made to show most modelling concepts so as make modelling concepts interesting and easy to learn. The demand for 3D technology skills is growing quickly in the job market. The demand for these skills is outpacing the growth of the labour market overall. 3D skills, best-known for rendering immersive experiences indistinguishable from real life, have become crucial in industries as diverse as manufacturing, architecture, health care, media, and entertainment. Thus, it is important to focus on 3d modelling concepts as they have a rising scope in the future and can make the future brighter. Making 3d models also mention the creative talent of many students and help they discover their creative side. This research aimed to make 3d modelling concepts easier for learners and bringing out the creative side of 3d modelling.

REFERENCES

Arayici, Y., & Hamilton, A. (2005). Modeling 3D Scanned Data to Visualize the Built Environment. *Proceedings of the Ninth International Conference on Information Visualisation*, 509-514. 10.1109/IV.2005.82

Brand, M., Kang, K., & Cooper, D. B. (2004). Algebraic solution for the visual hull. *Proceedings of the 2004 IEEE Computer Society Conference on Computer Vision and Pattern Recognition*, I33-I35. 10.1109/CVPR.2004.1315010

Castellani, U., Fusiello, A., Murino, V., Papaleo, L., Puppo, E., & Pittore, M. (2005). A complete system for on-line 3D modelling from acoustic images. *Signal Processing Image Communication*, *20*(9-10), 832–852. doi:10.1016/j.image.2005.02.003

De Luca, L., Veron, P., & Florenzano, M. (2006). Reverse engineering of architectural buildings based on a hybrid modeling approach. *Computers & Graphics*, *30*(2), 160–176. doi:10.1016/j.cag.2006.01.020

Dhenain, M., Ruffins, S. W., & Jacobs, R. E. (2001). Three-dimensional digital mouse atlas using high resolution MRI. *Developmental Biology*, *232*(2), 458–470. doi:10.1006/dbio.2001.0189 PMID:11401405

Esteban, C. H., & Schmitt, F. (2014). *Silhouette and stereo fusion for 3D object modeling. 3ds Max Projects: A Detailed Guide to Modeling, Texturing, Rigging, Animation and Lighting.*

Eyetronics. (2004). http://www.eyetronics.com

Gang, L., Wang, Z., & Quensheng, P. (2004). Generating Visual Hulls From Freely Moving Camera. *Journal of Computer-Aided Design & Computer Graphics*, *16*(11), 1501–1505.

Halim, S., & MohdSharuddin, I. (2004). Close Range Measurement and 3D Modeling. *1st International Symposium on Engineering Surveys for Construction Works and Structural Engineering.*

Hu, J. Y. (2004). The Application of Computer Software—3D Studio Max, Lightscape and V-Ray in the Environmental Artistic Expression. *Image Understanding*, *96*, 367–392.

Kajiya, J. T. (1986). *The rendering equation*. Academic Press.

Kriete, A., Breithecker, A., & Rau, W. (2001). 3D imaging of lung tissue by confocal microscopy and micro-CT. *Proceedings of SPIE - The International Society for Optical Engineering*, 469-476. 10.1117/12.434736

Levoy, M., Pulli, K., Curless, B., Rusinkiewicz, S., Koller, D., Pereira, L., Ginzton, M., Anderson, S., Davis, J., Ginsberg, J., Shade, J., & Fulk, D. (2000). The digital Michelangelo Project: 3D scanning of large statues. Siggraph 2000, 131-144.

Lian, Q., Li, D.-C., Tang, Y.-P., & Zhang, Y.-R. (2006). Computer modeling approach for a novel internal architecture of artificial bone. *CAD Computer Aided Design*, *38*(5), 507–514. doi:10.1016/j.cad.2005.12.001

Lin, T. H., Lan, C. C., Wang, C. H., & Chen, C. H. (2014). Study on realistic texture mapping for 3D models. *International Conference on Information Science, Electronics and Electrical Engineering (ISEEE)*, *3*, 1567-1571. 10.1109/InfoSEEE.2014.6946184

Montenegro, A. A., Carvalho, P. C. P., Velho, L., & Gattass, M. (2004). Space carving with a hand-held camera. *Proceedings of the XVII Brazilian Symposium on Computer Graphics and Image Processing (SIBGRAPI'04)*, 396-403. 10.1109/SIBGRA.2004.1352986

Mueller, Vereenooghe, Vergauwen, Van Gool, & Waelkens. (n.d.). Photo-realistic and detailed 3D modeling: the Antonine nymphaeum at Sagalassos (Turkey). *Computer Applications and Quantitative Methods in Archaeology (CAA): Beyond the artifact - Digital interpretation of the past*. http://www.vision.ee.ethz.ch/~pmueller/documents/caa04_pmueller.pdf

Murdock. (2014). *Autodesk 3ds Max 2014 Bible*. Academic Press.

Park, S.-Y., & Subbarao, M. (2005). A multiview 3D modeling system based on stereo vision techniques. *Machine Vision and Applications*, *16*(3), 148–156. doi:10.100700138-004-0165-2

Paul, Samanta, & Sanyal. (2011). Dynamic job Scheduling in Cloud Computing based on horizontal load balancing. *International Journal of Computer Technology and Applications, 2*(5), 1552-1556.

Paul, M., Samanta, D., & Sanyal, G. (2011). Dynamic job scheduling in cloud computing based on horizontal load balancing. *International Journal of Computer Technology and Applications*, 2(5), 1552–1556.

Paul, M., & Sanyal, G. (2011). Segmentation technique of SAR imagery using entropy. *International Journal of Computer Technology and Applications*, 2(5).

Sainz, M., Pajarola, R., Mercade, A., & Susin, A. (2004, July/August). A Simple Approach for Point-Based Object Capturing and Rendering. *IEEE Computer Graphics and Applications*, 24(4), 33. doi:10.1109/MCG.2004.1 PMID:15628083

Samanta, D. (2011). A novel statistical approach for segmentation of SAR Images. *Journal of Global Research in Computer Science*, 2(10), 9–13.

Samanta, D., & Paul, M. (2011). A Novel Approach of Entropy based Adaptive Thresholding Technique for Video Edge Detection. *Threshold (x, y)*, 1, 1.

Samanta, D., & Sanyal, G. (2011a). Automated Classification of SAR Images Using Moment. *International Journal of Computer Science Issues*, 8(6), 135.

Samanta, D., & Sanyal, G. (2011b). *Development of Adaptive Thresholding Technique for Classification of Synthetic Aperture Radar Images*. Academic Press.

Samanta, D., & Sanyal, G. (2011c). Development of edge detection technique for images using adaptive thresholding. *International Conference on Information Processing*, 671–676. 10.1007/978-3-642-22786-8_85

Samanta, D., & Sanyal, G. (2011d). SAR image segmentation using Color space clustering and Watersheds. *International Journal of Engineering Research and Applications*, 1(3), 997–999.

Samanta, D., & Ghosh, A. (2012). Automatic obstacle detection based on gaussian function in robocar. *J. Res. Eng. Appl. Sci*, 2(2), 354–363.

Samanta, D., & Sanyal, G. (2012). Segmentation technique of SAR imagery based on fuzzy c-means clustering. *IEEE-International Conference On Advances In Engineering, Science And Management (ICAESM-2012)*, 610–612.

Samanta, D., & Sanyal, G. (2012a). A novel approach of SAR image classification using color space clustering and watersheds. *2012 Fourth International Conference on Computational Intelligence and Communication Networks*, 237–240. 10.1109/CICN.2012.27

Samanta, D., & Sanyal, G. (2012c). An Approach of Segmentation Technique of SAR Images using Adaptive Thresholding Technique. *International Journal of Engineering Research & Technology (Ahmedabad)*, *1*(7).

Samanta, D., & Sanyal, G. (2012f). Novel Shannon's entropy based segmentation technique for SAR images. *International Conference on Information Processing*, 193–199. 10.1007/978-3-642-31686-9_22

Samanta, D., & Sanyal, G. (2012g). *SAR image classification using fuzzy CMeans*. Academic Press.

Samanta, D., & Sanyal, G. (2012h). Statistical approach for Classification of SAR Images. *International Journal of Soft Computing and Engineering (IJSCE)*, 2231–2307.

Samanta, D., & Sanyal, G. (2013). An Approach of Tabu Search for Unsupervised Classification for SAR Images. *Seven International Conference on Image and Signal Processing*.

Samanta, D., & Sanyal, G. (2012b). A novel approach of SAR image processing based on Hue, Saturation and Brightness (HSB). *Procedia Technology*, *4*, 584–588. doi:10.1016/j.protcy.2012.05.093

Samanta, D., & Sanyal, G. (2012d). Classification of SAR Images Based on Entropy. *Int. J. Inf. Technol. Comput. Sci*, *4*(12), 82–86. doi:10.5815/ijitcs.2012.12.09

Samanta, D., & Sanyal, G. (2012e). Novel approach of adaptive thresholding technique for edge detection in videos. *Procedia Engineering*, *30*, 283–288. doi:10.1016/j. proeng.2012.01.862

Sarti, S. T. (2002). Image based multiresolution implicit object modeling. *EURASIP Journal on Applied Signal Processing*, *10*, 1053–1066.

Sun, W., & Lal, P. (2002). Recent development on computer aided tissue engineering—A review. *Computer Methods and Programs in Biomedicine*, *67*(2), 85–103. doi:10.1016/S0169-2607(01)00116-X PMID:11809316

Sun, W., Starly, B., Nam, J., & Darling, A. (2005). Bio-CAD modeling and its applications in computer-aided tissue engineering. *Computer Aided Design*, *37*(11), 1097–1114. doi:10.1016/j.cad.2005.02.002

Tavares, J., Dutta, P., Dutta, S., & Samanta, D. (n.d.). *Cyber Intelligence and Information Retrieval*. Academic Press.

Toshihiro, A., Masayuki, K., & Naokazu, Y. (2005). 3D Modeling of Outdoor Environments by Integrating Omnidirectional Range and Color Images. *Proceedings of the Fifth International Conference on 3-D Digital Imaging and Modeling (3DIM'05)*.

Woop, S., Schmittler, J., & Slusallek, P. (2005). RPU: A Programmable Ray Processing Unit for Realtime Ray Tracing. *Siggraph 2005*.

Yang, Lee, Kim, & Kim. (2005). Adaptive Space Carving with Texture Mapping. *LNCS, 3482*, 1129-1138.

Yılmaz, Mülayim, & Atalay. (2002). Reconstruction of Three Dimensional Models from Real Images. *Proceedings of the First International Symposium on 3D Data Processing Visualization and Transmission (3DPVT.02)*.

Chapter 2
Constructive Outlook of Cafeteria Using Autodesk 3ds Max 3D Modelling and Rendering

Dinesh Sharma
DXC Technology, Bangalore, India

ABSTRACT

In this modern world, we intend to modernize everything and try to get everything at the tip of our fingers. It has been changed with technology based on individual creativity. In this chapter, we see a cafeteria that has been rendered to a new version with the help of Autodesk 3ds max. Autodesk 3ds Max is a professional 3D computer graphics program for making 3D animations, models, games, and images. As we all know, eye-catching visuals, ambiance attracts all kinds of crowds. The structure of the architecture, menu format, lighting effects, seating arrangement, serving ideas have been rendered here. Keeping the world crisis in mind, an approach to the same issue is shown. This chapter aims at designing a cafeteria with enhanced models with material effects. The process of rendering the cafeteria is shown in detail.

INTRODUCTION

Advanced technology has been a boon in many ways to humans. We construct various things according to our wants and needs. When we talk about this paper, we can see that rendering the cafeteria through Autodesk 3Ds Max is a process that gives a neat interior planning of a cafeteria. This includes manual planning and technology

DOI: 10.4018/978-1-6684-4139-8.ch002

processing through which a model of the cafeteria is created (A. S. Baskoro et al. 2015)(H. Esmaeili et al. 2014). Autodesk 3Ds Max is a professional 3D computer graphics tool for creating 3D animations models, games, and photographs (Natephra, W. et al. 2017). It was previously known as the 3D studio and 3D studio Max. Autodesk Media and Entertainment created and produced it. Video game makers, various TV commercial studios, and architectural visualization studios all use it (L. L. Khoroshko et al. 2018) (Samanta, Debabrata, & Sanyal, G. (2011b)).

This paper aims to give a broader perspective of a cafe that is designed for all kinds of crowds as in from teens to adults, for example, college students who want to chill and have a group discussion or a bunch of people who wants to do friendly chat with their colleagues or friends, for couples, every kind of a crowd can have their way. Ambiance and visuals support everything (Samanta, Debabrata, & Sanyal, G. (2012g))(S. Vu et al. 2018). Indeed, we know small details also play major roles in designing a cafe. Due to COVID-19, there is no manual menu that is given to customers to place an order they can just look at the wall and order whatever they wish to choose from the menu, this can be a unique way of having the menu, many people have their websites or apps to order but this can be hustle free. After the rendering effect, these are the changes available (Deryabin, N.B. et al. 2017) (Samanta, Debabrata, & Sanyal, G. (2011a)).

OBJECTS CREATED FOR CAFETERIA

Flooring: Created using the plane under Standard Primitives and drag it around on the surface as required. Then, using the material editor, select and import the required texture and select Satin Varnished Wood finishing (W. Sun et al. 2005) (Samanta, Debabrata, Paul, M., & Sanyal, G. (2011)). Then, by using the UVM Map select the length and the width as required.

Lighting: The lights used on the roof are created using a target light and the brightness / luminosity is adjusted so that the lights, after rendering gives a realistic view. The lights on the left wall have been created using free light so that it shouldn't interfere with the lights on the roof. Hence, we create a more realistic view (Hegazy, M. et al. 2022) (Samanta, Debabrata, & Paul, M. (2011)).

Mirror: Created using an ellipse under splines and has been extruded and modified using editable poly. To top it off, another ellipse has been added on top of the first ellipse to give it a realistic view (Soon-Yong Park et al. 2005)(Samanta, Debabrata, & Sanyal, G. (2012f)).

Seating: Created using a box and edited using editable poly and the look has been modified by adjusting the edge, polygon and vertex function. Finally, it has been cloned as to the required numbers. The single seat near the counter of the shop has been created using a cone under Standard Primitives and modified it using editable poly. The circular seat is created using a circle and adjusting it to its desired size and has been cloned to its required numbers (YeeWa Choy et al. 2012)(Z. Pezeshki et al. 2017).

Wall: Created using 2D box under Standard Primitives and adjust the height and length as required. Then, change the color as per the required choice. The wall which is seen right in front of the camera has been decorated as a menu option using material editor and matte paint as a finisher (Wei Sun et al. 2002)(Samanta, Debabrata, & Sanyal, G. (2012h)).

CONFIGURING THE REFERENCE IMAGE

To construct a complex model given in this paper it is a cafeteria, it requires a lot of changes for which Fig.1 shows Flowchart diagram of the 3D Animation Model. Fig.2 shows 3D Animated Mirror with a wooden frame.

CREATING AN ELLIPTICAL MIRROR WITH A SQUARE SHAPED FRAME

The Mirror is created using the rectangle object which is available under Splines. Select the Left view amongst the four view quadrants, and then create a rectangle. The thickness of the wooden frame is created depending on the thickness which usually an average photo frame has. It can be modified as per the requirement (D. Tsipotas et al. 2015)(Samanta, Debabrata, & Ghosh, A. (2012)). But it is recommended to keep it to an average size. Then, to create the mirror inside the frame, select the same view and create a sphere under Splines. Select the line which has been created as a sphere and create an exact instance of that sphere. The second sphere should be placed inside the first one. Once that is done, enable the rendering option for both the spheres as it is just a line (M. T. Valdez et al. 2016)(Samanta, Debabrata, & Sanyal, G. (2012e)). Then, select the second sphere and extrude it, adjust the size and alignment of the spherical mirror so that it should be placed at the center. Once, that is completed. Select the Rectangular frame and the Spherical Mirror and make an exact instance of it four times (D. Fritsch et al. 2017)(Ulaş Yılmaz et al. 2002). Select the material editor tab by pressing 'm' key and choose the unused sphere. Select the standard material and on the maps roll out, click the map button for reflection. In the material browser, select the flat mirror and click 'ok'. The mirror material has been created and it will be added on the sphere by using assign on selection. The spherical mirror has been created (Samanta, Debabrata, & Sanyal, G. (2012d))(M. R. Filho et al. 2011).

Figure 1. Flowchart diagram of the 3D animation model

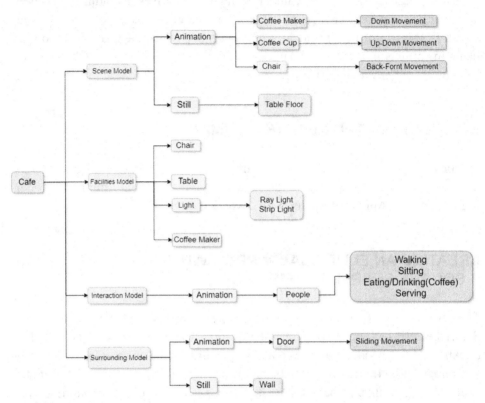

CREATING A CHAIR

The design of a chair should be appropriate to fit in the model which has been created. In this case, it's a cafeteria. To create a chair, you must follow these steps as mentioned or change the setting/modify as per your requirements (H. Esmaeili et al. 2017)(Samanta, Debabrata, & Sanyal, G. (2011c)). The steps are- Create a square box using the box option under standard primitives. Modify the box creating various segments and removing and adjusting the segments to get the required shape as shown in the above figure. After the desired shape has appeared of the chair, remove the remaining edges / segments (Yoo-Kil Yang et al. 2005)(Samanta, Deababrata, & Sanyal, G. (2012)). For the foot of the chair create the shape of four legs of a chair using line under splines section. Fig.3 shows 3D Animated Chair with wooden legs and a plastic seating space.

Figure 2. 3D animated mirror with a wooden frame

CREATING A WALL LAMP

The wall lamp has been created by combining different objects. The lamp support has been created by using the cone. The cone has been created and the shape has

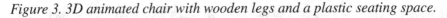

Figure 3. 3D animated chair with wooden legs and a plastic seating space.

been changed by using the edit mesh option. The cone segments have been removed alternatively so that the lamp can be seen. As for the lamp and the wall stand, the chamfer cylinder has been created and the sides has been modified using the edit poly (Günther-Diringer et al. 2016)(Samanta, Debabrata, & Sanyal, G., 2011d). Then the grills have been created using the freehand tool from splines and increased the radial thickness. As for the wall support, the sphere has been used and modified it into semi-hemisphere using the edit poly modifier. The cone has been created with similar shape to the lamp support and by using the self-illumination, the light has been produced (U. Castellani et al. 2005)(Samanta, Debabrata, & Sanyal, G., 2012b). The lighting effect is done by using the spotlight option and the target is given to the wall so that the lamp can show the light effect at rendering. Fig.4 shows 3D Animated Wall Lamp with a curved Design.

CREATING A TABLE

The table is created taking in consideration the design of the chair because the table and the chair design should match. Else, an odd object to design ratio will be there which will create an imbalance to the model. The chair has been created in three parts. The first part, the hexagonal head of the table is created under the extended primitive's section (Ardakani, H.K. et al. 2020)(Samanta, Debabrata, & Sanyal, G.,2013). Create a hexagon and divide it into the required segments such that the two blocks of the hexagon can be extruded to make the two legs of the table. Once, the desired shape and design of the hexagon (the head of the table is made). Extrude the feasible two segments from the hexagon to make the legs of the table. The third, part is the bottom stand of the table, to create that. Select the box under Standard Primitives and create a box with respect to the size of the hexagon (Head of the table) and the legs. Once, the base stand of the table is created (Kwon, Y.M. et al. 2017). Open the material editor and select the matte wood texture, upload a wooden image, and apply the texture to the object (Manson, A. et al. 2015)(Yusuf Arayici et al. 2005). Hence, the table has been created. Fig.5 shows 3D Animated Table with a wooden finish.

CREATING A DESIGNER CABINET

The Designer Cabinet is created using a box which is available under Standard primitives. Select the top view in one of the four quadrants, and then increase the length of the box according to the required choice. Divide the height segments of the box into 20 segments. Then, in the parameters section, check the Limit Effect section and bend the box using the bend option under the modifier. Change the upper limit of the object as it is required to get a roof type texture (Nadeem, A. et al. 2015). Once the roof is popped out. Decrease the angle to such an extent that the extended roof part of the object is at a completely right angle to the straight object. Once the desired shape has been acquired, select the object as editable poly, and select

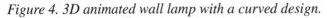

Figure 4. 3D animated wall lamp with a curved design.

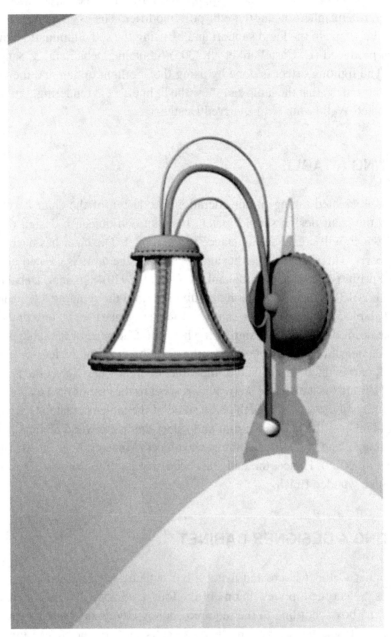

the vertex. Then either extend or reshape a particular vertex as the roof is required (Lungershausen, U. et al. 2013). For the cutout, which is visible in the picture, as the object has already been divided into segments? Select the following segment, where you want an empty space and extrude it so that, the object in that section disappears. After that is done using material editor, select the kind of texture, i.e., Ceramic, Matte, Rubber, etc., which is required. Apply the material and choose the pattern which is required by importing a texture from the desktop. Then once, the material pattern has been applied to the object, select the UVM Map in the modifier and modify the texture of design of the pattern imported (Samanta, Debabrata, & Sanyal, G. (2012c)). Fig.6 shows 3D Animated Designer Cabinet.

Figure 5. 3D animated table with a wooden finish.

Figure 6. 3D animated designer cabinet

RENDERED MODEL

All the objects that are complicated have been explained above. This rendered image above is a complete showcase of the model and it is a real-life example of how it can be created. There are a lot of steps that has to be followed and the creation of objects also needs to be followed in a serial wise. First, the walls and the floor need to be created. After which the designer cabinet the reception desk should be done. As, these are the items which are complicated to create, after which the wall mirrors

40

Figure 7. 3D animated rendered image

are to be created as assembling all these things will take time and is a very difficult task when done at the end (Samanta, Debabrata., 2011). The material texture of the floor should be kept as glossy wood and then add the texture, the walls are to be made as a matte rubber to prevent the shining affect to take place. As if it does, the brightness will be immense which will make a wrong impact on the rendered image (Samanta, Debabrata, & Sanyal, G, 2012a). After which the coffee machine, the high seater chairs, the wall lamps, and the ceiling lights are to created/add. The menu of this cafeteria is designed in a unique way such that the customer doesn't need to wait for the waiter to come. Finally, once these things are done and the materials have been added with the desired color and texture, the tissue stacks and the roof of the model is added (Toshihiro ASAI et al. 2005). Finally, the target camera is added in such a way that all the work put into the model and the detail should reflect in one rendered image/picture. Depending on the desired zoom/focus on the model, place the camera and use the Scale line Renderer for this model as the amount of texture and details are present (Van de Perre, G. et al. 2019). It will take a lot of time to render this model fully in the Arnold Renderer. Fig. 7 shows 3D Animated Rendered Image. Fig.8 shows 3D Animated Rendered Image.

The above displayed second rendered image is just a modified version of the first rendered image above. The only difference is that a bookshelf has been added to the model to make it look more professional and it would be more comfortable for the people who like reading books in the morning. The pattern of the designer cabinet has been changed and the tissues from the table have been removed (Woop, Sven

Figure 8. 3D Animated rendered image

et al. 2005). The target camera is places a little upwards than the previous rendered image. This image is viewed in the High-Quality feature and not rendered.

CONCLUSION

The given paper explains a cafeteria that serves the purpose of a cafe to all types of the crowd, which is rendered using 3ds Max. Its default rendering method is scanline rendering. Over time, advanced capabilities such as global lighting, radiosity, and ray tracing have been introduced to the scanline. Objects can be animated along curves with alignment, banking, velocity, smoothness, looping controls, and along surfaces with alignment controls. Animate the weight via a weight path-controlled animation between various curves. Objects can be forced to interact with other objects in a variety of ways, including by looking at them, orienting them in different coordinate spaces, and joining them at different times. These limits also allow for the animated weighing of several targets. This paper elaborates how and what components are required to complete a complex model of a cafeteria after that has been through the process of rendering.

REFERENCES

Arayici, Y., & Hamilton, A. (2005). Modeling 3D Scanned Data to Visualize the Built Environment. *Proceedings of the Ninth International Conference on Information Visualisation*, 509-514. 10.1109/IV.2005.82

Ardakani, H. K., Mousavinia, A., & Safaei, F. (2020). Four points: One-pass geometrical camera calibration algorithm. *The Visual Computer*, *36*(2), 413–424. doi:10.100700371-019-01632-7

Baskoro, A. S., & Haryanto, I. (2015). Development of travel speed detection method in welding simulator using augmented reality. *2015 International Conference on Advanced Computer Science and Information Systems (ICACSIS)*, 269-273. 10.1109/ICACSIS.2015.7415194

Castellani, U., Fusiello, A., Murino, V., Papaleo, L., Puppo, E., & Pittore, M. (2005). A complete system for on-line 3D modelling from acoustic images. *Signal Processing Image Communication*, *20*(9-10), 832–852. doi:10.1016/j.image.2005.02.003

Choy, Lim, Wang, & Chan. (2012). Development CT-based three-dimensional complex skull model for Finite element analysis. *2012 IEEE Conference on Sustainable Utilization and Development in Engineering and Technology (STUDENT)*, 135-139. 10.1109/STUDENT.2012.6408383

Deryabin, N. B., Zhdanov, D. D., & Sokolov, V. G. (2017). Embedding the script language into optical simulation software. *Programming and Computer Software*, *43*(1), 13–23. doi:10.1134/S0361768817010029

Esmaeili, H., Thwaites, H., & Woods, P. C. (2017). Workflows and Challenges Involved in Creation of Realistic Immersive Virtual Museum, Heritage, and Tourism Experiences: A Comprehensive Reference for 3D Asset Capturing. *2017 13th International Conference on Signal-Image Technology & Internet-Based Systems (SITIS)*, 465-472. 10.1109/SITIS.2017.82

Esmaeili, H., Woods, P. C., & Thwaites, H. (2014). Realisation of virtualised architectural heritage. *2014 International Conference on Virtual Systems & Multimedia (VSMM)*, 94-101. 10.1109/VSMM.2014.7136676

Filho, M. R., Negrão, N. M., & Damasceno, R. R. (2011). SwImax: A Web Tool Using Virtual Reality for Teaching the WiMAX Protocol. *2011 XIII Symposium on Virtual Reality*, 217-224. 10.1109/SVR.2011.27

Fritsch, D., & Klein, M. (2017). 3D and 4D modeling for AR and VR app developments. *2017 23rd International Conference on Virtual System & Multimedia (VSMM),* 1-8. 10.1109/VSMM.2017.8346270

Günther-Diringer, D. (2016). Historisches 3D-Stadtmodell von Karlsruhe. *J. Cartogr. Geogr. Inf., 66,* 66–71. doi:10.1007/BF03545207

Hegazy, M., Yasufuku, K., & Abe, H. (2022). An interactive approach to investigate brightness perception of daylighting in Immersive Virtual Environments: Comparing subjective responses and quantitative metrics. *Building Simulation, 15*(1), 41–68. doi:10.100712273-021-0798-3

Khoroshko, L. L., Ukhov, P. A., & Keyno, P. P. (2018). *Development of a Laboratory Workshop for Open Online Courses Based on 3D Computer Graphics and Multimedia. In 2018 Learning With MOOCS.* LWMOOCS. doi:10.1109/LWMOOCS.2018.8534678

Kwon, Y. M., Lee, Y. A., & Kim, S. J. (2017). Case study on 3D printing education in fashion design coursework. *Fash Text, 4*(1), 26. doi:10.118640691-017-0111-3

Lungershausen, U., Heinrich, C., & Duttmann, R. (2013). Turning Human-nature Interaction into 3D Landscape Scenes: An Approach to Communicate Geoarchaeological Research. *J. Cartogr. Geogr. Inf., 63,* 269–275. doi:10.1007/BF03546142

Manson, A., Poyade, M., & Rea, P. (2015). A recommended workflow methodology in the creation of an educational and training application incorporating a digital reconstruction of the cerebral ventricular system and cerebrospinal fluid circulation to aid anatomical understanding. *BMC Medical Imaging, 15*(1), 44. doi:10.118612880-015-0088-6 PMID:26482126

Nadeem, A., Wong, A. K. D., & Wong, F. K. W. (2015). Bill of Quantities with 3D Views Using Building Information Modeling. *Arabian Journal for Science and Engineering, 40*(9), 2465–2477. doi:10.100713369-015-1657-2

Natephra, W., Motamedi, A., Fukuda, T., & Yabuki, N. (2017). Integrating building information modeling and virtual reality development engines for building indoor lighting design. *Vis. in Eng., 5*(1), 19. doi:10.118640327-017-0058-x

Park, S.-Y., & Subbarao, M. (2005). A multiview 3D modeling system based on stereo vision techniques. *Machine Vision and Applications, 16*(3), 148–156. doi:10.100700138-004-0165-2

Paul, M., & Sanyal, G. (2011). Segmentation technique of SAR imagery using entropy. *International Journal of Computer Technology and Applications*, 2(5).

Pezeshki, Z., Soleimani, A., & Darabi, A. (2017). 3Ds MAX to FEM for building thermal distribution: A case study. *2017 3rd Iranian Conference on Intelligent Systems and Signal Processing (ICSPIS)*, 110-115. 10.1109/ICSPIS.2017.8311599

Samanta, D., & Paul, M. (2011). A Novel Approach of Entropy based Adaptive Thresholding Technique for Video Edge Detection. *Threshold (x, y)*, 1, 1.

Samanta, D. (2011). A novel statistical approach for segmentation of SAR Images. *Journal of Global Research in Computer Science*, 2(10), 9–13.

Samanta, D., & Sanyal, G. (2011a). Automated Classification of SAR Images Using Moment. *International Journal of Computer Science Issues*, 8(6), 135.

Samanta, D., & Sanyal, G. (2011b). *Development of Adaptive Thresholding Technique for Classification of Synthetic Aperture Radar Images*. Academic Press.

Samanta, D., & Sanyal, G. (2011c). Development of edge detection technique for images using adaptive thresholding. *International Conference on Information Processing*, 671–676. 10.1007/978-3-642-22786-8_85

Samanta, D., & Sanyal, G. (2011d). SAR image segmentation using Color space clustering and Watersheds. *International Journal of Engineering Research and Applications*, 1(3), 997–999.

Samanta, D., & Sanyal, G. (2012). Segmentation technique of SAR imagery based on fuzzy c-means clustering. *IEEE-International Conference On Advances In Engineering, Science And Management (ICAESM-2012)*, 610–612.

Samanta, D., & Ghosh, A. (2012). Automatic obstacle detection based on gaussian function in robocar. *J. Res. Eng. Appl. Sci*, 2(2), 354–363.

Samanta, D., & Sanyal, G. (2012a). A novel approach of SAR image classification using color space clustering and watersheds. *2012 Fourth International Conference on Computational Intelligence and Communication Networks*, 237–240. 10.1109/CICN.2012.27

Samanta, D., & Sanyal, G. (2012c). An Approach of Segmentation Technique of SAR Images using Adaptive Thresholding Technique. *International Journal of Engineering Research & Technology (Ahmedabad)*, 1(7).

Samanta, D., & Sanyal, G. (2012f). Novel Shannon's entropy based segmentation technique for SAR images. *International Conference on Information Processing*, 193–199. 10.1007/978-3-642-31686-9_22

Samanta, D., & Sanyal, G. (2012g). *SAR image classification using fuzzy CMeans*. Academic Press.

Samanta, D., & Sanyal, G. (2012h). Statistical approach for Classification of SAR Images. *International Journal of Soft Computing and Engineering (IJSCE)*, 2231–2307.

Samanta, D., & Sanyal, G. (2013). An Approach of Tabu Search for Unsupervised Classification for SAR Images. *Seven International Conference on Image and Signal Processing*.

Samanta, D., & Sanyal, G. (2012b). A novel approach of SAR image processing based on Hue, Saturation and Brightness (HSB). *Procedia Technology*, 4, 584–588. doi:10.1016/j.protcy.2012.05.093

Samanta, D., & Sanyal, G. (2012d). Classification of SAR Images Based on Entropy. *Int. J. Inf. Technol. Comput. Sci*, 4(12), 82–86. doi:10.5815/ijitcs.2012.12.09

Samanta, D., & Sanyal, G. (2012e). Novel approach of adaptive thresholding technique for edge detection in videos. *Procedia Engineering*, 30, 283–288. doi:10.1016/j.proeng.2012.01.862

Sun, W., & Lal, P. (2002). Pallavi Lal. Recent development on computer aided tissue engineering—A review. *Computer Methods and Programs in Biomedicine*, 67(2), 85–103. doi:10.1016/S0169-2607(01)00116-X PMID:11809316

Sun, W., Starly, B., Nam, J., & Darling, A. (2005). Bio-CAD modeling and its applications in computer-aided tissue engineering. *Computer Aided Design*, 37(11), 1097–1114. doi:10.1016/j.cad.2005.02.002

Tavares, J., Dutta, P., Dutta, S., & Samanta, D. (n.d.). *Cyber Intelligence and Information Retrieval*. Academic Press.

Toshihiro, A., Masayuki, K., & Naokazu, Y. (2005). 3D Modeling of Outdoor Environments by Integrating Omnidirectional Range and Color Images. *Proceedings of the Fifth International Conference on 3-D Digital Imaging and Modeling (3DIM'05)*.

Tsipotas, D., & Spathopoulou, V. (2015). An assessment of research on 3D digital representation of ancient Greek furniture, using surviving archaelological artefacts. *Digital Heritage*, 2015, 325–328. doi:10.1109/DigitalHeritage.2015.7419515

Valdez, M. T., Ferreira, C. M., & Barbosa, F. P. M. (2016). 3D virtual laboratory for teaching circuit theory — A virtual learning environment (VLE). *2016 51st International Universities Power Engineering Conference (UPEC),* 1-4. 10.1109/UPEC.2016.8114126

Van de Perre, G., De Beir, A., Cao, H. L., Esteban, P. G., Lefeber, D., & Vanderborght, B. (2019). Studying Design Aspects for Social Robots Using a Generic Gesture Method. *International Journal of Social Robotics, 11*(4), 651–663. doi:10.100712369-019-00518-x

Vu, S. (2018). Recreating Little Manila through a Virtual Reality Serious Game. *2018 3rd Digital Heritage International Congress (DigitalHERITAGE) held jointly with 2018 24th International Conference on Virtual Systems & Multimedia (VSMM 2018),* 1-4. 10.1109/DigitalHeritage.2018.8810082

Woop, S., Schmittler, J., & Slusallek, P. (2005). RPU: A Programmable Ray Processing Unit for Realtime Ray Tracing. *SIGGRAPH 2005.*

Yang, Lee, Kim, & Kim. (2005). Adaptive Space Carving with Texture Mapping. *LNCS, 3482,* 1129-1138.

Yılmaz, Mülayim, & Atalay. (2002). Reconstruction of Three Dimensional Models from Real Images. *Proceedings of the First International Symposium on 3D Data Processing Visualization and Transmission (3DPVT.02).*

Chapter 3
Editing Shapes With Meshes for 3D Modelling in Autodesk Platform

Ritwika Das Gupta
CHRIST University, India

Daksh Agarwal
University of Pennsylvania, USA

ABSTRACT

Setting up the sources, working with editable poly, information in the inside of the kitchen design, and applying turbo-smooth and symmetry modifiers are all detailed in the process for generating a 3D model. In addition to lighting the scene and setting up the renderer, the method materials are introduced to the model. Methods and techniques for rendering are also defined. The final rendering was created by combining several pictures. The research aims to create a design that incorporates materials to enhance models. The shapes used were cylinder, sphere, box, plane, and spline. Modifiers include editable poly, editable spline, and UVW map. Finally, the authors used a material editor and target lighting to improve the model. The method of using meshes to create model is also used in this research. A mesh is a type of three-dimensional geometric model.

INTRODUCTION

Autodesk 3Ds Max is a graphics program for making 3D models, animations, games, and images. Autodesk Media and Entertainment produced it. It has the capabilities

DOI: 10.4018/978-1-6684-4139-8.ch003

to model in 3D and has flexible plugin architecture. It is majorly used by video game developers and TV commercial studios (Guha, A., et al. 2021) (Anselmo Antunes Montenegro et al. 2004). It can also give movie effects to animations. It contains various tools and modifiers to modify a single standard object to different realistic models. It helps in creating natural textures for models and mapping them correctly to the objects. It helps in providing proper light and shadow effects to the models. It has different rendering options for making the models flexible to render. It has new icons, a customizable user interface, and its scripting language (Chatterjee, R. et al. 2021).

WORKING PROCEDURE OF MESHES IN AUTODESK MAX

A mesh is a type of three-dimensional geometric model. A basic shape in the mesh is made up of vertices and edges (Matthew Brand et al. 2004). The renderable surface is made up of faces or polygons. Examples of basic standard primitive meshes are sphere, teapot, etc. Each mesh can be edited to make a new realistic model using different modifiers and tools. Each face, vertices, edges, and polygons of a mesh can be edited separately (Althar, R. R. et al. 2021) (Kajiya, James T et al. 1986).

VARIOUS MODELS INCLUDED IN THE KITCHEN DESIGN

The complete kitchen design was achieved by using various modifiers and tools. The major target was to give realistic look to each object and that is done by various approaches mentioned below. Walls- The walls (shown in Figure 1) were made by three boxes aligning them properly and assigning different material using the material editor. Materials were fitted properly using UVW map modifier (Samanta, D. et al. 2022) (Podder, S. K. et al. 2022).

Refrigerator- Refrigerator is shown in figure 2. The refrigerator was made using a box, whose front face was divided into two faces using connect option of edit Poly modifier. These two faces where extruded and rescaled to form a fridge like structure. All the corner edges were chamfered using chamfer option in edit Poly modifier to make the corners smooth (Lin, T. H. et al. 2014) (Samanta, D. et al. 2022). The handle of the refrigerator was made using a box whose left and right faces were removed and shell modifier was used to give thickness to the handles. Turbo smooth modifier was used to make the handles smooth. The lock of the refrigerator was made using a cylinder which was extruded and rescaled to make a lock like structure. The topmost face of the lock was then extruded inwards to make the whole of the lock. To create a small design on the lock each edge of the

Figure 1. The final mesh of the walls.

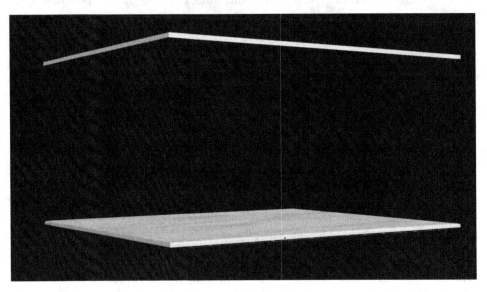

lock very extruded inwards. Turbo smooth modifier was used to smooth the final lock (Bhattacharya, A. et al. 2022). The legs of the refrigerator were made using a cylinder and by extruding and rescaling the cylinder. This leg was cloned to form four legs of the refrigerator (Biswal, A. K. et al. 2021).

Storage shelves and ingredients storage containers: The storage shelves and the ingredients storage containers (shown in Figure 3) are a part of kitchen storage models. The shelves were created by box which is a standard primitive. The top right shelf is a box. Firstly, the top face of the box was extruded and rescaled to make a design (Carlos Hernández Esteban et al. 2014) (Dhenain M et al. 2001). Each time after extruding the amount of rescaling was different in this way the top design was created. Similarly, the lower face was extruded and rescaled differently to create the design. The box was then divided into six segments using connect option of edit Poly modifier. Each segment of the division was extruded inwards and the corner of the shelf was extruded inwards as well. Then a square division was created in between each segmented area using connect option of edit Poly modifier, these square edges were extruded inwards and rescaled down to make the face smaller. This smaller face was then extruded outwards and rescaled down again. This process of extruding and rescaling was continued to create the designs on the shelves (Gurunath, R. et al. 2021). At the bottom center of the shelf, the bottom face was moved upwards using move tool to create the design. At the bottom front face of the shelf the edges were connected in such a way that it gets divided into two segments, one smaller segment at the top and one larger segment below. The edges of these segments were further

Figure 2. The final mesh of the refrigerator model.

connected using connect option of edit Poly modifier to create a square face. The square face in the larger partitioned area was extruded and rescaled in the similar way as mentioned above and square face on the smaller partitioned area was extruded inwards to create a hollow shelf. Similarly, the top left shelf was created using a box and extruding and re scaling faces which were divided using connect option of edit Poly modifier. The ingredients containers inside the hollow shelves were created using cylinder. The cylinder was extruded and rescaled to increase its size and then again extruded and re scaled down and then extruded bit by bit and re scaled down to create a container like shape (Kelly L. Murdock et al. 2014). Then an oil tank which was an extended primitive was used as cap of the container and oil tank along with the container was grouped together when the entire container was formed. This grouped container was then cloned several times to create many containers and they were properly set within the hollow shelves. The lower shelf was made by a single box which was extruded to create an L shape. This L shaped box was then divided into various segments using connect option of edit Poly modifier. The top face of the box was extruded upwards and each division on the box was connected by edges to create different square faces according to the design. These square faced edges were then extruded inwards an outwards and scaled appropriately to create shelf and drawer designs. A sphere was used to create the knobs of the shelves; this fear was rescaled according to the knob size and placed in correct position for creating knobs of the shelves (Kriete A. et al. 2001). The wood material and marble material was created as a standard material using the material editor tool (M Paul et al. 2011). These materials were images of a wood texture and marble texture which were added to the diffuse option present in the material editor tool. These materials were then assigned to each face of the shelves and properly aligned using UVW map modifier. In the UVW map modifier box option was used to align the wood texture. The glass material used at the shelves was made by ray caster material in material editor by increasing the glossiness, specular level and transparency to give a glass look. Then the entire rack of container was cloned to make many racks and placed in its perfect position. These racks were mapped with a wood texture, each container was mapped with the silver texture and the caps of the containers well mapped with shiny black texture (Yusuf Arayici et al. 2005).

Mixer grinder- The mixer grinder (shown in figure 4) is a part of working area model. It was created using a cylinder which was extruded using edit poly modifier and face extrude. The top face was extruded and rescaled have until a Dome shape was formed which was the base of the mixer grinder. The top utensil of the mixer grinder was again created using a cylinder and extruded to form a utensil structure. The cover of the utensil was created in the similar manner. The topmost face of the utensil was removed a shell modifier was used to give thickness to the utensil. The plug was made using a cylinder, by cutting the top face of the cylinder and creating edges so that it forms a handle of the plug. This face created by the cut edges is then extruded to form a plug like structure. The plug pins were made using cylinders and

Figure 3. The final mesh of the storage shelves and ingredients storage containers models.

these pins were grouped together with the plug (Ulaş Yılmaz et al. 2002). A line shape was used to create the wire of the plug. This line shape was then modified using lathe modifier to convert 2D line two or 3D wire (Soon-Yong Park et al. 2005). All these objects are aligned properly to make the final mixer structure. Turbo smooth modifier was used to smooth the entire mixer grinder model. The shiny gray and shiny white materials were made by ray caster material in material editor by increasing the glossiness and specular level. For reflection under maps option as reflection material fall off was used and its mix curve pointer was decreased to a certain level from the center, to create a proper reflection (W. Sun et al. 2005). The black shiny material for base of the mixer was made using the material editor. For this ray caster material was used, the glossiness and the specular level was increased to give it appropriate shine. The glass material which is the cover of the mixer utensil was made using recaster material that's shine and glossiness was increased and transparency was increased to a certain level along with the increase in level of illumination. For reflection, fall of texture was mapped do they reflect option. All these materials were mapped to their respective objects (Wei Sun et al. 2002) (Toshihiro ASAI et al. 2005).

Washbasin and hand towel- The washbasin and hand towel (shown in Figure 5). The washbasin was created by extrude option available in edit Poly modifier, the top face off the lower shelf was segmented and for the sub segmented to create a face which will fit to form a washbasin. This face was then extruded inwards and rescaled to reduce the size of its base (Samanta, D. et al. 2021). This was how the washbasin was designed. The tap of the washbasin was made using a cylinder which was extruded and bent using bend modifier. The top of the tap was made by a sphere

Figure 4. The final mesh of the mixer grinder model.

which was rescaled to form a top structure and combined with a cylinder to form a perfect taps' top (Sarti, S. Tubaro et al. 2002) (Eapen, N. G. et al. 2022). The holder of that tap was made my extruding a cylinder and re scaling it as well as combining it with oil tank, which is a compound primitive. All these objects were placed in a proper position and grouped together as a tap. The hand towel was made using a plane which was extruded as required. This extruded plane was then segmented into many segments. Each edge of the segments was moved outwards and inwards alternatively. Turbo smooth modifier was used to smooth these models. The shiny gray and shiny white materials were made by ray caster material in material editor by increasing the glossiness and specular level. All these materials were mapped to their respective objects (Raghavendra Rao, A. et al. 2022).

Dishes, cooking pans, and teapot: The dishes cooking pans and teapot (shown in Figure 6) are a part of utensils models (U. Castellani, et al. 2005). The dish rack was

Figure 5. The final mesh of the washbasin and hand towel models.

made using a box which was segmented using connects option of edit Poly modifier, each segmented face was alternatively removed. The back, front and the bottom face of the box was removed and shell modifier was used to give thickness to the entire rack (Miguel Sainz et al. 2004). A dish was made using a cylinder which was extruded and rescaled to form a dish like structure. This dish was then cloned into several dishes and placed appropriately within the rack (Liu Gang et al. 2004). The cooking pan was made using a cylinder, whose top face was extruded and rescaled to make it larger. This process of scaling and extruding continued until the base of the pan was formed. The cap of the pan was again formed by a cylinder, whose top face was extruded and re scaled to make it smaller until a cap like structure was formed. The teapot is a standard primitive used directly (Yoo-Kil Yang et al. 2005).

Drinking glasses, water bottles- The drinking glasses and the water bottles is shown in figure 7. The drinking glass was made using a cylinder which was extruded and rescaled to form a glass like structure. The top face of the glasses was then removed and shell modifier was used to give thickness to the glass. A single glass was then cloned to form several glasses as shown in the figure. The water bottles were made using a cylinder which was extruded and rescaled until it forms a water bottle structure. The cap of the water bottle was made by an oil tank which is a compound primitive (Hegde, D. S. et al. 2022). This cap and the bottle base were group together and cloned to form two water bottles. The glass material was made using recaster material that's shine and glossiness was increased and transparency was increased to a certain level along with the increase in level of illumination (Gurunath, R. et al. 2021). For reflection under maps option as reflection material fall off was used and its mix curve pointer was decreased to a certain level from the center, to create a proper reflection. Different colors were given to the object using the material editor tool and providing different color materials with slight shine onto the colors. The

Figure 6. The final mesh of the dishes, cooking pans, and teapot models.

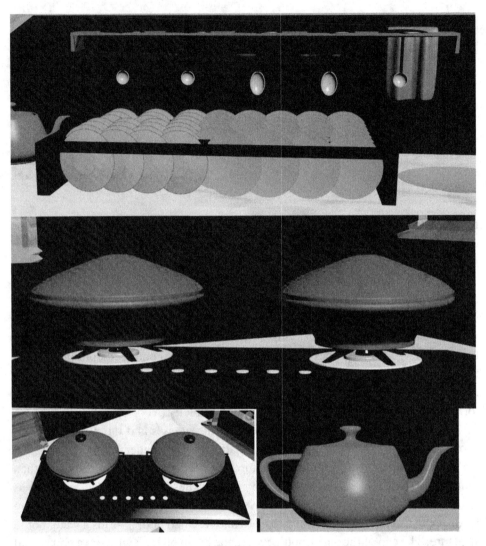

shine was given by using ray caster material and by increasing the glossiness and specular level. All these materials were mapped to their respective objects.

Cooking utensils, spoon set- The cooking utensils and spoon set (shown in Figure 8) are a part of utensils modifier. The rack for the cooking utensils was made by a box. The top, bottom, front and back faces were removed and the top face was segmented into several segments using connect option of edit Poly modifier. The alternative segmented faces were removed and shell modifier was used to give thickness to the rack structure. Square faces what created using connects option off

Figure 7. The final mesh of the drinking glasses, water bottles models.

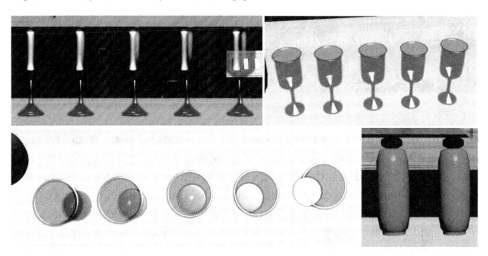

edit Poly modifier on the top of one segment of the rack (M. Levoy et al. 2000). These square faces were removed to create whole like structures on the rack. The utensils were made by a cylinder which was extruded to make a utensil handle and the top portion of the utensil was made by a sphere. By removing half of the sphere, a semi sphere was created and thickness was provided using shell modifier. The top area of the utensil was made by re scaling a sphere using a scale tool. All these objects are grouped together after placing them in correct position. A single utensil was then cloned to make many utensils. For making the spoon set, the cooking utensils were scaled down to make them smaller and look like spoons. These spoons were mirrored and cloned and align into correct position. The jar of the spoon set was made by extruding a cylinder and rescaling them accordingly so that it takes a jar shape. The top face of the jar was removed and shell modifier was used to give thickness to the jar. The shiny gray (steel material) was also made by ray caster material in material editor by increasing the glossiness and specular level (Halim SETAN et al. 2004). For reflection under maps option as reflection material fall off was used and its mix curve pointer was decreased to a certain level from the center, to create a proper reflection. The black shiny material for handles of the utensils was made using the material editor. For this, ray caster material was used, the glossiness and the specular level was increased to give it appropriate shine. All these materials were mapped to their respective objects (Hu, Jia Ying. et al. 2013).

Microwave oven- The microwave oven is shown in figure 9. The microwave open was made by extrude option available in edit Poly modifier, by extruding the face of the lower shelf inward. Then segments were created over the extruded face, using connect option, to connect edges, in edit Poly modifier. The small squares made

Figure 8. The final mesh of the cooking utensils, spoon set models.

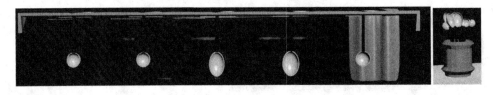

on top of the face using connect option were then extruded inwards and rescaled to form a microwave model. Cylinders were used as buttons of the microwave and they were smoothened by turbo smooth modifier. The handle of the microwave oven was made using a box (Livio De Luca et al. 2006). The top, bottom and back faces of the box were removed and then shell modifier was used to increase the thickness of the handle appropriately, to create a handle. The black shiny material for the first outer and second outer box faces of the microwave oven was made using the material editor. For this ray caster material was used, the glossiness and the specular level was increased to give it appropriate shine. The glass material mapped to the innermost square face of the micro wave was made using recaster material that's shine and glossiness was increased and transparency was increased to a certain level along with the increase in level of illumination. All these materials were mapped to their respective objects.

Gas stove- The gas stove (shown in Figure 10) is a part of the cooking area models. The base of the gas stove was made using a box which is a standard primitive. The topmost face of the box was extruded using extrude option in edit poly modifier and scaled down using scale tool. The buttons on the gas stove was made using cylinder and smoothen using turbo smooth modifier. The cooking top of the gas stove was made by a cylinder which was smoothen using turbo smooth modifier. Another cylinder was used over this cylinder an extruded to form the fire area of the cooking top. A box was used for making the utensil holder on the cooking top (Qin Lian et al. 2006). This box was bent using the bend modifier and cloned to form four more boxes and mirrored to its specific position. The entire cooking top was then grouped and cloned form two cooking tops. The shiny gray and shiny white materials were made by ray caster material in material editor by increasing the glossiness and specular level. The black shiny material for base of the mixer was made using the material editor. For this ray caster material was used, the glossiness and the specular level was increased to give it appropriate shine. All these materials were mapped to their respective objects.

Kitchen Chimney- The kitchen chimney is shown in figure 11. The kitchen chimney was made by a cylinder and a cone, which was combined together to form a chimney like structure. The bottom face of the cone was removed and shell modifier was used to give thickness to the cone (Tavares, J. M. R. S. et al. 2021). The shiny gray material was made by ray caster material, in material editor by increasing the glossiness and specular level and mapped to the chimney appropriately (Woop, Sven; et al. 2005).

Figure 9. The final mesh of the microwave oven model.

Figure 10. The final mesh of the gas stove model.

Figure 11. The final mesh of the kitchen chimney model.

CONCLUSION

The wood texture was aligned using the UVW map modifier box option. To give the shelves a glass appearance, the glossiness, specular level, and transparency were increased in the ray caster material in material editor. To make a proper reflection, the maps option's reflection material fall off were employed, and the mix curve pointer was dropped to a particular level from the centre. Multi-sub/object was used to map different textures to different faces of the shelves so that different faces could be given different ids and each id could be used to create a new material in the material editor. The shiny grey (steel material) was also created in the material editor by increasing the glossiness and specular level of the ray caster material. To make a proper reflection, the maps option's reflection material fall off were employed, and the mix curve pointer was dropped to a particular level from the centre. The material editor was used to create the black shiny material for container tops. The glossiness and specular level of this ray caster material were improved to give it an acceptable sheen. Then, using a move tool, a box in the shape of Iraq was produced and placed inside the glass covering of the shelf; on top of this box, a container was created by extruding a cylinder in the same manner as discussed earlier, and an oil tank was used as the container's cap. After grouping the entire container, the turbo smooth modifier was applied to smooth it out. This grouped container was cloned multiple times to create a large number of similar containers. The entire container rack was then cloned to create many racks and placed in its ideal location. The wood texture was applied to the racks, the silver texture was applied to each container, and the caps of the containers were well mapped with a shiny black texture.

REFERENCES

Althar, R. R., Samanta, D., Konar, D., & Bhattacharyya, S. (2021). *Software Source Code: Statistical Modeling*. Walter de Gruyter GmbH & Co KG. doi:10.1515/9783110703399

Arayici, Y., & Hamilton, A. (2005). Modeling 3D Scanned Data to Visualize the Built Environment. *Proceedings of the Ninth International Conference on Information Visualisation*, 509-514. 10.1109/IV.2005.82

Bhattacharya, A., Ghosh, G., Mandal, R., Ghatak, S., Samanta, D., Shukla, V. K., ... Mandal, A. (2022). Predictive Analysis of the Recovery Rate from Coronavirus (COVID-19). In *Cyber Intelligence and Information Retrieval*. Springer. doi:10.1007/978-981-16-4284-5_27

Biswal, A. K., Singh, D., Pattanayak, B. K., Samanta, D., Chaudhry, S. A., & Irshad, A. (2021). Adaptive Fault-Tolerant System and Optimal Power Allocation for Smart Vehicles in Smart Cities Using Controller Area Network. *Security and Communication Networks*, *2021*, 2021. doi:10.1155/2021/2147958

Brand, M., Kang, K., & Cooper, D. B. (2004). Algebraic solution for the visual hull. *Proceedings of the 2004 IEEE Computer Society Conference on Computer Vision and Pattern Recognition*, I33-I35. 10.1109/CVPR.2004.1315010

Castellani, U., Fusiello, A., Murino, V., Papaleo, L., Puppo, E., & Pittore, M. (2005). A complete system for on-line 3D modelling from acoustic images. *Signal Processing Image Communication*, *20*(9-10), 832–852. doi:10.1016/j.image.2005.02.003

Chatterjee, R., Roy, S., Islam, S. H., & Samanta, D. (2021). An AI Approach to Pose-based Sports Activity Classification. *2021 8th International Conference on Signal Processing and Integrated Networks (SPIN),* 156–161.

De Luca, L., Veron, P., & Florenzano, M. (2006). Reverse engineering of architectural buildings based on a hybrid modeling approach. *Computers & Graphics, 30*(2), 160–176. doi:10.1016/j.cag.2006.01.020

Dhenain, M., Ruffins, S. W., & Jacobs, R. E. (2001). Three-dimensional digital mouse atlas using high resolution MRI. *Developmental Biology, 232*(2), 458–470. doi:10.1006/dbio.2001.0189 PMID:11401405

Eapen, N. G., Rao, A. R., Samanta, D., Robert, N. R., Krishnamoorthy, R., & Lokesh, G. H. (2022). Security Aspects for Mutation Testing in Mobile Applications. In *Cyber Intelligence and Information Retrieval.* Springer. doi:10.1007/978-981-16-4284-5_2

Esteban. (2014). *Silhouette and stereo fusion for 3D object modeling. 3ds Max Projects: A Detailed Guide to Modeling, Texturing, Rigging, Animation and Lighting.*

Gang, L., & Wang, Z. (2004). Peng Quensheng. Generating Visual Hulls From Freely Moving Camera. *Journal of Computer-Aided Design & Computer Graphics, 16*(11), 1501–1505.

Guha, A., Samanta, D., Pramanik, S., & Dutta, S. (2021). Concept of Indexing and Concepts associated with Journal Publishing. In *Interdisciplinary Research in Technology and Management: Proceedings of the International Conference on Interdisciplinary Research in Technology and Management (IRTM, 2021).* CRC Press. 10.1201/9781003202240-3

Gurunath, R., Alahmadi, A. H., Samanta, D., Khan, M. Z., & Alahmadi, A. (2021). A Novel Approach for Linguistic Steganography Evaluation Based on Artificial Neural Networks. *IEEE Access: Practical Innovations, Open Solutions, 9,* 120869–120879. doi:10.1109/ACCESS.2021.3108183

Gurunath, R., Samanta, D., Dutta, S., & Kureethara, J. V. (2021). Essentials of Abstracting and Indexing for Research Paper Writing. In *Interdisciplinary Research in Technology and Management.* CRC Press.

Halim, S., & Mohd Sharuddin, I. (2004). *Close Range Measurement and 3D Modeling.* Presented at the 1st International Symposium on Engineering Surveys for Construction Works and Structural Engineering.

Hegde, D. S., Samanta, D., & Dutta, S. (2022). Classification Framework for Fraud Detection Using Hidden Markov Model. In *Cyber Intelligence and Information Retrieval*. Springer. doi:10.1007/978-981-16-4284-5_3

Hu, J. Y. (2004). The Application of Computer Software—3D Studio Max, Lightscape and V-Ray in the Environmental Artistic Expression. *Image Understanding, 96*, 367–392.

Kajiya, J. T. (1986). *The rendering equation*. Academic Press.

Kriete, A., Breithecker, A., & Rau, W. (2001). 3D imaging of lung tissue by confocal microscopy and micro-CT. *Proceedings of SPIE - The International Society for Optical Engineering*, 469-476. 10.1117/12.434736

Levoy, M., Pulli, K., Curless, B., Rusinkiewicz, S., Koller, D., Pereira, L., Ginzton, M., Anderson, S., Davis, J., Ginsberg, J., Shade, J., & Fulk, D. (2000). The digital Michelangelo Project: 3D scanning of large statues. Siggraph 2000, 131-144.

Lian, Q., Li, D.-C., Tang, Y.-P., & Zhang, Y.-R. (2006). Computer modeling approach for a novel internal architecture of artificial bone. *CAD Computer Aided Design, 38*(5), 507–514. doi:10.1016/j.cad.2005.12.001

Lin, T. H., Lan, C. C., Wang, C. H., & Chen, C. H. (2014). Study on realistic texture mapping for 3D models. *International Conference on Information Science, Electronics and Electrical Engineering (ISEEE), 3*, 1567-1571. 10.1109/InfoSEEE.2014.6946184

Montenegro, A. A., Carvalho, P. C. P., Velho, L., & Gattass, M. (2004). Space carving with a hand-held camera. *Proceedings of the XVII Brazilian Symposium on Computer Graphics and Image Processing (SIBGRAPI'04)*, 396-403. 10.1109/SIBGRA.2004.1352986

Murdock. (2014). *Autodesk 3ds Max 2014 Bible*. Academic Press.

Park, S.-Y., & Subbarao, M. (2005). A multiview 3D modeling system based on stereo vision techniques. *Machine Vision and Applications, 16*(3), 148–156. doi:10.100700138-004-0165-2

Paul, Samanta, & Sanyal. (2011). Dynamic job Scheduling in Cloud Computing based on horizontal load balancing. *International Journal of Computer Technology and Applications, 2*(5), 1552-1556.

Podder, S. K., & Samanta, D. (2022). Green Computing Practice in ICT-Based Methods: Innovation in Web-Based Learning and Teaching Technologies. *International Journal of Web-Based Learning and Teaching Technologies, 17*(4), 1–18. doi:10.4018/IJWLTT.285568

Raghavendra Rao, A., & Samanta, D. (2022). A Real-Time Approach with Deep Learning for Pandemic Management. In *Healthcare Informatics for Fighting COVID-19 and Future Epidemics*. Springer. doi:10.1007/978-3-030-72752-9_6

Sainz, M., Pajarola, R., Mercade, A., & Susin, A. (2004, July/August). A Simple Approach for Point-Based Object Capturing and Rendering. *IEEE Computer Graphics and Applications*, *24*(4), 33. doi:10.1109/MCG.2004.1 PMID:15628083

Samanta, D., Alahmadi, A. H., Karthikeyan, M. P., Khan, M. Z., Banerjee, A., Dalapati, G. K., & Ramakrishna, S. (2021). Cipher Block Chaining Support Vector Machine for Secured Decentralized Cloud Enabled Intelligent IoT Architecture. *IEEE Access: Practical Innovations, Open Solutions*, *9*, 98013–98025. doi:10.1109/ACCESS.2021.3095297

Samanta, D., Dutta, S., Galety, M. G., & Pramanik, S. (2022). A Novel Approach for Web Mining Taxonomy for High-Performance Computing. In *Cyber Intelligence and Information Retrieval*. Springer. doi:10.1007/978-981-16-4284-5_37

Samanta, D., Karthikeyan, M. P., Agarwal, D., Biswas, A., Acharyya, A., & Banerjee, A. (2022). Trends in Terahertz Biomedical Applications. *Generation, Detection and Processing of Terahertz Signals*, 285–299.

Sarti, S. (2002). Tubaro. Image based multiresolution implicit object modeling. *EURASIP Journal on Applied Signal Processing*, *10*, 1053–1066.

Sun, W., & Lal, P. (2002). Recent development on computer aided tissue engineering—A review. *Computer Methods and Programs in Biomedicine*, *67*(2), 85–103. doi:10.1016/S0169-2607(01)00116-X PMID:11809316

Sun, W., Starly, B., Nam, J., & Darling, A. (2005). Bio-CAD modeling and its applications in computer-aided tissue engineering. *Computer Aided Design*, *37*(11), 1097–1114. doi:10.1016/j.cad.2005.02.002

Tavares, J. M. R. S., Dutta, P., Dutta, S., & Samanta, D. (2021). Cyber Intelligence and Information Retrieval. *Proceedings of CIIR 2021*.

Toshihiro, A., Masayuki, K., & Naokazu, Y. (2005). 3D Modeling of Outdoor Environments by Integrating Omnidirectional Range and Color Images. *Proceedings of the Fifth International Conference on 3-D Digital Imaging and Modeling (3DIM'05)*.

Woop, S., Schmittler, J., & Slusallek, P. (2005). RPU: A Programmable Ray Processing Unit for Realtime Ray Tracing. *Siggraph 2005*.

Yang, Lee, Kim, & Kim. (2005). Adaptive Space Carving with Texture Mapping. *LNCS, 3482*, 1129-1138.

Yılmaz, U., Mülayim, A., & Atalay, V. (2002). Reconstruction of Three Dimensional Models from Real Images. *Proceedings of the First International Symposium on 3D Data Processing Visualization and Transmission (3DPVT.02)*. 10.1109/TDPVT.2002.1024117

Chapter 4
3D Image Creation With Standard Light Effects

Muskaan Jain
CHRIST University, India

ABSTRACT

The goal of this research work is to investigate the process of producing standard lighting for a bookshelf, as well as the process of rendering that scene. Lights in reality enable you to see things, and lights in 3ds Max do the same job. Furthermore, you may give characteristics to 3ds Max's lighting tools, allowing them to cast shadows and even control atmospheric lighting effects. If you haven't defined any lights, 3ds Max will use the default lighting. This allows you to observe any object you make without using any lights in the scene. The default lights vanish as soon as another light is added to the scene, and they mysteriously reappearance if all other lights in the area are removed. The 3D scene has comprised the boxes of varied parameters and a compound object named ProBoolean. Boxes of lesser length, width, and height are placed over the box of greater parameters, and smaller boxes are cut using ProCutter also named as ProBoolean compound object.

INTRODUCTION

Visuals play an important part in relaying a message and communicating things more quickly in a fast-paced society. The one element that has the potential to modify the game entirely is graphic design. Graphic design has the potential to transform the way businesses, individuals, and institutions are viewed (A. S. Baskoro et al. 2015) (Manson, A. et al. 2015). Graphic design uses special visual effects to keep the viewer's attention. Special visual effects are illusions employed in the theatre,

DOI: 10.4018/978-1-6684-4139-8.ch004

cinema, TV, and the simulating industries to reproduce imagined events in a narrative or a virtual situation are special visual effects. The graphical tools work miracles by giving all of the effects that make our items more appealing (Samanta, Debabrata, et al. (2011a)). Autodesk 3ds Max is a professional 3d modeling program for 3D animation development, games, and graphics. Autodesk designs and produces entertainment media. 3ds Max provides a comprehensive and versatile toolset for creating quality designs with complete artistic freedom (Tavares, J. et al.). It saves time by utilizing centralized creative tools for dynamic light mixing, color correction, and lens effects on generated images. It works more efficiently with an artist-friendly user interface and easy controls. It offers a fantastic collection of tools and instructions and unique features that make it a user-friendly piece of software. It has a variety of unique built-in Primitive forms, such as teapots, cones, cubes, and pyramids, intended as a basis for model building. Working with this becomes more accessible and more enjoyable when most of the tools and instructions are right in front of the user and do not confuse them (YeeWa Choy et al. 2012)(Samanta, Debabrata, et al., 2011). This application is also used to simulate mechanical parts since it includes the NURBS feature, which allows for smooth modeling through mathematical formulae. Character design is additionally simplified by including models for hair, skin, fur, and fabric in 3ds Max. These installed features shorten modeling time and improve detailing. It is compatible with the Material Editor, which allows users to create and manipulate materials and maps in their projects (Samanta, Debabrata, et al., 2013).

Autodesk provides a diverse range of 3D CAD software packages that may be used to explore and exchange ideas, visualize concepts, and model how designs will work before they are created. 3D CAD, or three-dimensional computer-aided design, is a design and technical documentation technique that substitutes human sketching with an automated procedure. 3D CAD software is used by architects, engineers, and other professionals to precisely represent and visualize things on a computer using a collection of three-dimensional points (U. Castellani et al. 2005).

CREATION OF 3D BOOKSHELF MODEL

The way we design 3D models has transformed. To help designers and end-users visualize the space requirements, 3D modeling enhances the efficiency and accuracy of the drawing. Creating in three-dimensional space has advantages over a traditional drawing in that it helps structural engineers to grasp the circumstances of a design better. Constructing system design is complicated, and it may be used to better clearly communicate projects to other designers, architects, and customers (Samanta, Debabrata, et al. (2012b))(L. L. Khoroshko et al. 2018).

Creating a three-dimensional Bookshelf model in 3Ds Max is a complicated procedure requiring familiarity with compound objects, especially ProBoolean. Compound objects are composed of two main or more existing objects that are grouped into a single component. It includes many types: Morph, Scatter, Conform, Connect, BlobMesh, ShapeMerge, Terrain, Loft, Mesher, Boolean, and ProBoolean, also called ProCutter compound objects. The ProCutter compound objects are design features that enable you to blend 2D and 3D shapes in ways that would be difficult or impossible to do otherwise. ProCutter supports Union, Intersection, Subtraction, Merge, Attach, and Insert. Figure 1 shows Object Type rollout, Figure 2 projects Box Parameters rollout, Figure 3 express A Box, Figure 4 shows A larger box with 6 smaller boxes., Figure 5 shows Compound Objects rollout., Figure 6 shows Pick boolean and Parameters rollout., Figure 7 says A ProBooleanated Object, Figure 8 shows Material editor window., Figure 9 express An object with the material assigned to it. Steps to create a bookshelf with materials:

1. Create panel -->Geometry --> Standard Primitives --> Object Type rollout --> Box button.

2. In the parameters rollout, enter 371cm, 74cm, and 189cm for length, breadth, and height, accordingly.

3. This is what your object will look like when you change the parameters.

4. Now, repeat step 1 to make 6 more boxes with lengths, widths, and heights of 67cm, 75cm, and 52cm, respectively.

5. Place each box as shown in the diagram below.

6. Select the larger box and then the ProBoolean compound object from the object type rollout.

7. Follow the steps below to choose the ProCutter compound object.
    Select an object--> Create panel --> (Geometry) --> Compound Objects--> Object Type rollout --> ProBoolean or ProCutter.

Figure 1. Object type rollout.

8. After you have picked the larger box, go to ProBoolean and, in the parameters rollout, select subtraction and click on start picking from pick boolean, then start selecting the smaller boxes one by one (Deryabin, N.B. et al. 2017).

Figure 2. Box parameters rollout.

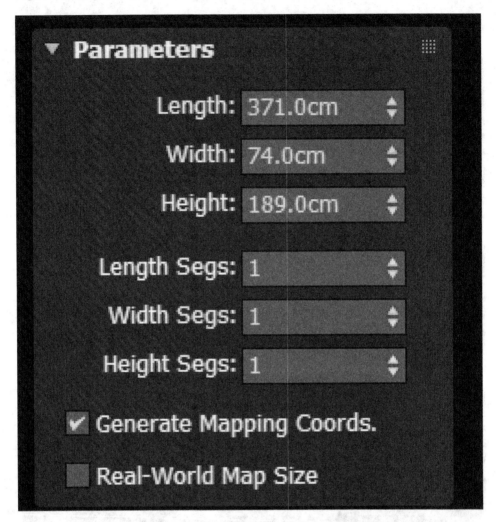

9. An object similar to the one illustrated below is generated.

10. Follow the steps below to assign material to the whole object (Material Editor): Compact--> Diffuse--> Bitmap--> (Select an image from your system)--> (Assign Material to Selection)

11. The object will appear somewhat like this when the scene has been rendered.

Figure 3. A box.

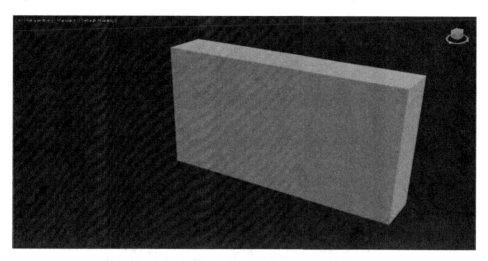

ENHANCING 3D MODELS WITH LIGHTS

A well-modeled 3D object may appear unconvincing to inadequate 3D lighting implementation (Samanta, Debabrata, et al., 2011c). A right selection of lighting methods, on the other hand, may substantially increase the value of the computer-generated scene. There are three types of lighting in 3ds Max: Photometric, Standard,

Figure 4. A larger box with 6 smaller boxes.

Figure 5. Compound objects rollout.

and Arnold (Lungershausen, U. et al. 2013). Figure 10 shows Photometric lights rollout, Figure 11says Photometric Target light properties, Figure 12 projects A refrigerator with photometric target light, Figure 13 express Photometric Free light properties., Figure 14 shows A refrigerator with photometric free light., Figure 15 shows Photometric Sun Positioner properties., Figure 16 says A tree with photometric sun positioner, Figure 17 projects Standard lights rollout.

Photometric Lights: Photometric lights employ photometric or light energy measurements to more precisely characterize lights as they would be in the actual world. Real-world lights' distribution, intensity, color temperature, and other properties may be customized (H. Esmaeili et al. 2017)(Kwon, Y.M. et al. 2017). To create lighting based on commercially available lights, you may also import particular photometric data available from lighting manufacturers. 3ds Max offers the following sorts of photometric light objects: Target Light (Photometric), Free Light (Photometric), and Sun positioned (Samanta, Debabrata, et al. (2011))(Samanta, Deababrata, et al. (2012)).

Let's look at an example of each category and see how they differ.

Figure 6. Pick boolean and parameters rollout.

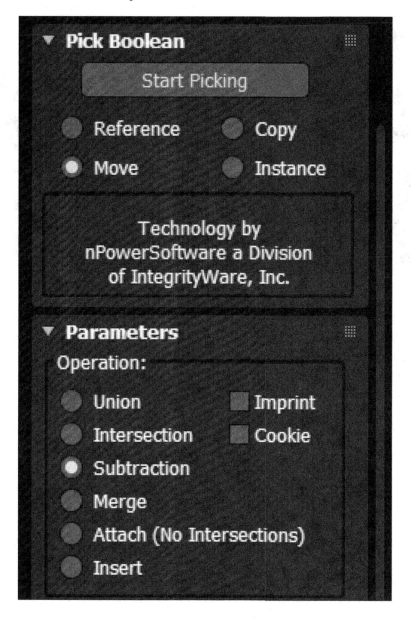

Target Light: A target light has a target sub-object that may be used to direct the light. It has many parameters, and they are shown in the below image.

I have designed a refrigerator and used a target light to check how it would appear after rendering. This is how it appears once the scene has been produced (S. Vu et al. 2018) (Samanta, Debabrata, et al. (2012g).

Figure 7. A ProBooleanated object.

Free Light: A free light does not have a target sub-object (D. Tsipotas et al. 2015) (Woop, Sven; et al. 2005). You may direct it with modifications. Free light has varied parameters, and they are shown in the image shown below.

I have designed a refrigerator and used a free light to check how it would appear after rendering. This is how it appears once the scene has been produced (Samanta, Debabrata, et al., 2012a).

Sun Positioner:

The new Sun Positioner, a simplified alternative to the Daylight System, enables a synchronized approach for customers of advanced physical renderers. Sun Positioner has various properties and they are shown in the below image (H. Esmaeili et al. 2014)(Soon-Yong Park et al. 2005).

I have designed a tree and used a sun positioner to check how it would appear after rendering. This is how it appears once the scene has been produced (Z. Pezeshki et al. 2017).

Standard Lights: Standard lights are computer-generated objects that replicate the lighting processes used in the theatre, in the movies, and in the sun itself, such as residential or workplace lights. Different types of light objects simulate diverse sorts of light sources, casting light in different ways (Samanta, Debabrata. (2011))(Samanta, Debabrata, et al. (2012)). Contrary to photometric lighting, the physiologically based intensity values of standard lights are not available (Hegazy, M. et al. 2022). 3ds Max offers the following sorts of standard light objects: Target

Figure 8. Material editor window.

spotlight, Target directional light, Free spotlight, Free directional light, Omni Light, and Skylight (M. R. Filho et al. 2011).

Let's look at an example of each category and see how they differ.

Target Spot: A spotlight, like a flashlight, emits a narrow beam of light on a particular object. A Free Spot, unlike a focused spotlight, has no particular object (UlaşYılmaz, et al. 2002)(Samanta, Debabrata, et al. (2012e)). Figure 18 says Standard Target Spot properties, Figure 19 shows an android with standard target spot, Figure 20 projects Standard Target Direct light properties, Figure 21express an android with standard target direct light, Figure 22 shows Standard Free Spot

Figure 9. An object with the material assigned to it.

properties, Figure 23 says A food court table with a standard free spot, Figure 24 projects Standard Free Direct light properties. You may drag and turn the free spot to target it at any angle. Target spotlight has various properties and they are:

I designed an android and used a targeted spotlight to check how it would appear after rendering. This is how it appears once the scene has been produced (Van de Perre, et al. 2019)(Yoo-Kil Yang et al. 2005).

Target Direct: Directional lights emit parallel light beams in a straight path on the target object. The primary purpose of directional lighting is to imitate sunshine. You may change the color of the light as well as position it and spin it in three-dimensional space. It has various parameters as mentioned below in the image (Ardakani, H.K. et al. 2020)(Samanta, Debabrata, et al., 2012c).

I have designed an android and used a targeted directional light to check how it would appear after rendering. This is how it appears once the scene has been produced.

Like a flashlight, free Spot: A spotlight emits a narrow beam of light in free space. A Free Spot, unlike a focused spotlight, has no particular object (D. Fritsch et al. 2017)(Natephra, W. et al. 2017). You may drag and turn the free spot to target it at any angle. It has properties as mentioned below.

Figure 10. Photometric lights rollout.

I have designed a food court table and used a free spotlight to check how it would appear after rendering. This is how it appears once the scene has been produced.

Free Direct: Directional lights emit parallel light beams in a straight path in free space, much like the sun does at the earth's surface (Wei Sun et al. 2002)(Yusuf Arayici et al. 2005). The primary purpose of directional lighting is to imitate sunshine. You may change the color of the light and position it and spin it in three-dimensional space. Free Directional light has many parameters, and they are:

I have designed a group of androids and used a free directional light to check how it would appear after rendering (Samanta, Debabrata, et al. (2011b)). This is how it appears once the scene has been produced. Figure 25 shows Many androids with a standard free direct light above one android, Figure 26 shows Standard Omni light properties, Figure 27 projects A food court table with standard omni light, Figure 28 express Standard Skylight properties, Figure 29 says A board with standard skylight, Figure 30 shows Arnold light rollout.

Omni: From a single source, an Omni light emits beams in all directions and can be used to create "fill lighting" to a scene or to simulate point source sources. Omni lights have varied properties namely: General, Intensity/Color/Attenuation, Advanced effects, shadow parameters, and Shadow Map parameters (Günther-Diringer et al. 2016)(Samanta, Debabrata, et al., 2012h).

Figure 11. Photometric target light properties.

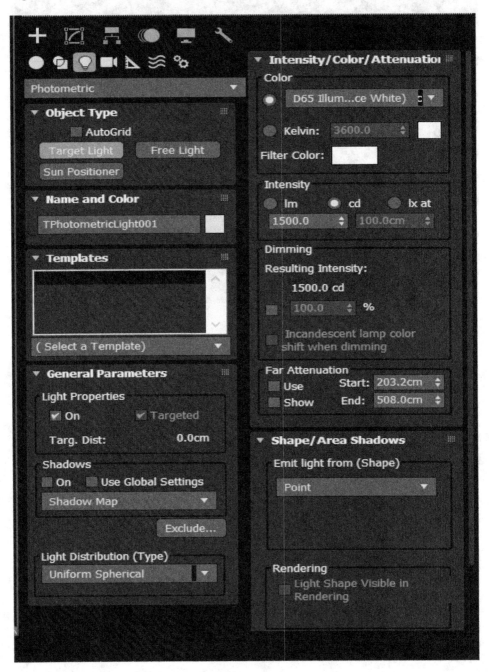

Figure 12. A refrigerator with photometric target light.

I have designed a food court table and used an Omni light to check how it would appear after rendering. This is how it appears once the scene has been produced.

Skylight: The Skylight light simulates natural light. You may change the color of the sky or apply a map to it. Above the scene, the sky is represented as a dome. Skylight has various sub-properties and they are:

I have designed a Board and used a skylight to check how it would appear after rendering. This is how it appears once the scene has been produced.

Arnold Lights: Arnold lights are intended for use with the Arnold renderer. 3ds Max offers the following sort of Arnold light object: Arnold light.

Arnold light has a list of properties namely: General, Shape, Color/Intensity, Rendering, Shadow, and Contribution. Figure 31 shows Arnold light properties, Figure 32 says A board with arnold light, Figure 33 projects General parameters rollout of lights, Figure 34 says Standard lights rollout, Figure 35 express A ProBooleanated object(bookshelf) with material assigned to it and with omni light, Figure 36 shows Bookshelf enhanced with omni lights, Figure 37 projects Bookshelf with additional objects.

Figure 13. Photometric free light properties.

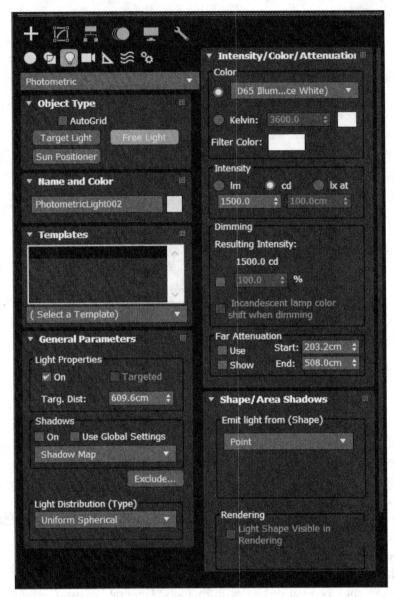

- In the General Properties rollout, you can switch the light on or off. You may also choose between free and focused lighting. By default, Targeted is cleared, which results in the light being created as a free light (M. T. Valdez et al. 2016).

Figure 14. A refrigerator with photometric free light.

- You may choose the form of the light in the Shape rollout. The chosen form determines how the light is emitted. The Quad option is used by default, which lights a rectangular area and only produces light in one direction. The Shape rollout's parameters are determined by the type of light picked. The chosen form determines how the light is emitted (Nadeem, A. et al. 2015).
- You may change the color of the light source in the Color/Intensity rollout. To achieve a nice render of a scene, you usually need to modify the Intensity or Exposure of the illumination. Exposure acts as an intensity amplifier, increasing the intensity in a series of leaps (Samanta, Debabrata, et al. (2011d)).
- The quality of specular highlights and shadows may be adjusted in the Rendering rollout. Raising the Samples value lowers noise in shadow spots while boosting render time.
- You can turn on or off the striking of rays from the light in the Shadow rollout. The Atmospheric Shadows option governs how volumetric shadows are computed.
- The advanced settings in the Contribution rollout allow you to customize the elements of light input in the ultimate rendering. For physically realistic results, leave the different parameters at their defaults of 1.0 and 999 for Max. Bounces. You may modify those options to give yourself more creative control.

Figure 15. Photometric sun positioner properties.

Let's look at an example of each category and see how they differ.

I have designed a board and used an Arnold light to check how it would appear after rendering. This is how it appears once the scene has been produced.

Figure 16. A tree with photometric sun positioner.

Shadow Types and Shadow Controls: The General Parameters rollout for both standard and photometric lights allows you to toggle shadow-casting on or off for the light and select the sort of shadow it casts. Create panel --> (Lights) --> Create a light --> General Parameters rollout --> Shadows group --> Shadow type.

The shadow type depends on the renderer chosen.

The Quicksilver hardware renderer always casts shadow map shadows. The Quicksilver renderer supports most shadow controls with light objects (Samanta, Debabrata, et al. (2012f)). The exception is that the shadow pattern is not supported (Shadow Parameters Map). Soft-edged shadows may cast area lighting. The scan renderer supports the following types of shadows: Ray-Traced, Advanced Ray-Traced, Area, and Shadow Map (Samanta, Debabrata, et al. (2012d)).

Bookshelf with Omni Lights:

Steps to add standard light and enhance the model are:

1. Steps to utilize standard lights: Create panel --> Lights --> Standard .

Figure 17. Standard lights rollout.

2. Varieties of standard lights:

3. Omni light under standard light enhances the bookshelf and gives the scene a more realistic appearance.
4. I have placed 8 Omni lights, 1 under every block and 2 on top of the bookshelf.
5. The image looks like this given below.

6. The object will appear somewhat like this when the scene has been rendered (W. Sun, et al. 2005).

7. The scene has been enhanced with the help of Omni lights.

8.   Additional objects(books, pen stand, and other necessary objects) are added to make the scene meaningful. Now the scene looks like this.

Figure 18. Standard target spot properties.

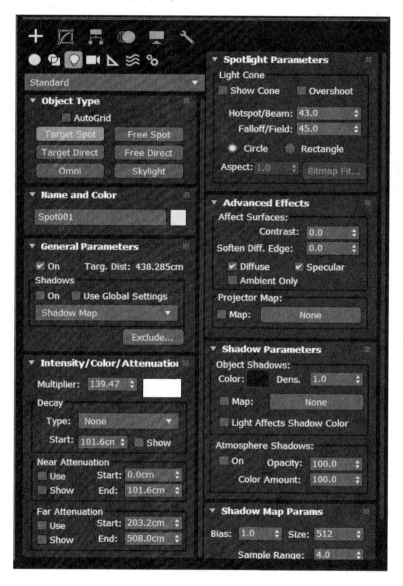

Figure 19. An android with standard target spot.

CONCLUSION

The project named "3D image creation with standard light effects" offers a thorough method for generating a bookshelf with standard lights, especially Omni lights. The goal of this thesis is to investigate the process of producing standard lighting for a bookshelf, as well as the process of rendering that scene. During the project, lights were placed after analyzing the different positions of light and which position will give a good effect on the bookshelf. Although this project just scratched the surface of standard lighting and rendering, it was quite informative as the first lighting and rendering focused project. Rendering improvements should also be studied to minimize rendering time. Other lights were not paid much attention as standard lights were in themselves very effective on the scene but the gist of other lights is also mentioned to understand other lights as well. The basic knowledge of the lights is assimilated by this project and now the focus can deviate to other complex concepts of lights. Now that the bookshelf is ready, the project can be extended to a study room containing other related objects or groups like a study table, comfortable chair, a laptop, various books, etc. Here are a few key takeaways from the project. We have learned to work with different photometric, standard, and Arnold lights. The proper position of the light in the scene makes a major difference in the scene while rendering. We have also learned how the position places major role in shadow parameters.

Figure 20. Standard target direct light properties.

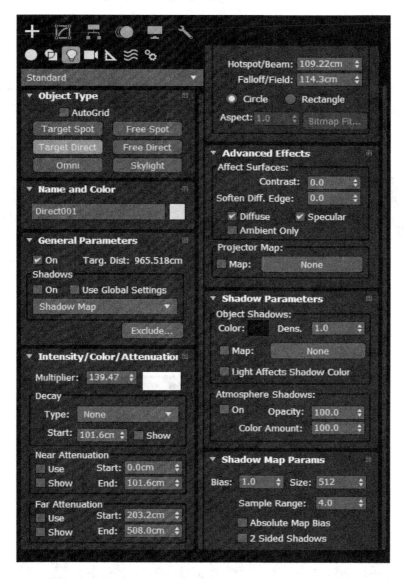

Figure 21. An android with standard target direct light.

Figure 22. Standard free spot properties.

Figure 23. A food court table with a standard free spot.

Figure 24. Standard free direct light properties.

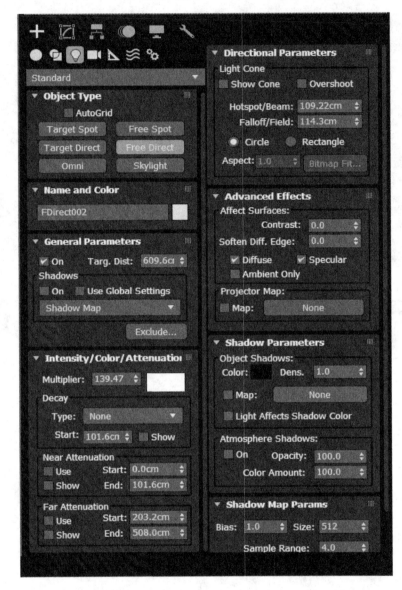

Figure 25. Many androids with a standard free direct light above one android.

Figure 26. Standard Omni light properties.

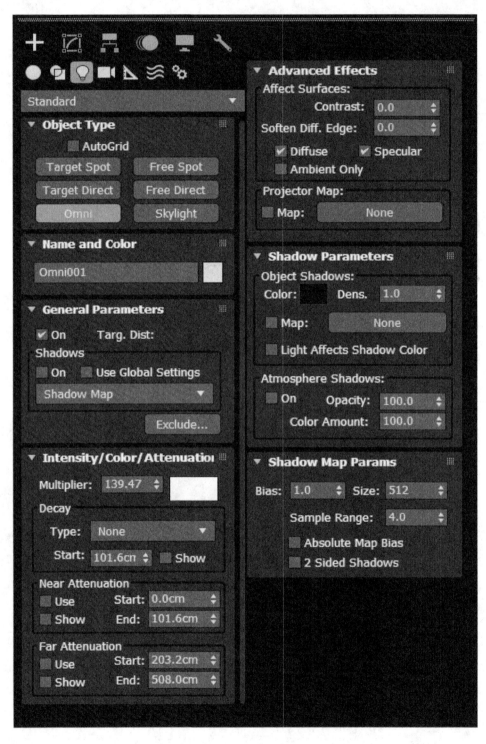

Figure 27. A food court table with standard omni light.

Figure 28. Standard skylight properties.

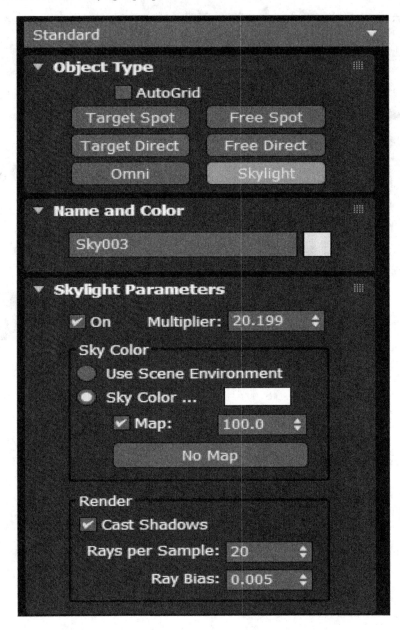

Figure 29. A board with standard skylight.

Figure 30. Arnold light rollout.

Figure 31. Arnold light properties.

Figure 32. A board with arnold light.

Figure 33. General parameters rollout of lights.

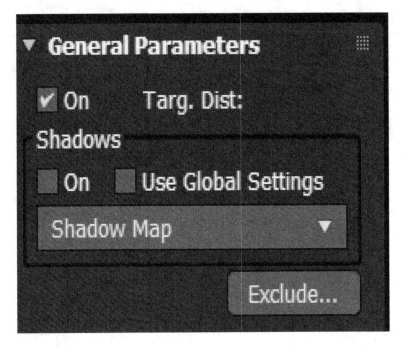

Figure 34. Standard lights rollout.

Figure 35. A ProBooleanated object(bookshelf) with material assigned to it and with omni light.

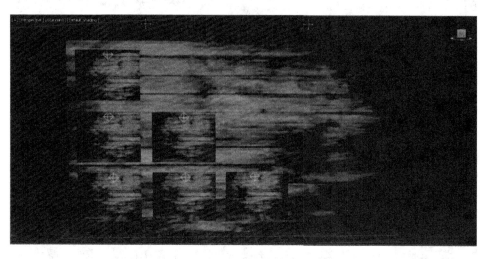

Figure 36. Bookshelf enhanced with omni lights.

Figure 37. Bookshelf with additional objects.

REFERENCES

Arayici, Y., & Hamilton, A. (2005). Modeling 3D Scanned Data to Visualize the Built Environment. *Proceedings of the Ninth International Conference on Information Visualisation*, 509~514. 10.1109/IV.2005.82

Ardakani, H. K., Mousavinia, A., & Safaei, F. (2020). Four points: One-pass geometrical camera calibration algorithm. *The Visual Computer*, *36*(2), 413–424. doi:10.100700371-019-01632-7

Baskoro, A. S., & Haryanto, I. (2015). Development of travel speed detection method in welding simulator using augmented reality. *2015 International Conference on Advanced Computer Science and Information Systems (ICACSIS)*, 269-273. 10.1109/ICACSIS.2015.7415194

Castellani, U., Fusiello, A., Murino, V., Papaleo, L., Puppo, E., & Pittore, M. (2005). A complete system for on-line 3D modelling from acoustic images. *Signal Processing Image Communication*, *20*(9-10), 832–852. doi:10.1016/j.image.2005.02.003

Choy, Lim, Wang, & Chan. (2012). Development CT-based three-dimensional complex skull model for Finite element analysis. *2012 IEEE Conference on Sustainable Utilization and Development in Engineering and Technology (STUDENT)*, 135-139. 10.1109/STUDENT.2012.6408383

Deryabin, N. B., Zhdanov, D. D., & Sokolov, V. G. (2017). Embedding the script language into optical simulation software. *Programming and Computer Software*, *43*(1), 13–23. doi:10.1134/S0361768817010029

Esmaeili, H., Thwaites, H., & Woods, P. C. (2017). Workflows and Challenges Involved in Creation of Realistic Immersive Virtual Museum, Heritage, and Tourism Experiences: A Comprehensive Reference for 3D Asset Capturing. *2017 13th International Conference on Signal-Image Technology & Internet-Based Systems (SITIS)*, 465-472. 10.1109/SITIS.2017.82

Esmaeili, H., Woods, P. C., & Thwaites, H. (2014). Realisation of virtualised architectural heritage. *2014 International Conference on Virtual Systems & Multimedia (VSMM)*, 94-101. 10.1109/VSMM.2014.7136676

Filho, M. R., Negrão, N. M., & Damasceno, R. R. (2011). SwImax: A Web Tool Using Virtual Reality for Teaching the WiMAX Protocol. *2011 XIII Symposium on Virtual Reality*, 217-224. 10.1109/SVR.2011.27

Fritsch, D., & Klein, M. (2017). 3D and 4D modeling for AR and VR app developments. *2017 23rd International Conference on Virtual System & Multimedia (VSMM)*, 1-8. 10.1109/VSMM.2017.8346270

Günther-Diringer, D. (2016). Historisches 3D-Stadtmodell von Karlsruhe. *J. Cartogr. Geogr. Inf., 66*, 66–71. doi:10.1007/BF03545207

Hegazy, M., Yasufuku, K., & Abe, H. (2022). An interactive approach to investigate brightness perception of daylighting in Immersive Virtual Environments: Comparing subjective responses and quantitative metrics. *Building Simulation*, *15*(1), 41–68. doi:10.100712273-021-0798-3

Khoroshko, L. L., Ukhov, P. A., & Keyno, P. P. (2018). *Development of a Laboratory Workshop for Open Online Courses Based on 3D Computer Graphics and Multimedia. In 2018 Learning With MOOCS*. LWMOOCS. doi:10.1109/LWMOOCS.2018.8534678

Kwon, Y. M., Lee, Y. A., & Kim, S. J. (2017). Case study on 3D printing education in fashion design coursework. *Fash Text*, *4*(1), 26. doi:10.118640691-017-0111-3

Lungershausen, U., Heinrich, C., & Duttmann, R. (2013). Turning Human-nature Interaction into 3D Landscape Scenes: An Approach to Communicate Geoarchaeological Research. *J. Cartogr. Geogr. Inf., 63*, 269–275. doi:10.1007/BF03546142

Manson, A., Poyade, M., & Rea, P. (2015). A recommended workflow methodology in the creation of an educational and training application incorporating a digital reconstruction of the cerebral ventricular system and cerebrospinal fluid circulation to aid anatomical understanding. *BMC Medical Imaging, 15*(1), 44. doi:10.118612880-015-0088-6 PMID:26482126

Nadeem, A., Wong, A. K. D., & Wong, F. K. W. (2015). Bill of Quantities with 3D Views Using Building Information Modeling. *Arabian Journal for Science and Engineering, 40*(9), 2465–2477. doi:10.100713369-015-1657-2

Natephra, W., Motamedi, A., Fukuda, T., & Yabuki, N. (2017). Integrating building information modeling and virtual reality development engines for building indoor lighting design. *Vis. in Eng., 5*(1), 19. doi:10.118640327-017-0058-x

Park, S.-Y., & Subbarao, M. (2005). A multiview 3D modeling system based on stereo vision techniques. *Machine Vision and Applications, 16*(3), 148–156. doi:10.100700138-004-0165-2

Paul, M., & Sanyal, G. (2011). Segmentation technique of SAR imagery using entropy. *International Journal of Computer Technology and Applications, 2*(5).

Pezeshki, Z., Soleimani, A., & Darabi, A. (2017). 3Ds MAX to FEM for building thermal distribution: A case study. *2017 3rd Iranian Conference on Intelligent Systems and Signal Processing (ICSPIS),* 110-115. 10.1109/ICSPIS.2017.8311599

Samanta, D., & Paul, M. (2011). A Novel Approach of Entropy based Adaptive Thresholding Technique for Video Edge Detection. *Threshold (x, y), 1,* 1.

Samanta, D. (2011). A novel statistical approach for segmentation of SAR Images. *Journal of Global Research in Computer Science, 2*(10), 9–13.

Samanta, D., & Sanyal, G. (2011a). Automated Classification of SAR Images Using Moment. *International Journal of Computer Science Issues, 8*(6), 135.

Samanta, D., & Sanyal, G. (2011b). *Development of Adaptive Thresholding Technique for Classification of Synthetic Aperture Radar Images.* Academic Press.

Samanta, D., & Sanyal, G. (2011c). Development of edge detection technique for images using adaptive thresholding. *International Conference on Information Processing,* 671–676. 10.1007/978-3-642-22786-8_85

Samanta, D., & Sanyal, G. (2011d). SAR image segmentation using Color space clustering and Watersheds. *International Journal of Engineering Research and Applications*, *1*(3), 997–999.

Samanta, D., & Sanyal, G. (2012). Segmentation technique of SAR imagery based on fuzzy c-means clustering. *IEEE-International Conference On Advances In Engineering, Science And Management (ICAESM-2012)*, 610–612.

Samanta, D., & Ghosh, A. (2012). Automatic obstacle detection based on gaussian function in robocar. *J. Res. Eng. Appl. Sci*, *2*(2), 354–363.

Samanta, D., & Sanyal, G. (2012a). A novel approach of SAR image classification using color space clustering and watersheds. *2012 Fourth International Conference on Computational Intelligence and Communication Networks*, 237–240. 10.1109/CICN.2012.27

Samanta, D., & Sanyal, G. (2012c). An Approach of Segmentation Technique of SAR Images using Adaptive Thresholding Technique. *International Journal of Engineering Research & Technology (Ahmedabad)*, *1*(7).

Samanta, D., & Sanyal, G. (2012f). Novel Shannon's entropy based segmentation technique for SAR images. *International Conference on Information Processing*, 193–199. 10.1007/978-3-642-31686-9_22

Samanta, D., & Sanyal, G. (2012g). *SAR image classification using fuzzy CMeans*. Academic Press.

Samanta, D., & Sanyal, G. (2012h). Statistical approach for Classification of SAR Images. *International Journal of Soft Computing and Engineering (IJSCE)*, 2231–2307.

Samanta, D., & Sanyal, G. (2013). An Approach of Tabu Search for Unsupervised Classification for SAR Images. *Seven International Conference on Image and Signal Processing*.

Samanta, D., & Sanyal, G. (2012b). A novel approach of SAR image processing based on Hue, Saturation and Brightness (HSB). *Procedia Technology*, *4*, 584–588. doi:10.1016/j.protcy.2012.05.093

Samanta, D., & Sanyal, G. (2012d). Classification of SAR Images Based on Entropy. *Int. J. Inf. Technol. Comput. Sci*, *4*(12), 82–86. doi:10.5815/ijitcs.2012.12.09

Samanta, D., & Sanyal, G. (2012e). Novel approach of adaptive thresholding technique for edge detection in videos. *Procedia Engineering*, *30*, 283–288. doi:10.1016/j.proeng.2012.01.862

Sun, W., & Lal, P. (2002). Pallavi Lal. Recent development on computer aided tissue engineering—A review. *Computer Methods and Programs in Biomedicine, 67*(2), 85–103. doi:10.1016/S0169-2607(01)00116-X PMID:11809316

Sun, W., Starly, B., Nam, J., & Darling, A. (2005). Bio-CAD modeling and its applications in computer-aided tissue engineering. *Computer Aided Design, 37*(11), 1097–1114. doi:10.1016/j.cad.2005.02.002

Tavares, J., Dutta, P., Dutta, S., & Samanta, D. (n.d.). *Cyber Intelligence and Information Retrieval.* Academic Press.

Toshihiro, A., Masayuki, K., & Naokazu, Y. (2005). 3D Modeling of Outdoor Environments by Integrating Omnidirectional Range and Color Images. *Proceedings of the Fifth International Conference on 3-D Digital Imaging and Modeling (3DIM'05).*

Tsipotas, D., & Spathopoulou, V. (2015). An assesment of research on 3D digital representation of ancient Greek furniture, using surviving archaelological artefacts. *Digital Heritage, 2015,* 325–328. doi:10.1109/DigitalHeritage.2015.7419515

Valdez, M. T., Ferreira, C. M., & Barbosa, F. P. M. (2016). 3D virtual laboratory for teaching circuit theory — A virtual learning environment (VLE). *2016 51st International Universities Power Engineering Conference (UPEC),* 1-4. 10.1109/UPEC.2016.8114126

Van de Perre, G., De Beir, A., Cao, H. L., Esteban, P. G., Lefeber, D., & Vanderborght, B. (2019). Studying Design Aspects for Social Robots Using a Generic Gesture Method. *International Journal of Social Robotics, 11*(4), 651–663. doi:10.100712369-019-00518-x

Vu, S. (2018). Recreating Little Manila through a Virtual Reality Serious Game. *2018 3rd Digital Heritage International Congress (DigitalHERITAGE) held jointly with 2018 24th International Conference on Virtual Systems & Multimedia (VSMM 2018),* 1-4. 10.1109/DigitalHeritage.2018.8810082

Woop, S., Schmittler, J., & Slusallek, P. (2005). RPU: A Programmable Ray Processing Unit for Realtime Ray Tracing. *Siggraph 2005.*

Yang, Lee, Kim, & Kim. (2005). Adaptive Space Carving with Texture Mapping. *LNCS, 3482,* 1129-1138.

Yılmaz, Mülayim, & Atalay. (2002). Reconstruction of Three Dimensional Models from Real Images. *Proceedings of the First International Symposium on 3D Data Processing Visualization and Transmission (3DPVT.02).*

Chapter 5
Virtual Kitchen Scene Modelling Based on 3ds Max With Rendering View

Raghav Sham Kamat
CHRIST University, India

Oruan Memoye Kepeghom
Federal College of Education, Technical, Omoku, Nigeria

ABSTRACT

With the quick improvement of modem innovation, representing objects and scenes virtually is one of those major considerations made in technological sectors. A virtual three-dimensional representation of objects is not just to have a glimpse of the structure, but also to have a realistic view of the scene. This chapter mainly describes the usage and applications of 3ds Max related to which creating a 3D model of a kitchen is briefed. The chapter also includes the methodologies of designing and implementing various features of 3ds Max like editors and materials. The manner in which patterns are applied to objects, lighting effects, usage of modifiers like edit poly, edit mesh, turbo-smooth, mesh smooth bend, etc. are briefly described. This chapter can guarantee a variety of usage on texture maps with the help of rendering material editors which improves the quality of the rendering image and the structure.

INTRODUCTION

Graphical representation and special visualizations are generally utilized to represent specific component to gradually increase the attention given to it. Just as difficult

DOI: 10.4018/978-1-6684-4139-8.ch005

as it is to find any film or any brand advertisement doesn't use any special visual effects, we can easily depict the importance and usage level of any animation tool (Anselmo Antunes Montenegro et al. 2004). 3ds Max created by Autodesk media and entertainment is an expert 3D PC designs program for making 3D movements, models, games and pictures. It has an astounding arrangement of instruments and orders and supports special elements that make it an easy to understand for creating various 3d models. It has different remarkable inherent Primitive shapes like tea kettles, cones, 3D squares, pyramids that are utilized as an establishment for modern turn of events (Samanta, Debabrata, & Sanyal, G. (2012c), Samanta, Debabrata, & Sanyal, G. (2012f)). Working with this turns out to be all the more simple and more fun when the majority of the instruments and orders are directly before the client and it doesn't confound those (Soon-Yong Park et al. 2005). This program is likewise utilized in the recreation of mechanical parts as it upholds the NURBS highlight that permits smooth displaying by utilizing numerical recipes (Matthew Brand et al. 2004, Sarti et al. 2002). Character demonstrating is likewise simplified as 3ds Max incorporates recreations for hair, skin, hide, and fabric. These inbuilt instruments diminish the time taken for demonstrating and improve the enumerating (W. Sun et al. 2005, Toshihiro ASAI et al. 2005.).

METHODOLOGY

1. Step 1: Select standard Parameters and drag Plane
2. Step 2: In Shapes select Boxes for creating wall
3. Step 3: Clone walls, keep proper scaling and Position on two suitable sidesfor adding further objects.
4. Step 4: Using Planes again, make suitable copies of it so as to stick it adjacent to the walls.
5. Step 5: Place the planes perfectly adjacent to the wall (Box) by a assigning the perfect scale and position.
6. Step 6: To add floor, again use plane and place it in ground level surface. And place multiple small planes just like walls.
7. Step 7: To make Lower Shelfs, select 5 boxes from standard primitives and place it together on the floor. Scale it by clicking the suitable axis using the cursor.
8. Step 8: Select boxes from standard Primitives and reduce the scale by clicking the X-axis and pushing it inward. Place it right ahead of the 5 boxes to create a door.
9. Step 9: To give a smooth texture, click on modifier list and select click mesh smooth. Increase the intensity.

10. Step 10: Click on modifier list ®chamfer and increase the Iterations to 3.

11. Step 11: Click on shapes from standard Primitives and change the viewport display to top view.

12. Step 12: Click on Line tool and draw a necessary handle pattern to create a handle for shelfs.

13. Step 13: After drawing a specific handle shape, click on Modifier list and select Lathe modifier.

14. Step 14: Once lathe modifier is clicked, scroll down to parameters alignment and click on max align to get a proper scaled handle.

15. Step 15: Adjust the size of the handle with respect to the shelf doors and place them in a proper position.

16. Step 16: Select the boxes 4 and 5, Drag a box from standard primitive. Adjust the scale of the new box such that it fits in box 4 and 5 like a sink.

17. Step 17: Right click on the boxes 4 and 5, Click on Standard primitives.

18. Step 18: Click on compound objects and select ProBoolen.

19. Step 19: Click on start picking and select the box placed on the inside of lower shelf boxes 4 and 5, by doing a hollow space with the scale of the box placed is created.

20. Step 20: Click boxes and draw a simple small rectangle.

21. Step 21: Create clones of the rectangle by clicking on any of the three axis and dragging them by holding the shift key (shift +drag (left click)).

22. Step 22: By creating 3 rectangles place a rectangle (1) horizontally and the remaining 2 rectangles (2,3) vertically to (1), position the rectangle (2,3) parallel to each other and vertical to rectangle (1).

23. Step 23:Click on cylinder and place it parallel to rectangle (2) so that they both are connected

24. Step 24: Click on boxes and drag one. Re scale them so as to fit in the wall right above the lower shelf.

25. Step 25: Make 4 copies of the box by (shift +drag (left click)).

26. Step 26: By keeping all the boxes together upper shelf is created. And make copies of the boxes and drag them ahead.

27. Step 27: The copies should be scaled such that it appears like a door to the upper shelves.

28. Step 28: To create a door with a hollow opening in its center drag 4 boxes and scale them accordingly so that it fits right in the center of the door with bezels.

29. Step 29: Once positioned, click standard primitives ®compound objects®Pro Boolean and click on start picking and select the boxes placed. This will create a hollow space in door to give it a realistic look.

30. Step 30: Click plane from standard primitives ®Right click on plane and click object properties®Increase Transparency to create a glass effect.

31. Step 31: Create copies of the transparent plane and place it respectively in the mid-point of upper shelves door.

32. Step 32: Click on lower shelves handle and (shift +drag (left click)). Make copies of the handle and place it respectively to upper shelves.

33. Step 33: Click boxes and reduce the scale holding the axis such that it fits right in the upper shelves.

34. Step 34: Make exactly 2 copies each such that every single upper shelve has exactly two boxes inside as a holder. Place it one upon each other such that there is sufficient space between them and should be visible through the door.

35. Step 35: To create wood pattern blocks for the wall, click on box and scale it to appear like a long rectangular box. Make 3 copies of the box and place it on the wall with shelves and to create a square within which the upper shelf lies.

36. Step 36: Click box and reduce the horizontal thickness. Increase the vertical scale and adjust it so that it fits right upon the lower shelves. For placing objects like stove.

37. Step 37: Click on box ®make a clone of it and reduce the scale to create a hollow space from the top view.

38. Step 38: Once the clone is created place it inside the main box ®using compound objects and Pro-Boolean start picking the box.

39. Step 39: Make 4 copies of the drawer so that it can be placed on both the opposite sides of the wall.

40. Step 40: Click and drag box form standard primitives and increase the scale such that the two drawers fits right into it.

41. Step 41: Click (shift +drag (left click)) and make 4 copies of upper shelf handle. Once copies of handles are made, place it at the center of the drawers.

42. Step 42: Click modifier list and apply chamfer effects to the drawer holders and the box placed on the lower shelves.

43. Step 43: Make copies of the box placed on lower shelves and place it on the drawers scaled on either side of the wall.

44. Step 44: (Fridge) Click and drag Box (1)®Clone two boxes that fits right in front of the Box (1) and increase the scale such that it looks like a door.

45. Step 45: Click and drag box ®place it just above the Box (1).

46. Step 46: Click box and place it horizontally to the right door with the part of it inside.

47. Step 47: Click Standard primitives®Compound objects ®Pro Boolean®Select door ®Start Picking ®Click start picking ®Select the box placed horizontally. It creates a hollow space where a digital display can be added.

48. Step 48: Click plane ®scale it so that it fits right in the hollow space.

49. Step 49: Click box ®Scale it to a rectangle ®Reduce thickness®Clone it and reduce the size.

50. Step 50: Place the cloned box right above the box®Modifier List® Smooth

51. Step 51: Select the box below the cloned object®Editable Poly®Chamfer®Increase Intensity

52. Step 52: (Stove)Click cylinder ®make 4 clones®place in just on top of the chamfered cloned box.

53. Step 53: Click cylinder ®reduce the scale to half the size of the cylinders.

54. Step 54:(Burnals) Click the small cylinders ®convert to editable poly®click polygon ®extrude®increase intensity®modifier list ®turbo smooth.

55. Step 55: Make 4 clones of the burnals ®place it right in between the cylinders.

56. Step 56: Click shapes®lines ®draw an 'S' like pattern®Enable in viewport®increase width (3%)®increase height (15%).

57. Step 57: Make 4 clones for each burnals®place it at the edge of the burnals parallel and opposite to each other.

58. Step 58: (Knobs) Click cylinder®Scale it so that it can be place on the vertical side of the stove's rectangular box.

59. Step 59: Click on the knobs ®convert to editable poly ®click polygon ®select polygons at the center ®extrude®increase intensity.

60. Step 60: Click knob ®make 4 clones ®place side by side vertically.

61. Step 61: (Wall-Clock) Click cylinder ®scale it to the size of a wall clock ®convert to editable poly

62. Step 62: Click wall clock® modifier list®polygon®inset (24%)®save.

63. Step 63: Click the wall clock®extrude (16%)®save.

64. Step 64: Click cylinder®make 12 clones ®reduce the size respectively so as to fit in to the cylinder like numbers.

65. Step 65: Position the cylinders with respect to numbers on a clock

66. Step 66: Click box®make 3 clones for minute hour hand, minute hand and seconds' hand.

67. Step 67: Reduce the size of the hands, Seconds bigger than hours and minutes, hours smaller than seconds and minutes.

68. Step 68: Place the 3 boxes (minute hour hand, minute hand and seconds' hand) right inside the cylinder horizontal to it and having size exactly half the diameter of the clock cylinder.

69. Step 69:(Chimney) Click box®scale it to a narrow rectangle and place it above the stove.

70. Step 70: Click two boxes (1,2)) and drag ®increase the width of the box (1) to and box (2) with more intensity with respect to width.

71. Step 71: Place box(2) just below the narrow box and above the stove ®place box (1) just below box (2).

72. Step 72: (Fridge attached Cupboards): Click box ®place it on the left side of the stove and chimney ®Convert to editable poly.

73. Step 73: Click box®modifier list®click edge®Increase spacing ®Increase lines to 2.

74. Step 74: Click modifier list ®click polygon ®select the area between the 2 lines and extrude it to the max i.e., towards the end of the respective wall to which it is attached.

75. Step 75: Select two edges on the opposite side ®connect®increase the lines with respect to the objects present below including the fridge.

76. Step 76: Click polygon in modifier list ®(ctrl+) select the polygons that can get right beside the objects like stove and fridge.

77. Step 77: After selecting the polygons extrude that part until it touches the ground.

78. Step 78: Click box and make 3 clones for inner racks besides the stove®place the boxes one below the other besides the stove on the right side with 80% of the box merged inside.

79. Step 79:(Racks) Select the (Fridge attached Cupboards)®standard primitives®compound objects ®Pro Boolean ®Start picking®click on the boxes merged inside, right besides the stove.

80. Step 80:Click boxes and make clones of it with respect to the boxes extruded on the side with objects (chimney, stove and fridge) ®Reduce the thickness to give a door like shape ®make clones of it and place it in front of the extruded box.

81. Step 81: Make clones of the handle created for upper and lower shelves ®Drag and place it to the doors created.

82. Step 82: Add necessary materials to the objects by using the following method.
    a. Click M/Rendering®Modifier List®Compact material editor.
    b. Click map®Standard®Bitmap
    c. Diffuse®Select Bitmap®Select a desired pattern/image/texture.
    d. Assign to material
    e. To view in viewport, select the option to view the material in viewport.

83. Step 83: RENDERING
    a. Rendering
    b. Render setup
    c. Iterative Rendering mood
    d. Scaline Rendering
    e. Render

CREATING A 3-D MODEL OF KITCHEN INTERIORS

As hectic as it is to design any interior, the difficulty doesn't seem any less when minute detailing is considered (M. Levoy et al. 2000, Samanta, Debabrata, & Sanyal, G. (2011c)). When one has the right knowledge and usage experience with Autodesk software using modifiers like Mesh modifiers, Mesh smooth, Chamfer, Edit Poly, etc. 3ds Max provides us a lot of Primitives like standard primitives, spline and compound objects would be the basic component used to create the base of a kitchen model (Samanta, Debabrata, & Sanyal, G. (2012e)). Provided, View- Ports like the top, bottom, right, left and perspective view gives a clear picture of the model which makes it easier to add even the smallest of details (Kajiya et al. 1986, Liu Gang et al. 2004, Tavares, J. et al. 2021).

MODELING THE WALLS

Using Standard Primitives like box and plane, walls were created by dragging the box placing them in the right position so various small objects can be placed easily within the desired place (Samanta, Debabrata, & Sanyal, G. (2012g)). The size of the wall can be easily resized using the scale feature by dragging the respective axis (x, y, z) (Halim SETAN et al. 2004). Figure 1 shows wall model.

WALL PATTERNS

Planes from Standard Primitives were dragged for usage, Copies of planes were made by holding any of the plane axis (x, y, x) and dragging them to the right position by holding the shift key. Planes were respectively resized and positioned to cover every inch of the wall (Kelly L. Murdock 2014, Samanta, Debabrata, & Sanyal, G. (2012b)). Material editors were made use to give a specific design (pattern). Material editor being a part of rendering is easily accessible and necessary maps can be chosen and are easily visible on the desired object once assigned (Hu, Jia Ying. 2013)(Lin, T. H. et al. 2014)(Samanta, Debabrata, & Sanyal, G. (2011a)). Figure 2 & 3 represents wall patterns and wall scaling respectively.

Figure 1. Perspective view of walls

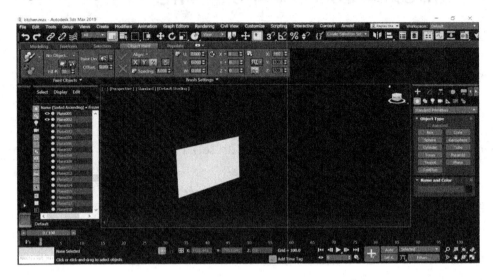

Figure 2. Adding sub planes on walls for giving material patterns

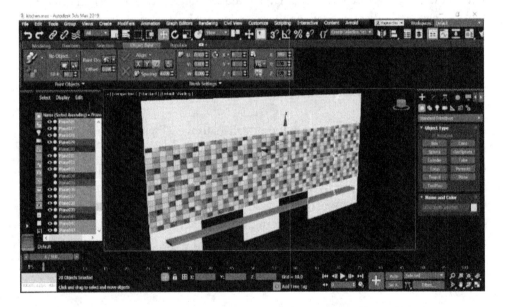

SHELF MODELLING (UPPER SHELF)

Using boxes as containers and compound objects to create hollow space. The shelf

Figure 3. Skeleton view of the planes

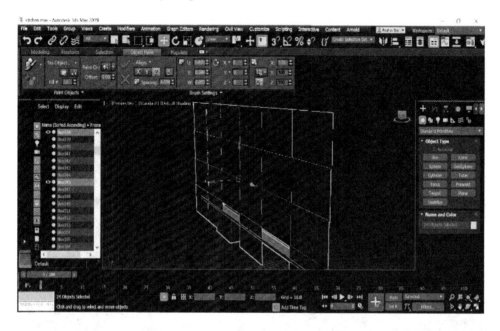

was created using Pro Boolean, a primitive of compound objects (Carlos Hernández Esteban et al. 2014)(Dhenain M et al. 2001, Eyetronics, 2004). The solid in were a hollow space had to be created was selected and a box with proper scaling and position was placed inside (Kriete A. et al. 2001, Samanta, Debabrata, & Paul, M. (2011)). After selecting the solid object placed inside the "start picking "option had to be selected and the hollow space was created by clicking the box placed inside, by clicking the necessary hollow space is created. Copies of shelf were created by dragging a shelf by holding any axis +shift key, number of copies can be created by just mentioning the number of copies required (Woop, Sven et al. 2005)(Yoo-Kil Yang et al. 2005).Figure 4 shows upper shelf modelling. Figure 5 projects upper shelf modelling (right angle) and Figure 6 express upper shelf copies and positioning.

SHELF MODELLING (LOWER SHELF)

The lower shelf has similar properties as the upper shelf. Boxes were used as containers and compound objects to create hollow space (Samanta, Debabrata, & Sanyal, G. (2012h)). And doors to all the shelves were created using boxes and proper scaling. The racks in the shelf were added using boxes and were duplicated and placed right inside the hollow space created using Pro Boolean (Yusuf Arayici et

Figure 4. Upper shelf with racks and door

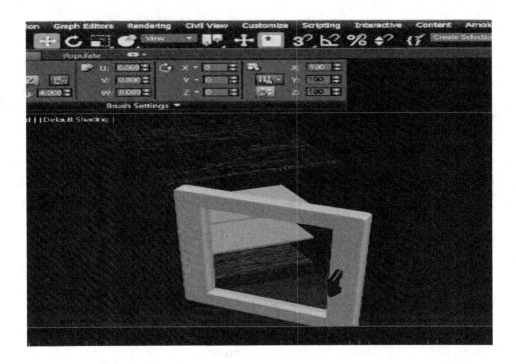

Figure 5. Interior view of upper shelf

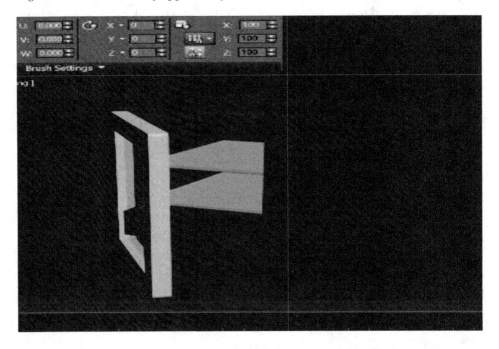

Figure 6. Upper shelf with clones and proper positioning

al. 2005, Samanta, Deababrata, & Sanyal, G. (2012)). The upper layer of the shelves was done quite easily by dragging boxes and cutting out a part using a box for sinks (U. Castellani et al. 2005). Fig. 7 shows Lower shelf completion with modifiers,Fig. 8 express Structural view of lower shelf sink, Fig. 9 projects Lower shelf placed in an apt position and Fig. 10 shows Top view of Lower shelf with sink opening.

FRIDGE

Using boxes and planes the basic structure of the fridge was made possible, using material editor different maps were assigned to the base structure to give it a realistic look. The filter in the fridge was again created using compound objects pro Boolean (Livio De Luca et al. 2006)(Samanta, Debabrata. (2011)). Fig. 11 says Front View of the fridge with LCD, Fig.12 shows Side View of the fridge with LCDand Fig. 13 projects Perspective view of the kitchen with maximum objects.

STOVE

Using standard primitives like boxes and cylinders the base of the stove was created. The burnal was made using cylinders and modifiers like Edit poly and mesh. The burnal holder was created using a line from shapes (Samanta, Debabrata, Paul, M., & Sanyal, G., 2011). Using lines, a 2d structure was drawn, and using Lathe modifier

Figure 7. Lower shelf completion with modifiers

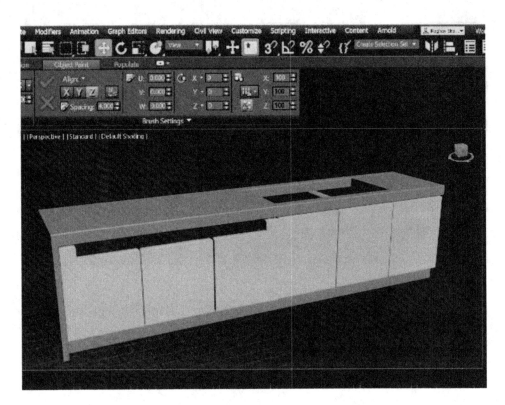

a 3d perspective was given to it (Miguel Sainz et al. 2004, Samanta, Debabrata, & Sanyal, G.,2011b). After minimizing and scaling the structure, it was properly positioned on the burnals. The stove knobs were created using cylinders (Ulaş Yılmaz et al. 2002)(Wei Sunet al. 2002). Fig. 14 shows Perspective view of the stove with elements attached and Fig. 15. express Top View of stove.

The structure was made using edit polymers which were done by enabling the edge faces to make use of grids for the structure. Properties like Extrude, Connect, and inset was used the most for creating the structure. A smooth interface was given to the whole structure using chamfer and turbosmooth (Samanta, Debabrata, & Sanyal, G.,2013).

WALL CLOCK

Wall clock was created using a cylinder and Edit poly, the hollow structure was created by applying the inset property and by making the extrude value negative.

Figure 8. Structural view of lower shelf sink

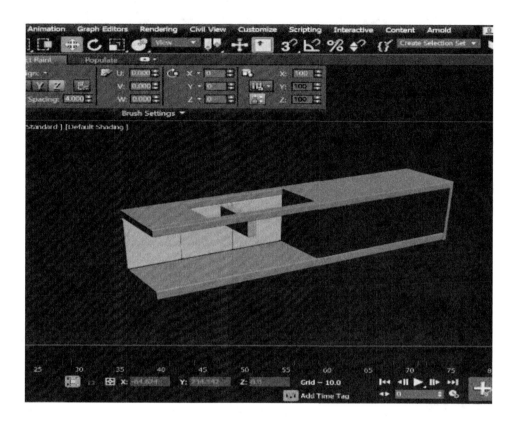

Figure 9. Lower shelf placed in an apt position

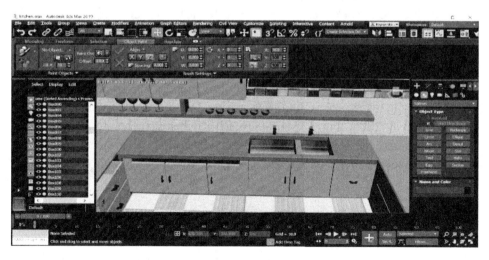

Figure 10. Top view of lower shelf with sink opening

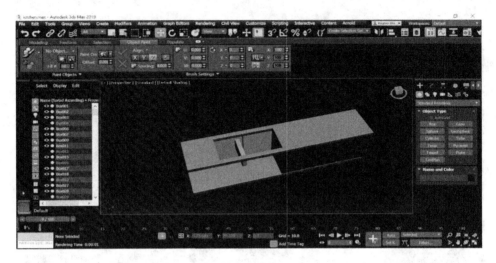

Numbers were done using cylinders by minimizing the scale and placing them in a proper position (Samanta, Debabrata, & Sanyal, G., 2012d), Paul, M., Samanta, D., & Sanyal, G., 2011). Fig. 16 shows Perspective View of wall Clock and Fig.17 projects Clock view (Upper perspective).

RENDERING

The process of converting any three-dimensional model to a 2d image is called rendering. By simulating the light rays the image formation is made possible when rendering is done (Qin Lian et al. 2006). A raster graphics image or a digital image is obtained as the result of rendering. Being the last step, rendering is one of the main sub-topics in computer graphics for having a final appearance of the created object (M Paul et al. 2011). The kitchen model is rendered via Arnold rendering after setting up the render to finalize the image. The view to render was kept at quad 4 – Perspective and target to Production rendering mode. The quality of the image is increased with respect to resolutions (Samanta, Debabrata, & Sanyal, G. (2012a)) (P. Mueller et al. 2005). Fig. 18 shows Overall Kitchen view before rendering and Fig. 19 shows Arnold Rendered image of Kitchen and Fig. 20 projects Front View of Arnold Rendered image of Kitchen.

Figure 11. Front View of the fridge with LCD

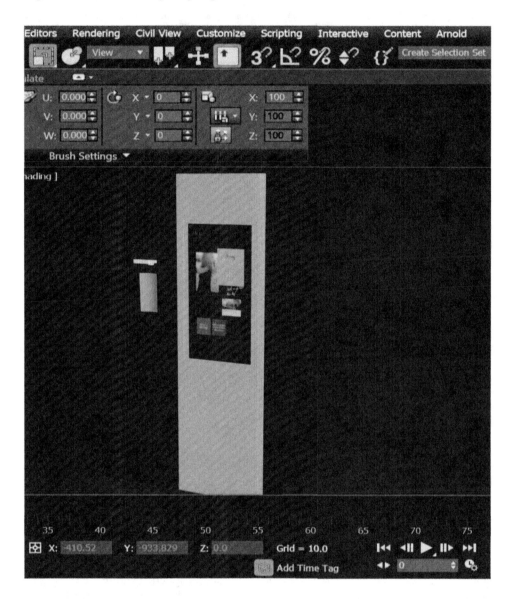

MATERIAL

The materials portray how an item mirrors or transmits the light (Samanta, Debabrata, & Sanyal, G.,2011d). They are information that are applied on the outside of an item and displayed in a certain way when the scene is delivered. Material maps were added to objects using the material editor in Rendering, a desired map should be

Figure 12. Side view of the fridge with LCD

selected and has to be assigned to the material. Once assigned, it should be viewed in the viewport for the change to reflect whilst rendering (Sarti et al. 2002) (Toshihiro ASAI et al.). By assigning maps, a realistic view is obtained when applied on objects. Material basically describes an objects visual property, it is one of those important factors with respect to visualization like color, pattern, diffuse, transparency etc. Standard material has its own property like highlighting controls, opacity and color. Maps can give a realistic view to any selected component and improve the quality of the material (Samanta, Debabrata, & Ghosh, A., 2012). Fig. 21 shows Kitchen

Figure 13. Perspective view of the kitchen with maximum objects

Figure 14 Perspective view of the stove with elements attached

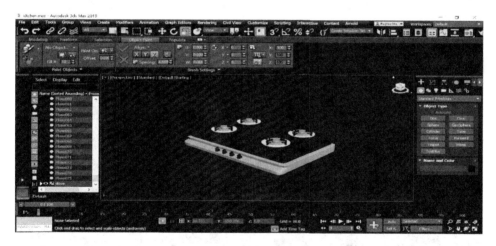

with materials enabled in viewport, Fig. projects 22 Kitchen view (Zoomed in), Fig. 23 express Productive Rendering Mode, Fig. 24 shows Iterative Rendering Mode with Scaline render, Fig. 25 shows Left view of Arnold Rendering, Fig.26 says Left view of Kitchen with Scaline Render, Fig. 27 projects Perspective view of Kitchen with all materials enabled.

Figure 15. Top view of stove

Figure 16. Perspective view of wall clock

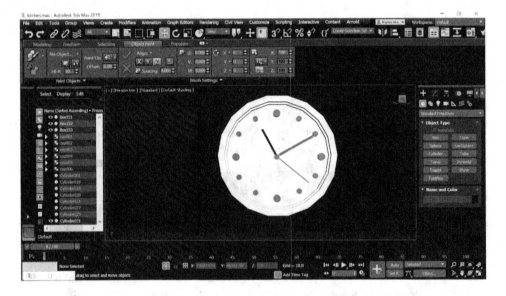

CONCLUSION

3ds Max is a powerful tool that helps us in creating objects of our own creativity for various purposes. Modelling a kitchen in 3ds Max was a complex task, the absence of reference image made it more challenging to place every object in place. As a beginner, learning the basic objects, standard primitives and modifiers like Edit poly and edit mesh was challenging and very much interesting. Adding minute details

122

to the kitchen like knobs, glasses, led, taps gave a realistic view to it. In this paper, various applications of 3ds max are being demonstrated; applications of Modifiers, Rendering, Standard Primitives, Compound objects, Material Editor and Edit poly are briefly mentioned about how useful these editors were to create a kitchen model.

Figure 17. Clock view (upper perspective)

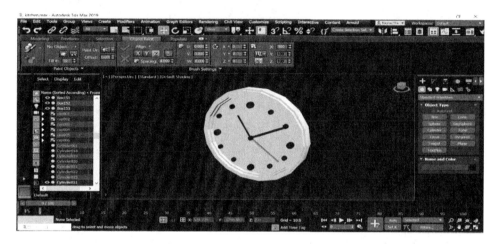

Figure 18. Overall kitchen view before rendering

Figure 19. Arnold rendered image of kitchen

Figure 20. Front view of Arnold rendered image of kitchen

Figure 21. Kitchen with materials enabled in viewport

Figure 22. Kitchen view (zoomed in)

Figure 23. Productive rendering mode

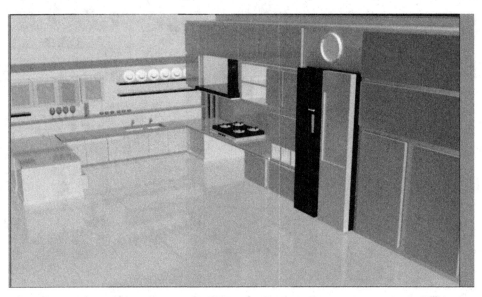

Figure 24. Iterative rendering mode with scaline render

Figure 25. Left view of Arnold rendering

Figure 26. Left view of kitchen with scaline render

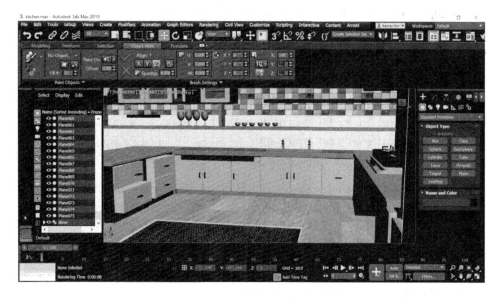

Figure 27. Perspective view of kitchen with all materials enabled

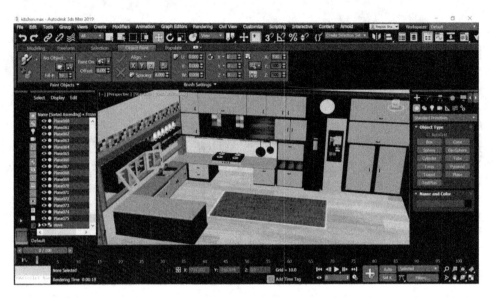

REFERENCES

Arayici, Y., & Hamilton, A. (2005). Modeling 3D Scanned Data to Visualize the Built Environment. *Proceedings of the Ninth International Conference on Information Visualisation*, 509~514. 10.1109/IV.2005.82

Brand, M., Kang, K., & Cooper, D. B. (2004). Algebraic solution for the visual hull. *Proceedings of the 2004 IEEE Computer Society Conference on Computer Vision and Pattern Recognition*, I33-I35. 10.1109/CVPR.2004.1315010

Castellani, U., Fusiello, A., Murino, V., Papaleo, L., Puppo, E., & Pittore, M. (2005). A complete system for on-line 3D modelling from acoustic images. *Signal Processing Image Communication*, *20*(9-10), 832–852. doi:10.1016/j.image.2005.02.003

De Luca, L., Veron, P., & Florenzano, M. (2006). Reverse engineering of architectural buildings based on a hybrid modeling approach. *Computers & Graphics*, *30*(2), 160–176. doi:10.1016/j.cag.2006.01.020

Dhenain, M., Ruffins, S. W., & Jacobs, R. E. (2001). Three-dimensional digital mouse atlas using high resolution MRI. *Developmental Biology*, *232*(2), 458–470. doi:10.1006/dbio.2001.0189 PMID:11401405

Esteban, C. H., & Schmitt, F. (2014). *Silhouette and stereo fusion for 3D object modeling. 3ds Max Projects: A Detailed Guide to Modeling, Texturing, Rigging, Animation and Lighting.*

Eyetronics. (2004). http://www.eyetronics.com

Gang, L., Wang, Z., & Quensheng, P. (2004). Generating Visual Hulls From Freely Moving Camera. *Journal of Computer-Aided Design & Computer Graphics*, *16*(11), 1501–1505.

Halim, S., & MohdSharuddin, I. (2004). *Close Range Measurement and 3D Modeling.* Presented at the 1st International Symposium on Engineering Surveys for Construction Works and Structural Engineering.

Hu, J. Y. (2004). The Application of Computer Software—3D Studio Max, Lightscape and V-Ray in the Environmental Artistic Expression. *Image Understanding*, *96*, 367–392.

Kajiya, J. T. (1986). *The rendering equation.* Academic Press.

Kriete, A., Breithecker, A., & Rau, W. (2001). 3D imaging of lung tissue by confocal microscopy and micro-CT. *Proceedings of SPIE - The International Society for Optical Engineering*, 469-476. 10.1117/12.434736

Levoy, M., Pulli, K., Curless, B., Rusinkiewicz, S., Koller, D., Pereira, L., Ginzton, M., Anderson, S., Davis, J., Ginsberg, J., Shade, J., & Fulk, D. (2000). The digital Michelangelo Project: 3D scanning of large statues. Siggraph 2000, 131-144.

Lian, Q., Li, D.-C., Tang, Y.-P., & Zhang, Y.-R. (2006). Computer modeling approach for a novel internal architecture of artificial bone. *CAD Computer Aided Design*, *38*(5), 507–514. doi:10.1016/j.cad.2005.12.001

Lin, T. H., Lan, C. C., Wang, C. H., & Chen, C. H. (2014). Study on realistic texture mapping for 3D models. *International Conference on Information Science, Electronics and Electrical Engineering (ISEEE)*, 3, 1567-1571. 10.1109/InfoSEEE.2014.6946184

Montenegro, A. A., Carvalho, P. C. P., Velho, L., & Gattass, M. (2004). Space carving with a hand-held camera. *Proceedings of the XVII Brazilian Symposium on Computer Graphics and Image Processing (SIBGRAPI'04)*, 396-403. 10.1109/SIBGRA.2004.1352986

Mueller, Vereenooghe, Vergauwen, Van Gool, & Waelkens. (n.d.). Photo-realistic and detailed 3D modeling: the Antonine nymphaeum at Sagalassos (Turkey). *Computer Applications and Quantitative Methods in Archaeology (CAA): Beyond the artifact - Digital interpretation of the past*. http://www.vision.ee.ethz.ch/~pmueller/documents/caa04_pmueller.pdf

Murdock. (2014). *Autodesk 3ds Max 2014 Bible*. Academic Press.

Park, S.-Y., & Subbarao, M. (2005). A multiview 3D modeling system based on stereo vision techniques. *Machine Vision and Applications, 16*(3), 148–156. doi:10.100700138-004-0165-2

Paul, Samanta, & Sanyal. (2011). Dynamic job Scheduling in Cloud Computing based on horizontal load balancing. *International Journal of Computer Technology and Applications, 2*(5), 1552-1556.

Paul, M., Samanta, D., & Sanyal, G. (2011). Dynamic job scheduling in cloud computing based on horizontal load balancing. *International Journal of Computer Technology and Applications, 2*(5), 1552–1556.

Paul, M., & Sanyal, G. (2011). Segmentation technique of SAR imagery using entropy. *International Journal of Computer Technology and Applications, 2*(5).

Sainz, M., Pajarola, R., Mercade, A., & Susin, A. (2004, July/August). A Simple Approach for Point-Based Object Capturing and Rendering. *IEEE Computer Graphics and Applications, 24*(4), 33. doi:10.1109/MCG.2004.1 PMID:15628083

Samanta, D. (2011). A novel statistical approach for segmentation of SAR Images. *Journal of Global Research in Computer Science, 2*(10), 9–13.

Samanta, D., & Paul, M. (2011). A Novel Approach of Entropy based Adaptive Thresholding Technique for Video Edge Detection. *Threshold (x, y), 1*, 1.

Samanta, D., & Sanyal, G. (2011a). Automated Classification of SAR Images Using Moment. *International Journal of Computer Science Issues, 8*(6), 135.

Samanta, D., & Sanyal, G. (2011b). *Development of Adaptive Thresholding Technique for Classification of Synthetic Aperture Radar Images*. Academic Press.

Samanta, D., & Sanyal, G. (2011c). Development of edge detection technique for images using adaptive thresholding. *International Conference on Information Processing*, 671–676. 10.1007/978-3-642-22786-8_85

Samanta, D., & Sanyal, G. (2011d). SAR image segmentation using Color space clustering and Watersheds. *International Journal of Engineering Research and Applications*, *1*(3), 997–999.

Samanta, D., & Ghosh, A. (2012). Automatic obstacle detection based on gaussian function in robocar. *J. Res. Eng. Appl. Sci*, *2*(2), 354–363.

Samanta, D., & Sanyal, G. (2012). Segmentation technique of SAR imagery based on fuzzy c-means clustering. *IEEE-International Conference On Advances In Engineering, Science And Management (ICAESM-2012)*, 610–612.

Samanta, D., & Sanyal, G. (2012a). A novel approach of SAR image classification using color space clustering and watersheds. *2012 Fourth International Conference on Computational Intelligence and Communication Networks*, 237–240. 10.1109/CICN.2012.27

Samanta, D., & Sanyal, G. (2012c). An Approach of Segmentation Technique of SAR Images using Adaptive Thresholding Technique. *International Journal of Engineering Research & Technology (Ahmedabad)*, *1*(7).

Samanta, D., & Sanyal, G. (2012f). Novel Shannon's entropy based segmentation technique for SAR images. *International Conference on Information Processing*, 193–199. 10.1007/978-3-642-31686-9_22

Samanta, D., & Sanyal, G. (2012g). *SAR image classification using fuzzy CMeans*. Academic Press.

Samanta, D., & Sanyal, G. (2012h). Statistical approach for Classification of SAR Images. *International Journal of Soft Computing and Engineering (IJSCE)*, 2231–2307.

Samanta, D., & Sanyal, G. (2013). An Approach of Tabu Search for Unsupervised Classification for SAR Images. *Seven International Conference on Image and Signal Processing*.

Samanta, D., & Sanyal, G. (2012b). A novel approach of SAR image processing based on Hue, Saturation and Brightness (HSB). *Procedia Technology*, *4*, 584–588. doi:10.1016/j.protcy.2012.05.093

Samanta, D., & Sanyal, G. (2012d). Classification of SAR Images Based on Entropy. *Int. J. Inf. Technol. Comput. Sci*, *4*(12), 82–86. doi:10.5815/ijitcs.2012.12.09

Samanta, D., & Sanyal, G. (2012e). Novel approach of adaptive thresholding technique for edge detection in videos. *Procedia Engineering*, *30*, 283–288. doi:10.1016/j.proeng.2012.01.862

Sarti, S. T. (2002). Image based multiresolution implicit object modeling. *EURASIP Journal on Applied Signal Processing, 10,* 1053–1066.

Sun, W., & Lal, P. (2002). Recent development on computer aided tissue engineering—A review. *Computer Methods and Programs in Biomedicine, 67*(2), 85–103. doi:10.1016/S0169-2607(01)00116-X PMID:11809316

Sun, W., Starly, B., Nam, J., & Darling, A. (2005). Bio-CAD modeling and its applications in computer-aided tissue engineering. *Computer Aided Design, 37*(11), 1097–1114. doi:10.1016/j.cad.2005.02.002

Tavares, J., Dutta, P., Dutta, S., & Samanta, D. (n.d.). *Cyber Intelligence and Information Retrieval.* Academic Press.

Toshihiro, A., Masayuki, K., & Naokazu, Y. (2005). 3D Modeling of Outdoor Environments by Integrating Omnidirectional Range and Color Images. *Proceedings of the Fifth International Conference on 3-D Digital Imaging and Modeling (3DIM'05).*

Woop, S., Schmittler, J., & Slusallek, P. (2005). RPU: A Programmable Ray Processing Unit for Realtime Ray Tracing. *Siggraph 2005.*

Yang, Lee, Kim, & Kim. (2005). Adaptive Space Carving with Texture Mapping. *LNCS, 3482,* 1129-1138.

Yılmaz, Mülayim, & Atalay. (2002). Reconstruction of Three Dimensional Models from Real Images. *Proceedings of the First International Symposium on 3D Data Processing Visualization and Transmission (3DPVT.02).*

Chapter 6
Text Modifier Based on Autodesk Platform

Guruprasad N.
CHRIST University, India

Muskaan Jain
CHRIST University, India

Tamanna Pramanik
CHRIST University, India

ABSTRACT

3ds Max is used in the video game industry for creating 3D character models, game assets, and animation. With an efficient workflow and powerful modeling tools, 3ds Max can save game artists a significant amount of time. 3ds Max fits into the animation pipeline at nearly every stage. From modeling and rigging to lighting and rendering, this program makes it easy to create professional-quality animations easier and simpler. Many industries use 3ds Max for generating graphics that are mechanical or even organic in nature. The engineering, manufacturing, educational, and medical industries all make use of 3ds Max for visualization needs as well. The real estate and architectural industries use 3ds Max to generate photorealistic images of buildings in the design phase. This way clients can visualize their living spaces accurately and offer critiques based on real models. 3ds Max uses polygon modeling which is a common technique in game design.

DOI: 10.4018/978-1-6684-4139-8.ch006

INTRODUCTION

The Bevel modifier extrudes shapes into 3D objects and applies a flat or round bevel to the edges. Bevel lets you extrude a shape up to four levels and specify a different outline amount for each level. A common use for this modifier is to create 3D text and logos, but you can apply it to any shape. Modifiers provide a way for you to sculpt and edit objects. They can change the geometry of an object, and its properties. Autodesk 3Ds Max is a graphics program for making 3D models, animations, games, and images. Autodesk Media and Entertainment produced it. It has the capabilities to model in 3D and has flexible plugin architecture. It is majorly used by video game developers and TV commercial studios (U. Castellani., et al. 2005) (Y. Arayici et al. 2005). It can also give movie effects to animations. It contains various tools and modifiers to modify a single standard object to different realistic models. It helps in creating natural textures for models and mapping them correctly to the objects. It helps in providing proper light and shadow effects to the models. It has different rendering options for making the models flexible to render. It has new icons, a customizable user interface, and its scripting language (V. Murino. et al. 2005).

PLACING AND BEVELING TEXT

The modifiers which help in making 3d text and Logos are called bevel modification. This modifier helps to view the actual text into 3d text. Figure 1 shows example of Beveling Text. (Livio De Luca et al. 2006)

WORKING PROCEDURE

1. Draw a shape using spline, Rectangle spline or Circle spline.
2. Select the shapes and then click on the Bevel modifier from the Modifier list.
3. On modifiers list, choose from the below options; (Debabrata Samanta et al. 2011)

   Capping: Select option called Start and/or End to cap with z value highest or lowest respectively. The end is open when either is off respectively.

   Cap type: Click on Morph to make cap faces which is suitable for morphing process, or Click on Grid to make cap faces in order to look like grid pattern, Grid is better than morphing.

   Surface: Click on liner sides for line intersect between segments, or select Curved sides for the segment intersection that gives a bezier curve.

Segments: Total number of segments which is made between the levels. Figure 2 shows Segment part of text.

Figure 1. Example of beveling text

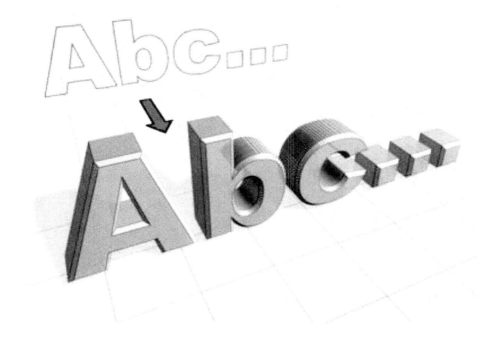

Smooth Across Levels: Which is applied to group of the edges of the beveled object to smoothen them?

Generate Mapping Coordinates: Which helps in the material mapping of the object. (C.H. Esteban et al. 2003)

Intersections: This prevents the lines intersecting within the objects(alphabets).this is achieved by adding one more vertex in the outline and transforming sharp corners into flat lines.

Bevel Values: This type of modifiers supports to achieve 2-4 levels of beveling of the objects

Figure 2. Segment part of text

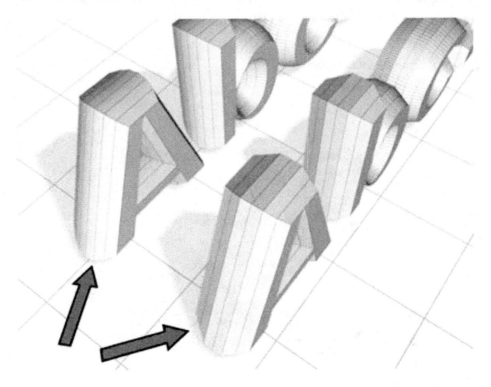

ADVANTAGES

With the help of Bevel modifier, we can give 3D design to text and 3D edge for the text as well. The Bevel Modifier has the ability to add bevel to the edges of the mesh which is selected. The Bevel modifier is a non-destructive alternative to the Bevel operation in edit mode. (C.H. Esteban et al. 2003). The main advantage of bevel modifier is that it is very much helpful in creating logos and 3D text.

COMPARATIVE

In the place of a bevel modifier we can also use extrude modifiers. But as an extrude modifier we need to select the edges, vertices, and face extrude the scanline object to achieve 3d edges, while in bevel modifier it has the in-built feature to add 3d design. We can also use editable poly and chamfer including with it to give 3D edges and smooth edges for the object, but as in bevel modifier

Figure 3. Adding text to viewport.

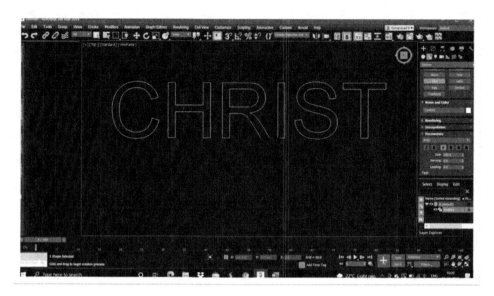

WORKING PROCEDURE

Figure 3 projects Adding Text to viewport. Figure 4 shows using edit spline modifiers and selecting vertex giving new shapes to Text. Figure 5 express Using fillet to tool to smoothen the edges. Figure 6 shows Using bevel modifiers and changing the values in level 1, 2 and 3. Figure 7 projects Editable poly is used to only middle layer of the text and inset that part to give better look. Figure 8 express Extrude modifier is used to other side of the polygon to given better look. Figure 9 shows Chamfer modifier is used to smoothen the polygons. Figure 10 projects adding material editor's bitmaps to give desired look. (Abhijit Guha et al. 2021)

LATTICE MODIFIER

The Lattice modifier transforms a shape's or object's edges into struts with joints at the vertices. This modifier helps us to generate geometry based on mesh topology and also works as an alternative to wireframe appearance. This modifier has the ability to affect the entire object or sub-object choices in the stack. This is ideal for making a cage since it is simple to do and yields excellent results. (M. Sainz et al. 2004)

Figure 4. Using edit spline modifiers and selecting vertex giving new shapes to text

Figure 5. Using fillet to tool to smoothen the edges.

Figure 6. Using bevel modifiers and changing the values in level 1,2 and 3. (Qin Lian et al. 2006)

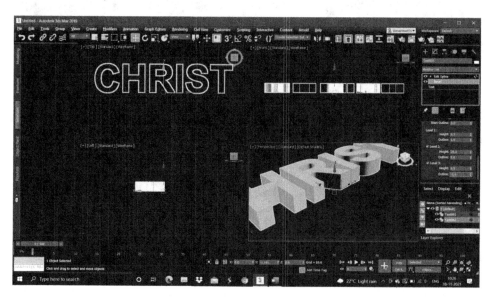

Figure 7. Editable poly is used to only middle layer of the text and inset that part to give better look

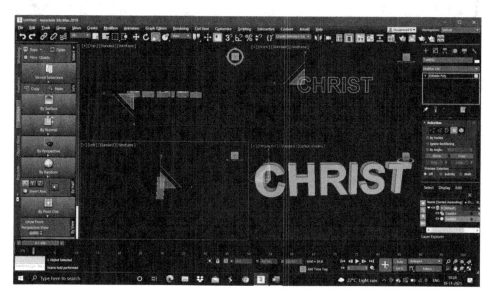

Figure 8. Extrude modifier is used to other side of the polygon to given better look

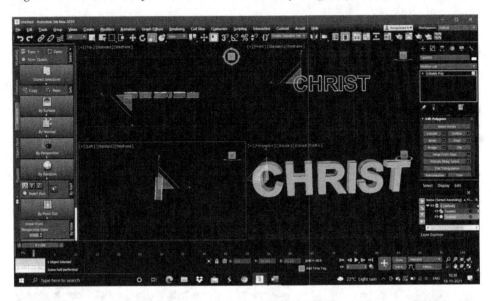

Figure 9. Chamfer modifier is used to smoothen the polygons(M. Maheswari et al. 2021)

Figure 10. Adding material editors bitmaps to give desired look

PROCEDURE

Given below is the procedure of selecting the lattice modifier in Autodesk 3ds Max 2019. Select the object-->Modify panel-->Modifier list-->lattice. (Debabrata Samanta et al. 2012). To begin with, be sure to convert the object or group to editable poly before applying the modification so that the lattice modifier may be applied to sub-objects.

PARAMETERS

Let's have a look at the lattice modifier's parameters. Upon creating an object and applying a lattice modifier on the object, we get a parameters rollout for the lattice modifier shown in figure 11.

DESCRIPTION OF THE PARAMETERS

Geometry class defines if the entire object or chosen sub-objects should be used, as well as which of the two main components i.e. struts and joints, should be presented. Apply To Entire Object: Applies Lattice to all of the object's edges or segments. When enabled, Lattice is applied only to sub-objects handed up the stack. Default it

Figure 11. Lattice modifier

is on. Joints Only From Vertices: This shows only the joints formed by the original mesh's vertices (shown in figure 12). Here is an example of the same:

Struts Only From Edges: This shows only the struts created by the initial mesh segments (shown in figure 13). Here is an example of the same:

Both: Shows (in figure 14) both the struts and the joints. Here is an example of the same:

The Struts group contains controls that influence the shape of the struts. Radius: This parameter controls the radius of the struts. Segments: Defines the number of segments that run along the struts. Modify this number when using the following modifications to deform the struts. Sides: Identifies the number of sides around the struts' circumference. Material ID: This parameter specifies the material ID for the struts. The struts and joints can all have distinct material IDs, so as to assign alternative materials to them. The struts are set to ID 1 by default. Ignore Hidden Edges: Only produces struts for visible edges. When disabled, it creates struts for

Figure 12. Mesh's vertices.

all edges, even unseen edges. By default, it is on. End Caps: Attaches end caps to struts. Smooth: It smoothens the struts.

The Joints group contains parameters that influence the design of the joints. Geodesic Base Type: The category of polyhedron utilized for the joints is specified. Tetra makes use of a tetrahedron. Octa makes use of an octahedron. Icosa An icosahedron is used. Radius: This parameter controls the radius of the joints. Segments: This parameter identifies the number of parts in the joints. The more segments there are, the more spherical the form of the joints. Material ID: The material ID that will be utilized for the joints. ID 2 is the default. Smoothing: Smoothens the joints.

The Mapping Coordinates group describes the characteristics of mapping that will be assigned to the item. None: No mapping is assigned. Reuse Existing: Uses the mapping that is presently allocated to the item. This could be the mapping specified by Generate Mapping Coords., in the creation parameters, or by a previously specified mapping modifier. When this option is selected, each joint inherits the mapping of the vertex it surrounds. New: It makes use of mapping created for the Lattice modifier. Cylindrical mapping is applied to each strut, while spherical mapping is applied to each joint. The lattice modifier simplifies the creation of a cage-like structure.

Figure 13. Mesh segment.

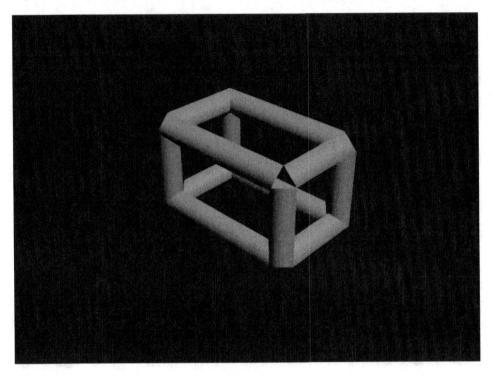

It has geometric settings that are useful, such as joints only from vertices, struts only from edges, and both. These characteristics aid in the creation of many sorts of structures, which would be difficult to do without the use of this modification. (Debabrata Samanta et al. 2012). There are several more characteristics and sub-parameters that allow a structure to be easily deformed.

MODELING

This is the 3ds Max software user-friendly interface. Our workplace is divided into multiple: viewports for our activity, a common panel in the right corner, as well as another tool at the top.

There are 4 major viewports in which we can draw our objects and they are: **Front, Left, Top, and Perspective viewport.**

To start with the mini-project, click on the Create tab on the right side --> geometry-->select Extended Primitive (shown in figure 15). Object type rollout will be visible.

Figure 14. Joined by mesh and vertices

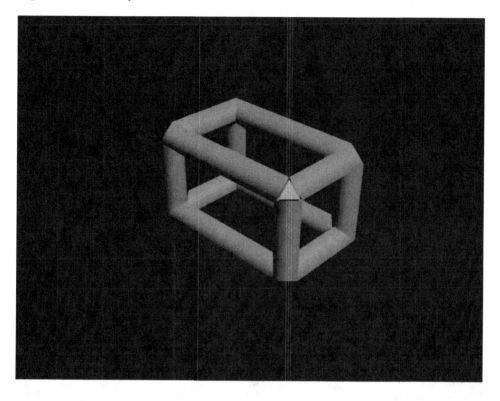

- Select **Capsule** from the object type rollout (shown in figure 16).

- Now convert the object to **editable poly** and cut the lower part of the capsule upon selecting vertices shown in figure 17.

- Select the object and choose the **lattice modifier** from the modifier list. Figure 18

- Click on **Struts Only from Edges** under the parameters rollout. Figure 19.

- The capsule will now look like this.

Figure 15. Extended primitive

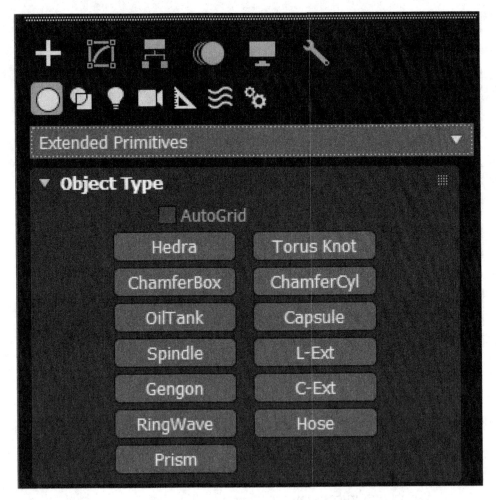

- **Decrease the radius of the struts** to give them a cage-like structure. Figure 21.

- The bars of the cage-like structure have corners. To make it circular in shape, **increase the sides of the struts** in the parameters rollout. Figure 22

- **Place a sphere** on top of the capsule. Figure 23.

Figure 16. Selection of capsule.

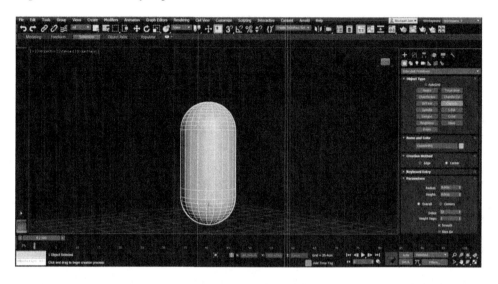

Figure 17. Convert the object to editable poly

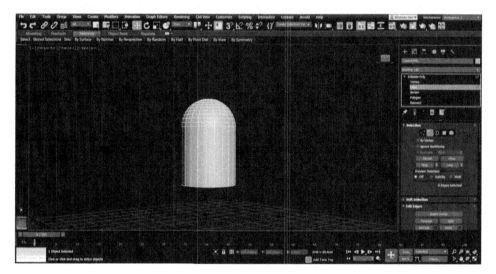

- Increase the **hemisphere to 0.5** and scale it on the z-axis. Figure 24.

- **Add a material** to the capsule and the sphere. Figure 25.

Figure 18. Using lattice modifier

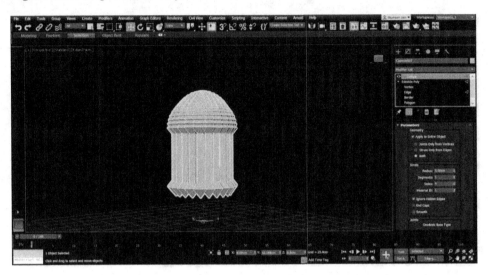

- Create a **2D circle** and check to enable in the renderer and enable in the viewport. This will look like the cage's holder. Figure 26. (V Kureethara et al. 2012)

- Add a **cylinder** below the cage for its support. Figure 27.

- Add a **tube** above the cylinder and of the same radius as the cylinder. Figure 28.

- Now we start with minor details of the cage, like the bird cup and seating.
- **Create a sphere** and increase the **hemisphere to 0.5**.
- Convert the sphere to **editable poly**. Select all the **upper polygons-->inset- ->delete**. Here we get a cup-like structure. Figure 29.

- To make a chain, **select text** under splines and **enter 0** in the text field in parameters rollout.
- Now **extrude** the text and make **clones** to make a chain-like structure.
- **Create a cylinder** to make the seat of the bird. (Anil Kumar et al. 2021)

Figure 19. Struts only from edges

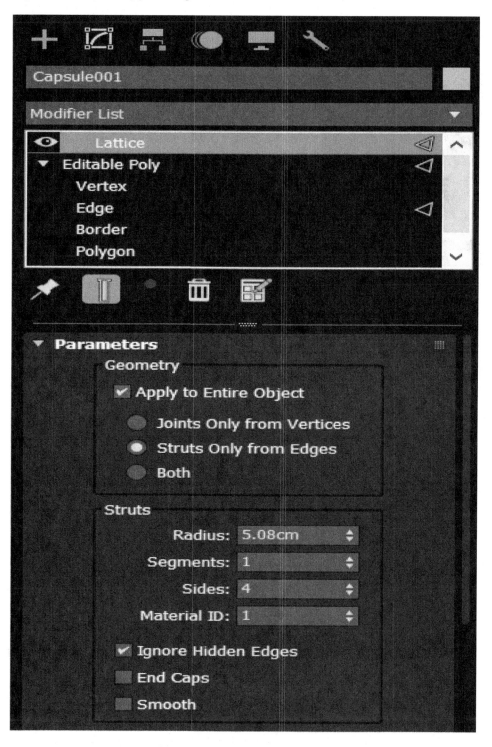

Figure 20. Final look

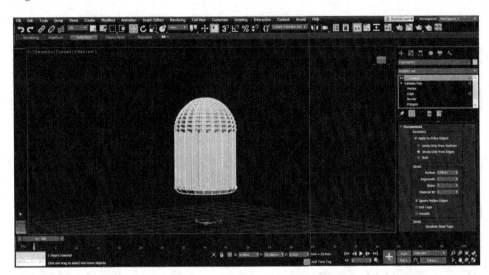

- **Merge the cylinder and the text** to make the actual seating of the bird. Figure 30.

Figure 21. Decrease the radius of the struts.

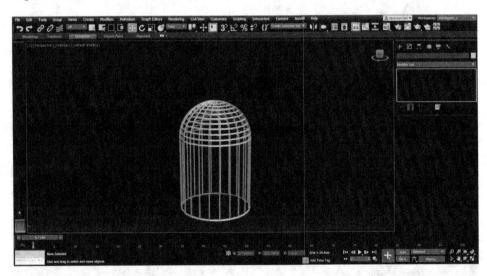

- The cage is ready with all minor objects.
- Let us see the rendered view of our cage.

Figure 22. Increase the sides of the struts.

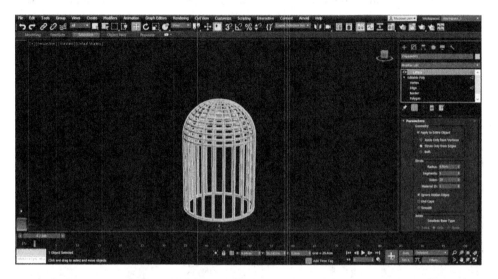

DEFINITION OF SKEW MODIFIER

The skew modifier helps the user to create a uniform offset in the geometry of the object. This can be achieved by using the amount and direction parameters of this modifier to control the direction of the skew along the three-axis and the degree of use of this modifier. In other words, The Skew create a uniform offset in the shape

Figure 23. Place a sphere.

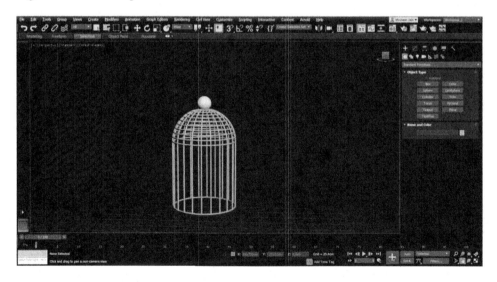

of an object that can be handled by using the amount and the direction parameters on any of the three-axis. (Anil Kumar et al. 2021)

Figure 24. Add hemisphere.

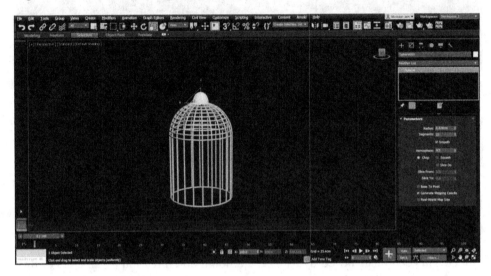

Figure 25. Add a material.

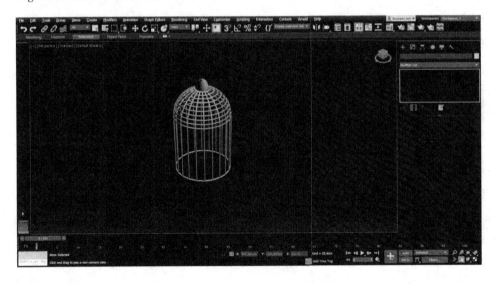

Figure 26. Create a 2D circle.

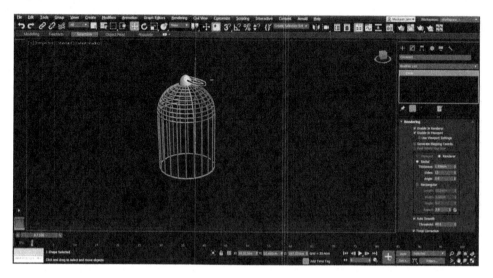

PARAMETERS

The parameters of Skew modifier are as follows Figure 32.

A spinbox to determine the degree and angle of use of the modifier from the vertical plane. Direction-A spinbox to determine the skew direction on any of the three-axis on the horizontal plane. To select the axis on which the skew will take

Figure 27. Add a cylinder.

Figure 28. Add a tube.

place. Limit Effect-Checkbox to apply limitations to the modifier. A spinbox to determine the upper limit boundary from the skew center point in world units. A spinbox to determine the lower limit boundary from the skew center point in world units (Anil Kumar et al. 2021)

Figure 29. Convert the sphere to editable poly.

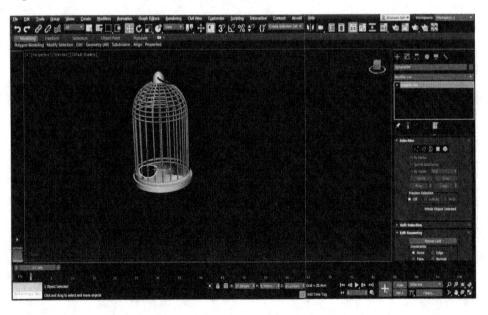

Figure 30. Merge the cylinder and the text.

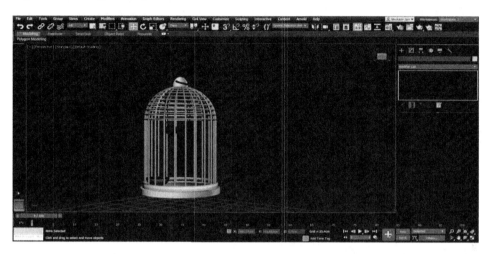

HOW TO USE

Step 1: Click on modify panel
Step 2: Make a selection
Step 3: Drop down the modifier list by clicking on it
Step 4: Move to object space Modifiers
Step 5: Select the Skew Modifier from the list

Procedure: The working procedure of the skew modifier is as follows:-

- Click on the object that you want to skew, then visit the modifiers panel and select Skew from the drop down modifiers list Figure 33.

- In the Parameters Rollout, select the gizmo axis X, Y, or Z of the skew. Figure 35.

- In the amount, spinbox set amount of the skew. The object skews to the amount set starting at the lower limit. Figure 36.

Figure 31. Final cage.

- In the direction, the spinbox set direction of the skew. The object pivots around the axis. By default, the center of the skew is the center of the object. Figure 37.

Set value in upper and lower limit. These determine the distance in current units over and under the center of the modifier, it rests at 0 on the Z-axis of the Gizmo. The skew offset is put in application between the limits. The neighboring geometry remains unaltered by the skew but it is translated to keep the object intact. At sub-object level, we can pick out and relocate the center of the modifier. The limitations remain on anyone side of the center of the skew as we move it to move the skew area to another of the object. Figure 38. (Anil Kumar et al. 2021)

Figure 32. Parameters of skew modifier.

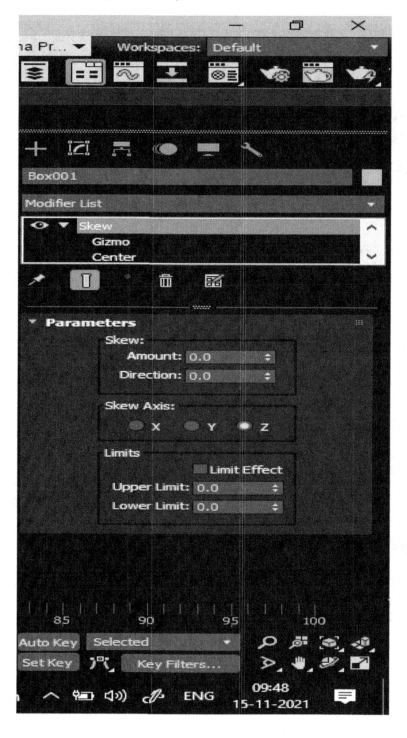

Figure 33. Adding skew.

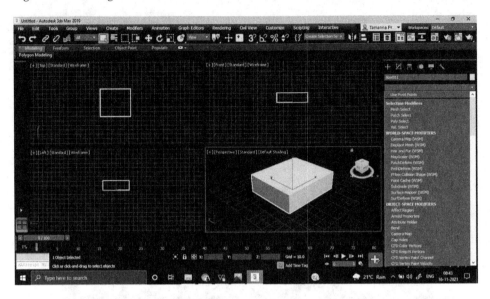

Figure 34. Applying skew.

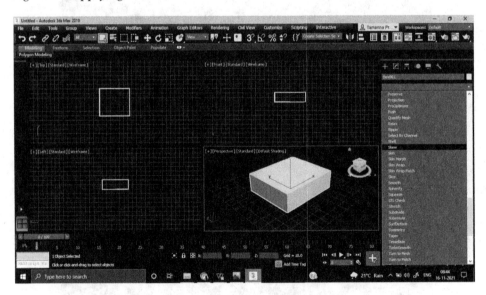

Figure 35. Select the gizmo axis X, Y, or Z of the skew.

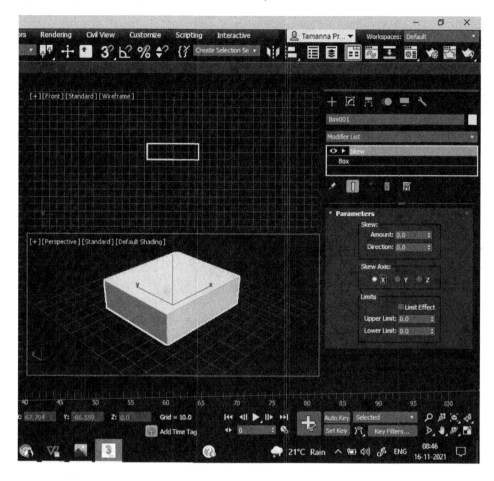

GIZMO

At a sub-object level, like any other object, we can transform and animate the gizmo by changing the result of the skew modifier. Moving the gizmo moves the center an equal distance and Scaling and Rotating the gizmo happens concerning the center of the gizmo. At sub-object level, we can move and animate the Skew effect at the center, The Advantages are as follows, The skew modifier helps the user to create a uniform offset in the geometry of the object. The amount and direction of the skew modifier can be changed according to the will of the user providing them with a greater option to achieve a more realistic view. The skew can be performed on any desired axis. It can prove to be very useful while creating chimney pipes, stone tools, the top of a tower, etc. Comparative study (Binod Kumar et al. 2021)

Figure 36.Set amount.

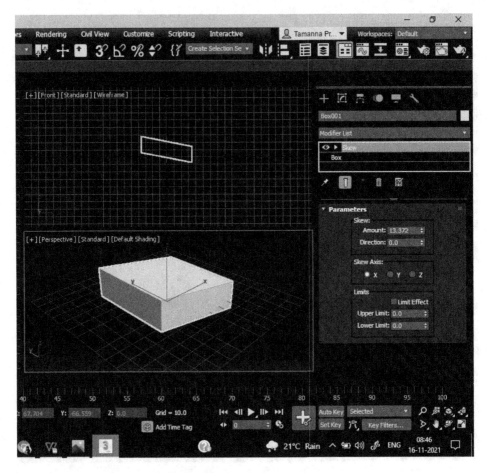

SKEW VS SHELL MODIFIER

The Skew Modifier creates a uniform offset in the geometry of the object whereby default the center of the skew is the center of the object. Whereas, The shell modifier gives thickness to an object by adding a set of extra faces.

The Shell Modifier does not have a sub-object level. Whereas, The Skew modifier has a sub-object level. Figure 39.

Figure 37. The center of the skew is the center of the object.

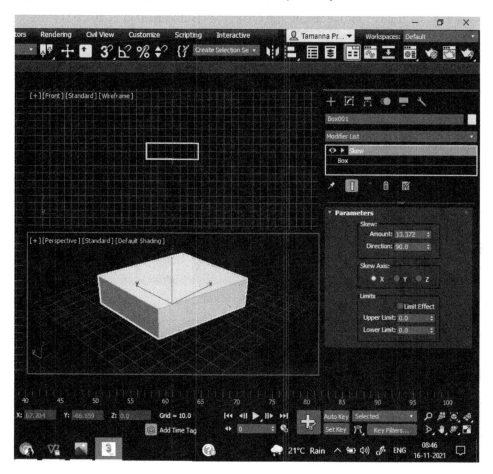

BEND MODIFIER

The Bend Modifier bends the object up to 360* over an axis. There is no provision to change direction or the amount of bend. Like Shell Modifier Bend Modifier does not have a sub-object level. Figure 40.

FFD

FFD is Free Form Deformation. It is used in animation for gas tanks and dance scenarios and also to model rounded shapes like chairs and sculptures

1.2*2*2 - It has a lattice resolution on 2*2*2

2.3*3*3 - It has a lattice resolution on 3*3*3

3.4*4*4 - It has a lattice resolution on 4*4*4 (Binod Kumar et al. 2021)

Figure 38.The interface.

Figure 39.Comparision skew vs shell.

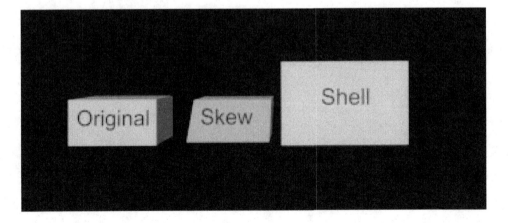

Figure 40. Comparision skew vs bend.

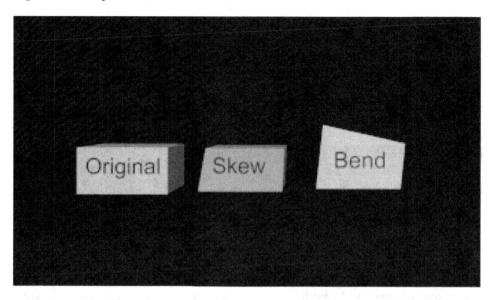

The FFD modifier margin the chosen geometry with a grid by adjusting the different control points, The circumscribed geometry is deformed. Whereas Skew modifier works on any of the X Y Z axes

The FFD modifier has Control Points, Lattice, and Set the volume in its Interface but the Skew modifier has Gizmo and Center.

Figure 41. Comparison skew vs FFD.

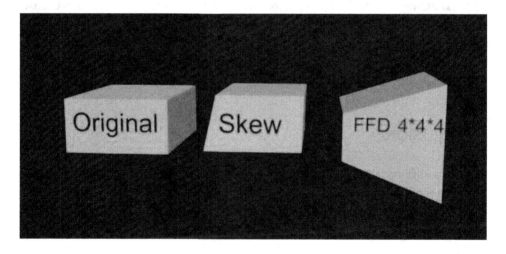

Figure 42. Comparison skew vs edit poly.

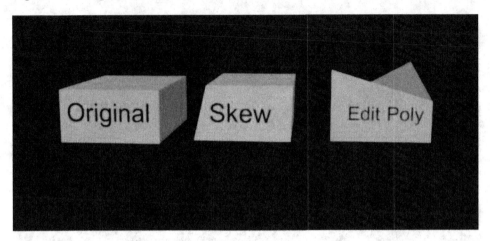

The skew modifier has a simpler parameter roll out with less number of parameters whereas, FFD modifiers have a more laid out parameter roll out with many parameters. Figure 41.

EDIT POLY

The edit Poly gives a choice of several editing tools for performing different modifications at the sub-object level of the selected object. Which are vertex, edge,border, and element. A wider range of modifications can be performed with the help of Edit Ploy on a different sub-object level. (Manu M K et al. 2018). The Edit Poly modifier incorporates most capacities of the fundamental Editable Poly item, excluding Vertex Color data, Subdivision Surface Rollout, Weight and Crease settings, and Subdivision Displacement Rollout. Alter poly allows us to invigorate sub-item changes and boundary changes. Likewise,we can hold the item creation boundaries and change them later. A handful number of modifications can be done with it. Figure 42 shows Comparison Skew Vs Edit Poly.

CONCLUSION

Lattice modifier made it very easy to make a cage which would get hard to make it with other modifiers. We can use many modifiers instead of bevel modifier but in order to achieve bevel we should spend more time, because we need to select edges, vertices and faces and modify while if we use bevel modifier it is easy to achieve the beveling of text as it has all the in built in feature in order to Bevel text.

REFERENCES

Arayici, Y., & Hamilton, A. (2005). Modeling 3D scanned data to visualize the built environment. *Ninth International Conference on Information Visualisation (IV'05),* 509-514.

Biswal, A. K., Singh, D., Pattanayak, B. K., Samanta, D., & Yang, M.-H. (2021). IoT-Based Smart Alert System for Drowsy Driver Detection. Wireless Communications and Mobile Computing. doi:10.1155/2021/6627217

Castellani, U., Fusiello, A., Murino, V., Papaleo, L., Puppo, E., & Pittore, M. (2005, October). A complete system for on-line 3D modelling from acoustic images. *Signal Processing Image Communication, 20*(9-10), 832–852. doi:10.1016/j.image.2005.02.003

De Luca, L., Veron, P., & Florenzano, M. (2006, April). Reverse engineering of architectural buildings based on a hybrid modeling approach. *Computers & Graphics, 30*(2), 160–176. doi:10.1016/j.cag.2006.01.020

Esteban, C. H., & Schmitt, F. (2003). Silhouette and stereo fusion for 3D object modeling. *Fourth International Conference on 3-D Digital Imaging and Modeling, 2003. 3DIM 2003. Proceedings,* 46-53.

Guha, A., Samanta, D., Banerjee, A., & Agarwal, D. (2021). A Deep Learning Model for Information Loss Prevention From Multi-Page Digital Documents. *IEEE Access: Practical Innovations, Open Solutions, 9,* 80451–80465. doi:10.1109/ACCESS.2021.3084841

Kureethara, V., Biswas, J., & Debabrata Samanta, N. G. (n.d.). Balanced Constrained Partitioning of Distinct Objects. *International Journal of Innovative Technology and Exploring Engineering.* doi:10.35940/ijitee.K1023.09811S19

Lian, Q., Li, D.-C., Tang, Y.-P., & Zhang, Y.-R. (2006, May). Computer modeling approach for a novel internal architecture of artificial bone. *Computer Aided Design, 38*(5), 507–514. doi:10.1016/j.cad.2005.12.001

Maheswari, M., Geetha, S., & Selva Kumar, S. (2021). PEVRM: Probabilistic Evolution Based Version Recommendation Model for Mobile Applications. *IEEE Access: Practical Innovations, Open Solutions, 9,* 20819–20827. doi:10.1109/ACCESS.2021.3053583

Manu, Roy, & Samanta. (2018). Effects of Liver Cancer Drugs on Cellular Energy Metabolism in Hepatocellular Carcinoma Cells. *International Journal of Pharmaceutical Research, 10*(3). . doi:10.31838/ijpr/2018.10.03.079

Park & Subbarao. (2005). A multiview 3D modeling system based on stereo vision techniques. *Machine Vision and Applications, 16*(3), 148-156.

Sainz, Pajarola, Mercade, & Susin. (2004). A simple approach for point-based object capturing and rendering. *IEEE Computer Graphics and Applications, 24*(4), 24-33.

Samanta & Sanyal. (2012a). Segmentation technique of sar imagery based on fuzzy c-means clustering. Academic Press.

Samanta & Sanyal. (2012b). A novel approach of sar image classification using color space clustering and watersheds. Academic Press.

Sanyal & Samanta. (2011). Segmentation technique of sar imagery using entropy. *International Journal of Computer Technology and Applications*, 2, 1548–1551.

Sun, W., Starly, B., Nam, J., & Darling, A. (2005, September). Bio-CAD modeling and its applications in computer-aided tissue engineering. *Computer Aided Design*, *37*(11), 1097–1114. doi:10.1016/j.cad.2005.02.002

Chapter 7
Lights and Camera Rendering for Living Room Modeling in 3ds Max Platform

Raghav Sham Kamat
CHRIST University, India

Oruan Memoye Kepeghom
Federal College of Education, Technical, Omoku, Nigeria

ABSTRACT

Rapid demands for the representation of various scenes and objects have bought in an evolution that ought to bring in the applications, usage, and development of various 3D modeling software. One would have the interest to have a glimpse of a sample (i.e., a 3D model of any structure to be created in the future). This chapter describes the usage and applications of 3ds Max with lights and camera view rendering related to which creating a 3D virtual scene of a living room is briefed. The chapter also includes the methodologies of designing and implementing various features of 3ds Max like editors, materials, lights, modifiers, and camera rendering. Usage of modifiers like edit poly, edit mesh, turbo-smooth, mesh smooth bend, etc. are briefly described. This chapter can assure a variety of map usages like texture maps with various camera angles to have a clear perspective of every object and scene in detail.

DOI: 10.4018/978-1-6684-4139-8.ch007

INTRODUCTION

As important as it is to make any object or a scene look convincing, at most importance should be given in implementing lights in a good fashioned way, by having the right selection of lights and placing them in an accurate position can always give a satisfying output to the scene. Lighting is not just to make any object or a scene visible, it gives just the amount of enhancement and appearance which eventually adds a realistic feel and colorization (Van de Perre, G. et al. 2019). 3D Lighting for any demonstration has a likeness between lighting i.e. cinematography or photography. The craftsman builds up a mix of light sources to cause to notice an exceptional piece of the stage, or to address the any properties of the scene. The job of lighting can be considerably more significant when it is applied for any commercial purposes (Nadeem, A. et al. 2015). Moreover, it can feature various details of any 3D model or a scene that are pertinent to set up an upper hand for various proposals and competitive submissions (M. T. Valdez et al. 2016). 3D lighting gives us a set of techniques and tools with which various scenarios can be created and demonstrated. 3D modelers can browse a wide assortment of light types, instruments and methods that attempt to cover their whole range of requirements (Samanta, Deababrata, et al. (2012)).

Considering 3D visualization, 3ds Max provides us a set of camera tools with which viewing a 3D model or a scene can be much easier with a lot of time being saved at the time of rendering (Samanta, Debabrata, et al. (2012c)). Different cameras like Physical cameras and Legacy cameras give us a variety of perspective to view any object or a scene (Deryabin, N.B. et al. 2017). 3ds Max uses various tools for providing different lighting conditions. Important concepts like aperture and shutter speed are very much important to understand for implementation (Lungershausen, U. et al. 2013). The amount of light can be easily controlled over the scene to just get the right amount of focus effects needed (Samanta, Debabrata, et al. (2012f)). This paper covers the maximal usage of various lights and cameras to enhance an object or a scene environment.

CREATING A VIRTUAL LIVING ROOM

Creating a living room with as many as lights and camera can be harder than it seems but with the large availability of modifiers and primitives such as standard and compound object, 3ds Max provides us various options to modify lights and its properties (Samanta, Debabrata, et al. (2012g)). Adding lights to objects gives more justification to the material and bitmaps added to it. Making use of modifiers can improvise the detailing of any object or a scene at the time of rendering, with the presence of lights the scene can be improvised and justified to give a realistic view (Tavares, J. et al.)(YeeWa Choy et al. 2012). Fig 1 shows Living room rendered image with lights.

Figure 1. Living room rendered image with lights

BASE STRUCTURE

Walls were created using boxes from standard primitives, after attaining three boxes it was places in a square shaped manner with a side open for editing purpose like placing objects in an accurate position and moving them (Samanta, Debabrata, et al., 2013)(H. Esmaeili et al. 2014). The walls are respectively scaled to appear as a wall by adjusting their axis (X, Y, Z). Planes were used as floor (Samanta, Debabrata, et al., 2012a). Fig 2 shows Rendered image of window mounted wall

Figure 2. Rendered image of window mounted wall

WINDOW

- Step 1: Select a wall of any side where window has to be placed®Convert to Editable poly.
- Step 2: Standard Primitives ®Box ®Scale it to a size of a window.
- Step 3: Place the box inside the wall where window has to be created.
- Step 4: Select wall®Compound objects®Pro-Boolean®Start Picking ®Select the box placed. This creates a hollow opening in the wall which can later be covered with plane as glass.
- Step 5: Select wall ®Modifier list®Polygon® Select the inner sides of the wall where a hollow opening was created.
- Step 6: Edge (Manually create line segments to extrude)® Select edges on corresponding opposite sides where the line segment has to be created.
- Step 7: Increase segments (range between 0.6333-2.11111) ®Create line segments on all 4 inner sides (Yoo-Kil Yang et al. 2005).
- Step 8: Editable poly®Polygon®Select the area between created line segments®Extrude ®Increase the extrude value until it intersects with each other and touches the opposite sides.

- Step 9: By doing the above steps, grills for the windows are created. Repeat the above steps on any other side where windows are required.
- Step 10: (Glass for windows) Standard primitives®Plane®Scale the plane just small so that it fits right inside the window area®Place the plane in the window area submerged in the wall.
- Step 11: Once placed, select plane®Color® Blue®Object properties ®Visibility ®Reduce visibility to 3. By doing this step we h=give a transparent effect to the plane that appears as a glass for the windows.

STEPS TO CREATE TABLE

- Step 1:Using cylinders and boxes from standard primitives and scaling the box upon each other to form a proper shape to place objects (U. Castellani et al. 2005).
- Step 2: Use material editor to give a realistic design to the table.
- Step 3: (Vase) Cylinder®Convert to editable poly®Increase line segments®Bend.
- Step 4: Vase®Bevel®Editable poly®Polygon ®Drag upward®Reduce thickness
- Step 5: Vase®Editable Poly®Vertex®Move.
- Step 6: Group all the object of table and placed the vase on top of it.

WINDOWS

Once the walls are placed, choose a relevant side to mount the window. Using the Pro Boolean under compound objects create an opening for the window to extrude grills from the walls. Select the wall and place a box thick enough to pass through the wall and to a size of a window. Once the box is placed go to modify Boolean properties, click on start picking and select the box passing through the wall (Kwon, Y.M. et al. 2017). By doing this, a hollow opening is created to create a window. Then select the wall and convert it to editable poly. Using an edge modifier, we can select the sides exactly opposite to the surface where the grill has to be extruded. When all required lines are drawn on the inner surface of the wall with the window opening, click polygon and select all the divided surface (ctrl+left click) and apply extrude effect to the selected portion, Increase the extrude amount until it touches the opposite surface. Add a plane and scale it in such a way that it fits right into the opening made for a window (Samanta, Debabrata, et al. (2011)). Reduce the visibility of the plane so that it becomes transparent (D. Fritsch et al. 2017)(Samanta, Debabrata, et al. (2012b)). Make a clone of the transparent plane and add an image of

Figure 3. Rendered image focusing sofa

any scenery using compact material editor. Apply bitmaps of any downloaded image and enable in viewport if real time view is required (Toshihiro ASAI et al. 2005) (Samanta, Debabrata, et al. (2011c)). Fig 3 shows Rendered image focusing sofa.

SOFA STRUCTURE

The structure was created using basic objects like boxes, Smoothening edges was done using modifiers like mesh smooth and increasing the noise intensity in noise modifier properties (Ardakani, H.K. et al. 2020)(Samanta, Debabrata, et al. (2011a)). Pillow shapes were created using FFD 4x4x4 modifier, apply the modifier to pillow sized boxes. Select check points from FFD 4x4x4 modifier properties and select the points in the edges and push it towards the inside (Z. Pezeshki et al. 2017). Apply noise modifier to the pillow and increase the noise intensity as mentioned above. Make clones of the pillows and place it on the sofa at different angles and position (Wei Sun et al. 2002). Fig 4 shows Rendered image of the sofa with modifiers.

Figure 4. Rendered image of the sofa with modifiers

SOFA

- Step 1: (Base) Standard primitives®Box ®Scale it to as of a rectangle.
- Step 2: Select box®Right Click ®Convert to editable poly ®Modifier List®Chamfer.
- Step 3: Select box®Modifier properties®Increase line segments.
- Step 4: Editable Poly ®Edge ®Select the edges of the rectangle ®Bevel.
- Step 5: (Back) New Box®Adjust the width of the new box same as the size of (Base)
- Step 6: Select Box (Back) ®Convert to editable poly ®Polygon®Select the opposite diagonal sides of the box ®Use arrows to move it in a U-Shaped direction.
- Step 7: Repeat step (54) on both corresponding sides that produces a horse shoe shaped object that has to be placed on the sofa.
- Step 8: (Pillows) Box®Convert to editable poly®Turbo smooth.
- Step 9: Modifier list ®FFD 4*4*4 Modifier ® Point selection (Vertex) ®Select end points on each diagonal sides ®Move the selected points in on each side.
- Step 10: Select Pillow® Modifier list®Mesh smooth®Noise®Increase noise amount.
- Step 11: (Pillows) Make sufficient clones (shift +drag (left click)) ® Place it on the Base in an upright position with each pillow in a different direction (L. L. Khoroshko et al. 2018).
- Step 12: Group the base, back and pillows together and place them in a right position suiting the scene.

BOX SOFAS (SMALL)

- Step 1: Standard Primitives®Box®Convert to editable poly ®Increase Line segments.
- Step 2: Vertex® Select Alternate points on all 6 sides of the square.
- Step 3: Extrude®Reduce the value to be Negative (-)
- Step 4: Bevel ®Reduce the value to be Negative (-)®Turbo smooth®Noise ®Increase noise amount (W. Sun et al. 2005).

SHOWCASE LIGHTS

Showcase lights creates a really well-balanced ambience to the living room as it makes it more attractive and the presence of lights casts shadows when activated providing a realistic view. Using cylinders, clones of it were made and was scaled big enough to place a free light inside (D. Tsipotas et al. 2015). Using Compound objects (Pro Boolean) a hollow space was created and holes were made using smaller cylinder scaled and placed inside the cylinder so that it passes through the cylinders. Again, make clones of the smaller cylinders and place it through the cylinder with hollow spaces, Using Pro Boolean the smaller cylinders and its clone were removed which creates pores for the light to pass through it and cast shadows (M. R. Filho et al. 2011). Fig 5 shows Rendered image of Showcase lights casting shadows. Fig 6 shows Rendered image of Showcase lights casting shadows on the wall, Fig 7 shows Rendered image of Showcase lights casting shadows on the shelves.

TV AND SPEAKERS

Speakers were created using boxes and applying basic modifiers like Bend on the object. The speaker box was bent towards the x- axis and a clone of it was made. Sleek speakers were created using capsules (Günther-Diringer et al. 2016)(Natephra, W. et al. 2017). The capsules were converted to editable poly and using polygon, with the increase in line segments parts of the capsule were extruded, using cylinders and Pro Boolean hollow spaces were created to the capsules and speaker box to place cords with the help of extrude modifier (S. Vu et al. 2018)(Samanta, Debabrata, et al. (2012e)). Stands for the speaker were created using boxes and scaling them irrespective of the speaker size so that the speakers can be placed on them (Samanta, Debabrata, et al. (2012h))(Yusuf Arayici et al. 2005).TV was created using flat boxes and planes. A flat scaled box was places on the furniture side of the wall and using editable polygon a larger surface big enough to place a plane to represent a

Figure 5. Rendered image of showcase lights casting shadows

screen was extruded with a negative value (Samanta, Debabrata, et al. (2011d))(H. Esmaeili et al. 2017). A plane was placed at the negatively extruded area. Using material editor, a bitmap was added to the plane to give a real TV display like appearance. Modifiers like Bevel were used on a box to create an amplifier system with knob attached to it created using a cylinder. Fig 8 shows Rendered image of the speaker and TV.

STEPS TO CREATE SPEAKERS

- Step 1: Box®Bend modifiers for giving a slant shape®Scale the boxes well enough to place it above the lower shelf and below the racks ®Drag Sphere from standard primitives and position it right into the speaker box®Pro-Boolean®Select Sphere ®Pick Operand and start picking (Samanta, Debabrata, et al. (2011)).
- Step 2: Sphere®Melt®Plastic®Z-Axis®Increase Sensitivity®Inset®Extrud e®Position

- Step 3(Amplifier): Box®Convert to Editable Poly®Increase line segments®Select necessary Polygon®Extrude and inset according to any design that has to be created.
- Step 4: (Speaker air vents) Cylinder®Place in the speaker box®Pro-Boolean®Select Sphere ®Pick Operand and start picking the sphere places.
- Step 5:(Sleek Speakers):Drag Capsule from compound objects® Sphere®Position the sphere one below another adjacent to the capsule®Pro-Boolean®Select capsule®Pick Operand and start picking the sphere placed adjacent to the capsule.
- Step 6: (AMPLIFIER KNOB)Cylinder®Melt®Z-Axis®Plastic®Increase Sensitivity.
- Step 7: (AMPLIFIER SCREEN) Edge Faces®Edit Poly®Select Area ®Inset ®Extrude®Color.

Figure 6. Rendered image of showcase lights casting shadows on the wall

Figure 7. Rendered image of showcase lights casting shadows on the shelves

ROOF AND LIGHTS

Make an exact clone of the floor plane and drag it upwards. Using boxes, scale it with the proper width and height with any desired roofing furniture structure (Samanta, Debabrata, et al. (2012d)). Make sufficient clones and form a uniform roofing structure with sufficient space for lights. Use a box and create two hollow spaces inside it to place free lights inside (A. S. Baskoro et al. 2015)(Samanta, Debabrata, et al. (2012)). Enable shadow to the free light and change the color to an ambience that gives yellow lighting. Make clones of the lights and place it in the roofing structure (Woop, Sven et al. 2005). Using target lights the whole hall was lit by placing it in multiple places with roof being the source and object like sofa and floor being the focal points (Samanta, Debabrata. (2011)). Fig 9 shows Rendered image of roof with lighting, Fig 10 says Zoomed image of roof lights, Fig 11 projects Rendered image of photo frames, Fig 12 express Rendered image of TV furniture, Fig 13 shows Lighting rendered image of TV furniture, Fig 14 says Home theatre focused rendered image.

Figure 8. Rendered image of the speaker and TV

Figure 9. Rendered image of roof with lighting

Figure 10. Zoomed image of roof lights

Figure 11. Rendered image of photo frames

METHODOLOGY

- Step 1: Click on Standard Primitives ®Shapes ®Plane ®Place the plane (1) on downward plane position to create a floor.
- Step 2: Standard Primitives ®Shapes ®Box ®Drag 2 – 3 sufficient boxes

Figure 12. Rendered image of TV furniture

Figure 13. Lighting rendered image of TV furniture

Figure 14. Home theatre focused rendered image

- Step 3: Right click on the boxes ®Scale ®Adjust the size of the boxes by selecting and dragging the axis (x-axis, y-axis and z-axis).
- Step 4: Place the boxes perpendicular to the plane (1) on all required adjacent sides.
- Step 5: Drag plane (2) from standard primitives ® shapes and place the plane (2) on plane (1) to create a carpet.
- Step 6: Drag a box ®Scale it such that it fits right into the wall.
- Step 7: Drag another box and scale it to be just as any rack of a shelf.
- Step 8: Make copies of the racks by (shift +drag (left click))
- Step 9: After making clones, place the racks perpendicular to the box that is placed adjacent to the walls.
- Step 10: Position the racks one after the other on both sides(opposite) adjacent to the wall.
- Step 11: To make Lower Shelfs, select boxes from standard primitives and place it together on the floor just below the racks with proper scaling.
- Step 12: Select boxes from standard Primitives and reduce the scale by clicking the any point of axis and pushing it inward to the object. Place it right ahead of the lower shelf to create doors.

- Step 13: Use modifiers like mesh smooth to give a smooth texture and are done by increasing the intensity (UlaşYılmaz, AdemMülayim et al. 2002).
- Step 14: Objects can also be given sufficient smoothness by using modifiers like chamfer.
- Step 15: Shapes® Line ® draw a U-Shaped pattern to create a handle for shelfs.
- Step 16: After creating a handle pattern, select modifier list and apply Lathe modifier.
- Step 17: Just after the lathe modifier is applied, change parameters like max alignment to the line to get a full scaled handle.
- Step 18: Adjust the size of the handle with respect to the shelf doors and place them in a proper position.
- Step 19: Box ®Convert to Editable Poly®Polygon ®Select a wider side of the box to create a display ®Inset®Extrude (decrease the value) to create bezels.
- Step 20: Drag a plane and place it adjacent to the TV box, right inside the bezels.
- Step 21: To give a scene running in the TV display use Material Editor.
- Step 22: Rendering ®Compact Material Editor® Standard ®Bitmap ®Select an image to appear as a scene ®Assign to material ®Show in Viewport (if wanted to be viewed by default)®Render.

STEPS TO CREATE SHELVES

- Step 1: Boxes ® Make clones ®Scale boxes with any desired or random sizes.
- Step 2: Place the boxes in any required pattern and group them ® Make an exact copy of the shelf boxes.
- Step 3: Cloned shelfs ®Scale such that the size is reduced to 80% ® Merge it with the shelves.
- Step 4: Select the grouped shelf®Compound Objects®Pro Boolean ®Pick operand®Start picking ®Select the cloned shelf.
- Step 5: By picking the cloned shelf a, hollow space that off the cloned shelf will be created in the original shelf where different objects like books and case can be placed.
- Step 6: (Books) Box®Scale the box to a size of a book ®Make a copy of the box ®Reduce scale of the clone to 80% of the book.
- Step 7: Merge the clone with the book with a different color(white).
- Step 8: Book®Convert to editable poly ®Modifier list®Chamfer/Mesh Smooth

- Step 9: Make clones of the books and apply different bitmaps using compact material editor to give a realistic look.
- Step 10: (Android) Cylinder®Edge Faces®EditMesh®Mesh-Smooth ®Edit Poly ®Chamfer®Increase Edge Sensitivity in Base.
- Step 11: Sphere®Edit poly®Select Half circle®Delete®Position sphere above cylinder
- Step 12: Cylinder®Placein sphere®Compound Object®Pro Boolean®Select Cylinder®Pick Operand® Start Picking.
- Step 13: Capsules®Edit Mesh®Turbo smooth®Position
- Step 14: (Shelf Pole) Standard primitives ® Cylinder ®Reduce Width ® Make Clones®Place the clones at different places connecting the shelf boxes.
- Step 15: Box®Make 3 clones ®Place a box adjacent to the wall ®Another box perpendicular to the box fixed to the wall.
- Step 16: (Lower rack) Fix the shelf to the box adjacent to the wall and to boxes below the shelf, one perpendicular and adjacent.
- Step 17: (Wall frames) Shapes ® Line ®Rectangle®Draw 3 layers of rectangle placed together.
- Step 18: Select lines ® Convert to Editable Poly ®Enable in Viewport® Increase thickness.
- Step 19: Make 3 clones of the frames, each of different sides and place the together adjacent to any side of the wall.
- Step 20: (Giving image to frames) Standard primitives ®Plane ®Make three clones ®Scale them with the size same as of the three frames.
- Step 21: Select planes ®Compact Material editor ®Select Bitmap®Choose image®Assign to material ® Enable in viewport (Optional). Repeat the step for all the planes that are to be placed in the frame (Manson, A. et al. 2015).
- Step 22: Attach planes with images to all 3 frames.

PLACING LIGHTS IN THE SCENE

- Step 1: Lights ®Photometric Lights®Target light
- Step 2: Use cursor and drag it towards pointing towards the object or any scene that has to be lit (Samanta, Debabrata, et al. (2011b)).
- Step 3: In the living room choose target spot lights ®Drag it from the floor to the roof such that the focal point is towards the roof and the light source is towards the floor or object.
- Step 4: Select the light source®Modifier list®Activate shadows.
- Step 5: Select light ®Properties®Saturation®Color.

- Step 6: Choose light yellow for a good living room ambiance or any color of your choice.
- Step 7: After modifying the light properties place it in the right position.
- Step 8: Make clones of the lights and place it in different places.
- Step 9: Drag a box from standard Primitives ®Compound objects®Pro Boolean ®Create two hollow spaces in the dragged box.
- Step 10: Lights ®Photometric lights®Free light.
- Step 11: Make clones of the free light and place it in the hollow space created in the box.
- Step 12: Select free lights® Properties®Activate shadows®Intensity®Reduce value to 800.
- Step 13: Group the box and lights together and place it near the shelves besides the television.
- Step 14: Standard Primitives®Cylinder®Scale it with increase in the amount of thickness.
- Step 15: Using compound objects and Pro Boolean create a hollow space inside the cylinder.
- Step 16: Cylinder ®Reduce thickness®Make clones of the cylinder®Place the clones in such a way that it passes trough the cylinder with hollow space.
- Step 17: Compound objects ®Select cylinder with hollow space®Pro Boolean ®Start Picking®Select small cylinders passing through it. It creates small spaces that allow the light to pass through when light placed inside.
- Step 18: Place free light inside the cylinder ®Activate shadow®Reduce light intensity®Change color to pink

PLACING CAMERAS

- Step 1: Cameras®Target camera® Alt+w ® Change viewport angle®Front view of any object or scene that has to be focused.
- Step 2: Hold the cursor to a point where the camera should be placed and drag towards the object or a scene.
- Step 3: Select Physical camera and repeat the same step as placing target camera for focusing a scene.
- Step 4: Select camera®Properties ®Adjust camera position®Adjust camera focal point.
- Step 5: Closer the camera is bought to the focal point, the size of the focal frame is reduced and vice versa (Hegazy, M. et al. 2022).

Repeat the above steps and place cameras at required places focusing the required object or scene.

MATERIAL AND RENDERING

- Step 1: Select object®Rendering ®Material editor®Compact material editor®Bitmap®Select required image ®Assign material ® Enable in viewport for real time view.
- Step 2: Rendering® Render setup®Iterative Rendering ®Scaline render® Render.

When rendered, the materials along with the objects and lights appear in a new window with all the properties (Soon-Yong Park et al. 2005).

CONCLUSION

Lights can be of great importance in 3ds max, not just to enhance the scene but also to justify the amount of accuracy and detailing to any object or a scene. Materials and colors can rightly be visible at its best instance which gives the best justification to it. Rendering can take up some time but end result with lights would be interesting. Adding cameras can be of great use to have a different perspective over the scene and also creating path animations using auto key frames.

REFERENCES

Arayici, Y., & Hamilton, A. (2005). Modeling 3D Scanned Data to Visualize the Built Environment. *Proceedings of the Ninth International Conference on Information Visualisation*, 509-514. 10.1109/IV.2005.82

Ardakani, H. K., Mousavinia, A., & Safaei, F. (2020). Four points: One-pass geometrical camera calibration algorithm. *The Visual Computer*, *36*(2), 413–424. doi:10.100700371-019-01632-7

Baskoro, A. S., & Haryanto, I. (2015). Development of travel speed detection method in welding simulator using augmented reality. *2015 International Conference on Advanced Computer Science and Information Systems (ICACSIS)*, 269-273. 10.1109/ICACSIS.2015.7415194

Castellani, U., Fusiello, A., Murino, V., Papaleo, L., Puppo, E., & Pittore, M. (2005). A complete system for on-line 3D modelling from acoustic images. *Signal Processing Image Communication*, *20*(9-10), 832–852. doi:10.1016/j.image.2005.02.003

Choy, Lim, Wang, & Chan. (2012). Development CT-based three-dimensional complex skull model for Finite element analysis. *2012 IEEE Conference on Sustainable Utilization and Development in Engineering and Technology (STUDENT)*, 135-139. 10.1109/STUDENT.2012.6408383

Deryabin, N. B., Zhdanov, D. D., & Sokolov, V. G. (2017). Embedding the script language into optical simulation software. *Programming and Computer Software*, *43*(1), 13–23. doi:10.1134/S0361768817010029

Esmaeili, H., Thwaites, H., & Woods, P. C. (2017). Workflows and Challenges Involved in Creation of Realistic Immersive Virtual Museum, Heritage, and Tourism Experiences: A Comprehensive Reference for 3D Asset Capturing. *2017 13th International Conference on Signal-Image Technology & Internet-Based Systems (SITIS)*, 465-472. 10.1109/SITIS.2017.82

Esmaeili, H., Woods, P. C., & Thwaites, H. (2014). Realisation of virtualised architectural heritage. *2014 International Conference on Virtual Systems & Multimedia (VSMM)*, 94-101. 10.1109/VSMM.2014.7136676

Filho, M. R., Negrão, N. M., & Damasceno, R. R. (2011). SwImax: A Web Tool Using Virtual Reality for Teaching the WiMAX Protocol. *2011 XIII Symposium on Virtual Reality*, 217-224. 10.1109/SVR.2011.27

Fritsch, D., & Klein, M. (2017). 3D and 4D modeling for AR and VR app developments. *2017 23rd International Conference on Virtual System & Multimedia (VSMM)*, 1-8. 10.1109/VSMM.2017.8346270

Günther-Diringer, D. (2016). Historisches 3D-Stadtmodell von Karlsruhe. *J. Cartogr. Geogr. Inf.*, *66*, 66–71. doi:10.1007/BF03545207

Hegazy, M., Yasufuku, K., & Abe, H. (2022). An interactive approach to investigate brightness perception of daylighting in Immersive Virtual Environments: Comparing subjective responses and quantitative metrics. *Building Simulation*, *15*(1), 41–68. doi:10.100712273-021-0798-3

Khoroshko, L. L., Ukhov, P. A., & Keyno, P. P. (2018). *Development of a Laboratory Workshop for Open Online Courses Based on 3D Computer Graphics and Multimedia. In 2018 Learning With MOOCS*. LWMOOCS. doi:10.1109/LWMOOCS.2018.8534678

Kwon, Y. M., Lee, Y. A., & Kim, S. J. (2017). Case study on 3D printing education in fashion design coursework. *Fash Text, 4*(1), 26. doi:10.118640691-017-0111-3

Lungershausen, U., Heinrich, C., & Duttmann, R. (2013). Turning Human-nature Interaction into 3D Landscape Scenes: An Approach to Communicate Geoarchaeological Research. *J. Cartogr. Geogr. Inf., 63*, 269–275. doi:10.1007/BF03546142

Manson, A., Poyade, M., & Rea, P. (2015). A recommended workflow methodology in the creation of an educational and training application incorporating a digital reconstruction of the cerebral ventricular system and cerebrospinal fluid circulation to aid anatomical understanding. *BMC Medical Imaging, 15*(1), 44. doi:10.118612880-015-0088-6 PMID:26482126

Nadeem, A., Wong, A. K. D., & Wong, F. K. W. (2015). Bill of Quantities with 3D Views Using Building Information Modeling. *Arabian Journal for Science and Engineering, 40*(9), 2465–2477. doi:10.100713369-015-1657-2

Natephra, W., Motamedi, A., Fukuda, T., & Yabuki, N. (2017). Integrating building information modeling and virtual reality development engines for building indoor lighting design. *Vis. in Eng., 5*(1), 19. doi:10.118640327-017-0058-x

Park, S.-Y., & Subbarao, M. (2005). A multiview 3D modeling system based on stereo vision techniques. *Machine Vision and Applications, 16*(3), 148–156. doi:10.100700138-004-0165-2

Paul, M., & Sanyal, G. (2011). Segmentation technique of SAR imagery using entropy. *International Journal of Computer Technology and Applications, 2*(5).

Pezeshki, Z., Soleimani, A., & Darabi, A. (2017). 3Ds MAX to FEM for building thermal distribution: A case study. *2017 3rd Iranian Conference on Intelligent Systems and Signal Processing (ICSPIS),* 110-115. 10.1109/ICSPIS.2017.8311599

Samanta, D., & Paul, M. (2011). A Novel Approach of Entropy based Adaptive Thresholding Technique for Video Edge Detection. *Threshold (x, y), 1,* 1.

Samanta, D. (2011). A novel statistical approach for segmentation of SAR Images. *Journal of Global Research in Computer Science, 2*(10), 9–13.

Samanta, D., & Sanyal, G. (2011a). Automated Classification of SAR Images Using Moment. *International Journal of Computer Science Issues, 8*(6), 135.

Samanta, D., & Sanyal, G. (2011b). *Development of Adaptive Thresholding Technique for Classification of Synthetic Aperture Radar Images.* Academic Press.

Samanta, D., & Sanyal, G. (2011c). Development of edge detection technique for images using adaptive thresholding. *International Conference on Information Processing*, 671–676. 10.1007/978-3-642-22786-8_85

Samanta, D., & Sanyal, G. (2011d). SAR image segmentation using Color space clustering and Watersheds. *International Journal of Engineering Research and Applications*, 1(3), 997–999.

Samanta, D., & Sanyal, G. (2012). Segmentation technique of SAR imagery based on fuzzy c-means clustering. *IEEE-International Conference On Advances In Engineering, Science And Management (ICAESM-2012)*, 610–612.

Samanta, D., & Ghosh, A. (2012). Automatic obstacle detection based on gaussian function in robocar. *J. Res. Eng. Appl. Sci*, 2(2), 354–363.

Samanta, D., & Sanyal, G. (2012a). A novel approach of SAR image classification using color space clustering and watersheds. *2012 Fourth International Conference on Computational Intelligence and Communication Networks*, 237–240. 10.1109/CICN.2012.27

Samanta, D., & Sanyal, G. (2012c). An Approach of Segmentation Technique of SAR Images using Adaptive Thresholding Technique. *International Journal of Engineering Research & Technology (Ahmedabad)*, 1(7).

Samanta, D., & Sanyal, G. (2012f). Novel Shannon's entropy based segmentation technique for SAR images. *International Conference on Information Processing*, 193–199. 10.1007/978-3-642-31686-9_22

Samanta, D., & Sanyal, G. (2012g). *SAR image classification using fuzzy CMeans*. Academic Press.

Samanta, D., & Sanyal, G. (2012h). Statistical approach for Classification of SAR Images. *International Journal of Soft Computing and Engineering (IJSCE)*, 2231–2307.

Samanta, D., & Sanyal, G. (2013). An Approach of Tabu Search for Unsupervised Classification for SAR Images. *Seven International Conference on Image and Signal Processing*.

Samanta, D., & Sanyal, G. (2012b). A novel approach of SAR image processing based on Hue, Saturation and Brightness (HSB). *Procedia Technology*, 4, 584–588. doi:10.1016/j.protcy.2012.05.093

Samanta, D., & Sanyal, G. (2012d). Classification of SAR Images Based on Entropy. *Int. J. Inf. Technol. Comput. Sci*, 4(12), 82–86. doi:10.5815/ijitcs.2012.12.09

Samanta, D., & Sanyal, G. (2012e). Novel approach of adaptive thresholding technique for edge detection in videos. *Procedia Engineering, 30*, 283–288. doi:10.1016/j.proeng.2012.01.862

Sun, W., & Lal, P. (2002). Recent development on computer aided tissue engineering—A review. *Computer Methods and Programs in Biomedicine, 67*(2), 85–103. doi:10.1016/S0169-2607(01)00116-X PMID:11809316

Sun, W., Starly, B., Nam, J., & Darling, A. (2005). Bio-CAD modeling and its applications in computer-aided tissue engineering. *Computer Aided Design, 37*(11), 1097–1114. doi:10.1016/j.cad.2005.02.002

Tavares, J., Dutta, P., Dutta, S., & Samanta, D. (n.d.). *Cyber Intelligence and Information Retrieval*. Academic Press.

Toshihiro, A., Masayuki, K., & Naokazu, Y. (2005). 3D Modeling of Outdoor Environments by Integrating Omnidirectional Range and Color Images. *Proceedings of the Fifth International Conference on 3-D Digital Imaging and Modeling (3DIM'05)*.

Tsipotas, D., & Spathopoulou, V. (2015). An assessment of research on 3D digital representation of ancient Greek furniture, using surviving archaelological artefacts. *Digital Heritage, 2015*, 325–328. doi:10.1109/DigitalHeritage.2015.7419515

Valdez, M. T., Ferreira, C. M., & Barbosa, F. P. M. (2016). 3D virtual laboratory for teaching circuit theory — A virtual learning environment (VLE). *2016 51st International Universities Power Engineering Conference (UPEC)*, 1-4. 10.1109/UPEC.2016.8114126

Van de Perre, G., De Beir, A., Cao, H. L., Esteban, P. G., Lefeber, D., & Vanderborght, B. (2019). Studying Design Aspects for Social Robots Using a Generic Gesture Method. *International Journal of Social Robotics, 11*(4), 651–663. doi:10.100712369-019-00518-x

Vu, S. (2018). Recreating Little Manila through a Virtual Reality Serious Game. *2018 3rd Digital Heritage International Congress (DigitalHERITAGE) held jointly with 2018 24th International Conference on Virtual Systems & Multimedia (VSMM 2018)*, 1-4. 10.1109/DigitalHeritage.2018.8810082

Woop, S., Schmittler, J., & Slusallek, P. (2005). RPU: A Programmable Ray Processing Unit for Realtime Ray Tracing. *Siggraph 2005*.

Yang, Lee, Kim, & Kim. (2005). Adaptive Space Carving with Texture Mapping. *LNCS, 3482*, 1129-1138.

Yılmaz, Mülayim, & Atalay. (2002). Reconstruction of Three Dimensional Models from Real Images. *Proceedings of the First International Symposium on 3D Data Processing Visualization and Transmission (3DPVT.02).*

Chapter 8

Object 3D Effect With Photometric Lighting With Real-Time View

Guruprasad N.
CHRIST University, India

ABSTRACT

In the rapid developing of modern technology, the digital information management and the virtual reality simulation technology have become the research center. Virtual living room 3D model can not only express the real-world objects of natural, real, and vivid, and can expand the living room of the reality of time space dimensions, the combinations of living room environment and information. This chapter uses 3ds Max technology to create three-dimensional model of wall, floor, and television, etc. This research focuses on 3D objects effect with photometric lighting and living room scene modeling technology and the scene design process in a variety of real-time processing technology optimization strategy. Finally, the result of virtual living room scene with the help of photometric lights is summarized.

INTRODUCTION

Along with the rapid growth of computer and internet technology as well as geographic information industry in the global range, virtual reality technology (VR) is becoming one of the main researches in the current computer domain (A. S. Baskoro et al. 2015) (Samanta, Debabrata et al. 2011). Virtual living room is through the virtual reality technology, to realize the function of the photometric in the form of 3D visualization on computer, which can show a variety of realistic living room scene information in

DOI: 10.4018/978-1-6684-4139-8.ch008

the form of virtual angle. This paper developed a living room virtual reality system, the use of 3ds Max for living room scene's 3D modeling (Kwon, Y.M. et al. 2017) (Samanta, Debabrata et al. 2011a). As we know we have three types of lighting system in 3ds max i,e Standard lights, Arnold lights and Photometric. In order to achieve the best rendered image while using standard lights and Arnold lights we are supposed to change the render setup, but while we are using Photometric lights it applies to any render platform. In photometric lights it using light energy values as it helps us to alter the light in order to give real world experience. We have four different distribution capabilities of photometric lights, ie Uniform spherical, Uniform Diffuse, Spotlight, Photometric web which help us to create best scene in viewport. We have multiple distribution options in light spread throughout the scene and the light shape which leads in the cast shadow of objects in the viewport. We have six options in light shape. Point shape in this option object emits the shadows as the light is coming from single geometric point. Line, in this option the object emits shadows as the light emitted in straight line. Rectangle, here object emits shadow as light is coming from rectangle surface. Likewise Disc, Sphere, Cylinder options helps objects to emit shadow in different form and shapes according.

METHODOLOGY

Creating a living room scene with Autodesk 3ds max was not easy, but was made simpler with the right knowledge on how to use various components of 3ds max like modifiers, primitives, objects and materials etc. Maximum usage of standard primitive objects like box and photometric lights is used in this work (Deryabin, N.B. et al. 2017)(Samanta, Debabrata et al. 2012a). With the drag and drop feature, interaction with objects like scaling, positioning and rotation was done with ease (Tavares, J. et al.)(W. Sun et al. 2005). Lines were drawn at the first then the points are connected using spline shape, then using mesh editor select the polygon of the lines then with the help of extrude modifier increase the wall height that u desire. Follow the below steps to build a wall in viewport

Step 1: To create a wall outline click on splines and select lines, then with the help of lines draw an outline of a map (Yoo-Kil Yang et al. 2005) as shown in below figure1.

Step 2: In the Modifier list select edit mesh, Select the polygon and click the spline so that the outline of maps are getting selected (Samanta, Debabrata et al. 2012g). And using extrude modifier try to increase the wall height that u desire. Figure 2 shows the structure of Edit mesh with select polygon. Figure 3 shows extrude with Increase the values.

Figure 1. Close the spline

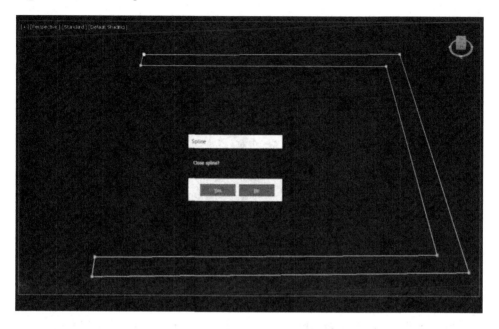

Figure 2. Edit mesh with select polygon

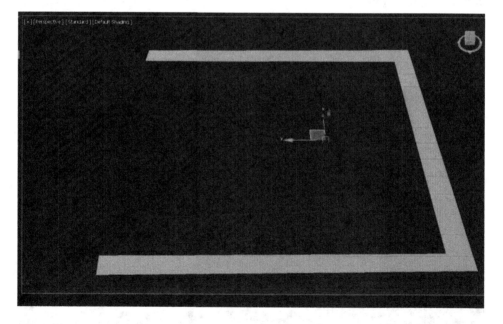

Figure 3. Extrude with increase the values

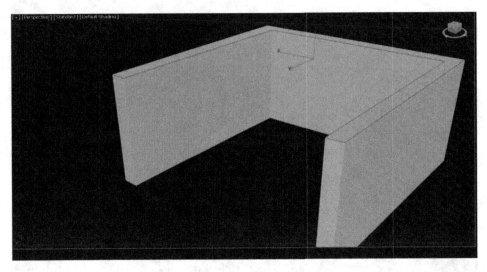

Step 3: To create hollow in wall, select box from standard primitives drag it on viewport of your desired length and width, place the box into the wall where you want to get hollow space to place a Television (H. Esmaeili et al. 2014) (D. Tsipotas et al. 2015). Figure 4 shows how the Pro-Boolean is used to select the object for eliminating from other.

Figure 4. Pro-Boolean is used to delete box from spline

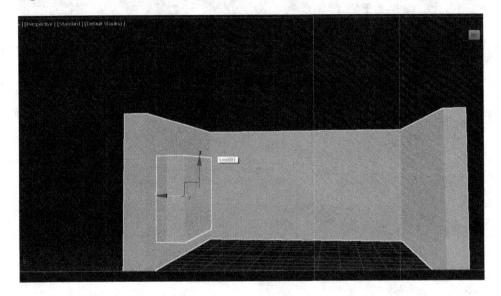

Step 3(Continues): Click on Compound object in that click on Pro-Boolean and select the wall, Then you will find the option called start picking select the Box which you want to delete, this will create a hollow in the wall (Samanta, Deababrata et al. 2012)(Nadeem, A. et al. 2015). Figure 5 shows the final view of the wall including with the hallow space.

Figure 5. Final view of the wall

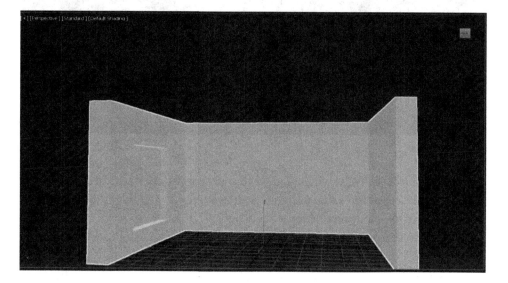

CREATION OF CEILING

Dragging the box from standard primitives, making clone with dragged boxes and using mesh modifiers, all boxes are connected to give a ceiling like structure. Inset and extrude modifiers were made use to give hollow spacing at the sides and extruded structure in the between for lights (UlaşYılmaz et al. 2002)(Samanta, Debabrata et al. 2012f). Figure 6 shows the ceiling design which is done in the scene.

Step 1: Drag a box from standard primitives increase the width of box as it should cover most part of ceiling. To create a above type of design we need add few more boxes (Woop, Sven et al. 2005)(Samanta, Debabrata et al. 2012h). Figure 7 shows the cloning of the boxes and aligning them for ceiling.

Step 2: To create specific design in the ceiling we can use Edit mesh modifier in the modifier list. Before that we need to create number of segments in the box (Ardakani, H.K. et al. 2020)(M. R. Filho et al. 2011). We should enable the edge faces visible in the viewport.

Figure 6. Ceiling design.

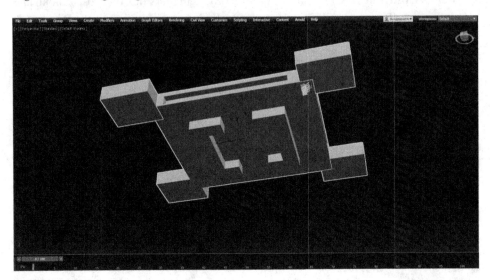

Step 3: Select the faces which you want to design the click on extrude modifier increase or decrease the values. Figure 8 shows that how to select the box's face and using extrude modifiers increase the values.

Step 4: To create a hollow design in the ceiling we can use Pro-Boolean from compound objects, as we in the wall construction (YeeWa Choy et al. 2012). Figure

Figure 7. Cloning boxes and aligning them

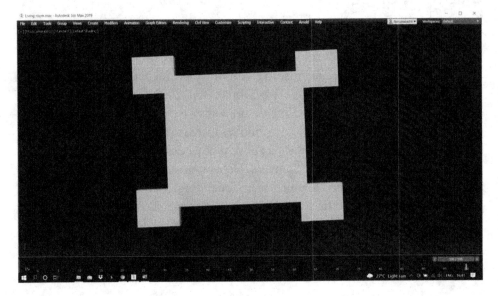

Figure 8. Extrude the selected faces increase the value.

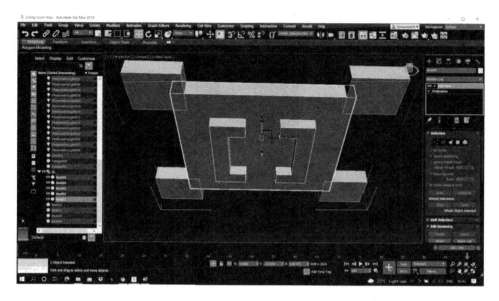

9 gives the complete understanding about the ceiling design and hallow space for the photometric light.

CREATION OF SOFA

Dragging chamfer box from extended primitives, making clone with dragged chamfer box and aligning the entire chamfer box to with sofa structure. Using material editor bitmaps are assigned to give a real-life pattern to the object (Samanta, Debabrata et al. 2011).

Step1: Drag a multiplechamfer boxes from extended primitives (i.e, Extended primitives>>Chamfer box). Figure 10 shows the alignment of the chamfer boxes.

Step 2: With the help of move tool and the rotate tool we can align the chamfer boxes to give a real time sofa feel (Samanta, Debabrata et al. 2011c)(Günther-Diringer et al. 2016). Figure 11 is the final view of the sofa with material editor bitmaps.

WINDOW CREATIONS

Dragging a box and cylinder from the standard primitives and using pro-Boolean operator window is created. Box is used to create as a frame of window, Cylinders are used as steel rod in between the Frames (Manson, A. et al. 2015)(Samanta,

Figure 9. Hallow space in ceiling using Pro-Boolean

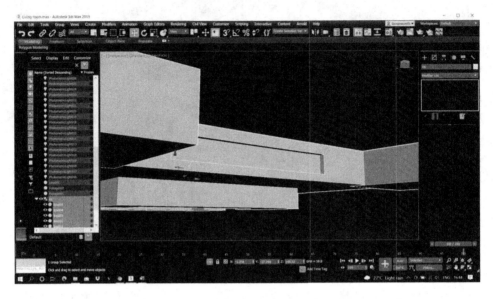

Debabrata et al. 2011b). Using material editor bitmaps are assigned to give a real-life pattern to the object. Figure 12 gives the finale view of the window.

Step 1: Drag a Box from standard primitives, and using pro-Boolean operator (as we did in wall creation) created hollow space in Box as shown in the below figure

Figure 10. Placing Chamfer boxes according.

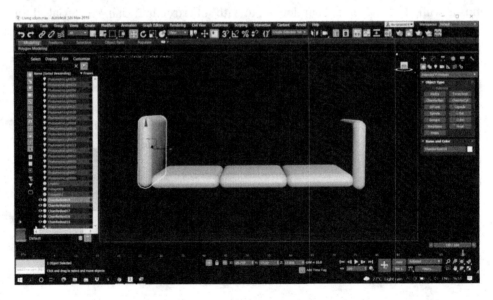

Figure 11. Final scene of sofa.

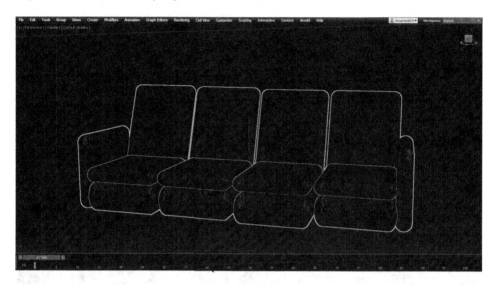

(Samanta, Debabrata et al. 2013). Figure 13 gives the better understanding about the window frame with bitmaps assign to it.

Step 2: Drag cylinder from the standard primitives, place horizontally in between the wooden frames (L. L. Khoroshko et al. 2018). Figure 14 shows how to place the cylinder across the frame.

Figure 12. Window scene.

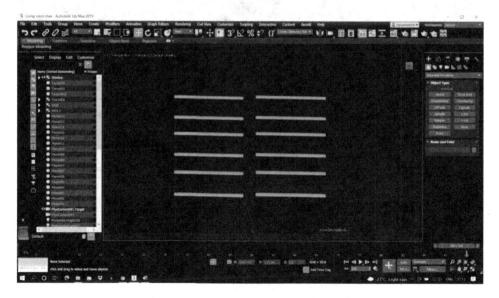

Figure 13. Window frame using Pro-Boolean.

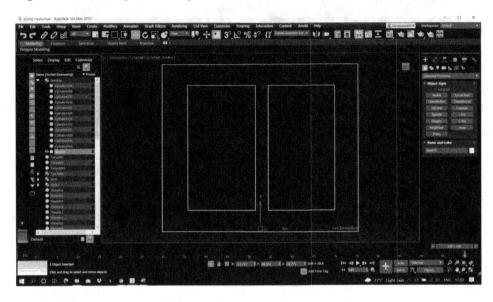

Figure 14. Placing Cylinder horizontally.

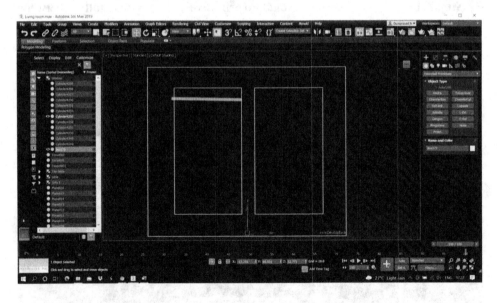

Step3: With the help of material editor bitmap we can assign real-time look of the window.

Figure 15. Final view of tea/coffee holder.

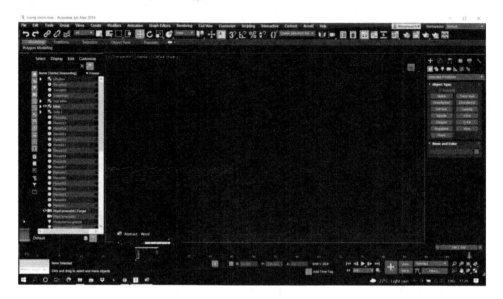

CREATION OF TEA HOLDER

Dragging a cylinder from standard primitives, and design using splines to give tea table texture (Soon-Yong Park et al. 2005). Figure 15 gives the final view of the Tea/Coffee holder.

Step 1: Drag a cylinder from standard primitives (Van de Perre, G. et al. 2019). Figure 16 shows the table top design and the table leg which is done using cylinder with bitmap assign to it.

Step 2: Splines design also known as 2D to 3D conversion, to create design as shown in the figure, first we need to select line from splines, and in the rendering section (we can see when we scroll down from splines object) select the check box which says "Enable in Viewport", as we scroll down again we can see creation method in that select the checked boxes which says smooth (Samanta, Debabrata et al. 2011d)(Samanta, Debabrata et al. 2012c)(D. Fritsch et al. 2017). So, that we draw according. (Tip: Try to draw lines in top view port so that it will be much easier). Figure 17 shows how to design the spline by drawing the lines manually.

Step 3: Using a move tool and rotate tool we can align all the line and Cylinder to give tea holder structure (U. Castellani et al. 2005)(Samanta, Debabrata et al. 2012e). And with help of material editor bitmap we can give real-life gesture to the tea table (in above figures the objects already have material editor in the as it is created earlier).

Figure 16. Base shapes using cylinder standard primitives.

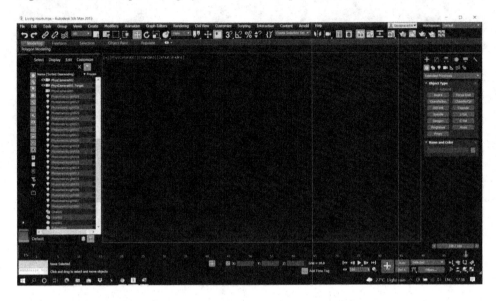

CREATION OF TEA TABLE WITH CLOTH MODIFIER

Figure 18 shows the final design of the table.

Figure 17. Spline is used for table design.

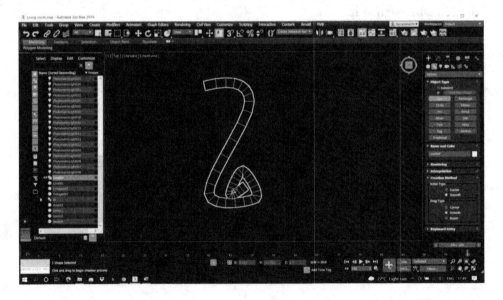

Figure 18. Table with cloth.

Figure 19. Box Standard primitive with Material editor bitmap.

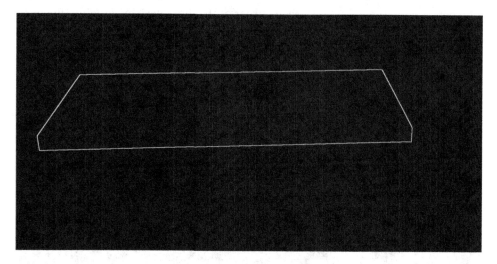

Step 1: To create a tea table first we need to select box from standard primitives and change dimension to give a table to look. Figure 19 shows the size and material used for the box.

Step 2: After the table top creation we need add the legs to tables for that, select cylinder from standard primitives and changes dimensions as we need (M. T. Valdez et al. 2016). Figure 20 shows the size and material used for the cylinder.

Figure 20. Cylinder primitives with material editor bitmap.

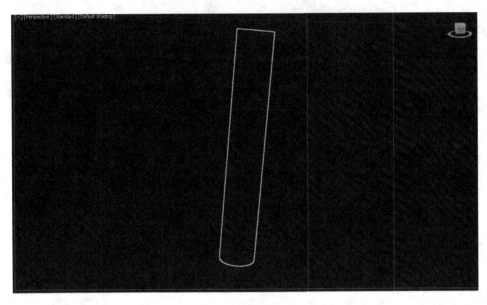

Then cloning the cylinder to each corner of the table we can get table finish (S. Vu et al. 2018). Figure 21 shows how the cloning is done and placing the box on top of those cloned legs.

Figure 21. Cloned cylinders with placing box on top.

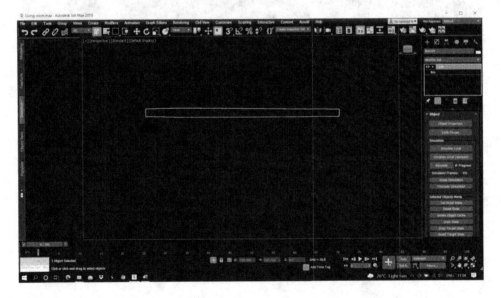

Figure 22. Placing plane on top of box.

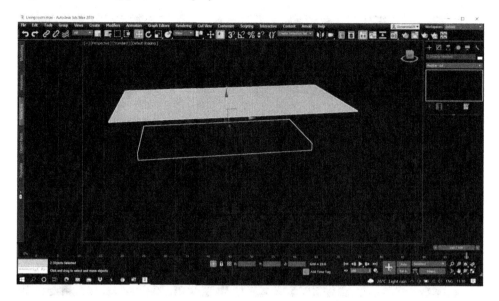

Step 3: To create a table cloth we need drag plane from standard primitives then we need to align the plane above the table top box (only top box not with the legs) (H. Esmaeili et al. 2017). Figure 22 tell how we should align the plane for better result in cloth.

Step 3:

Figure 23. Cloth modifier and with Material editor

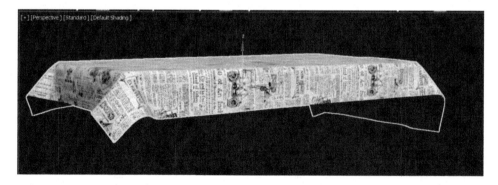

- To give cloth finish to the plane select plane first then in the modifier list select cloth modifier (Toshihiro ASAI et al. 2005).

Figure 24. Final view of table.

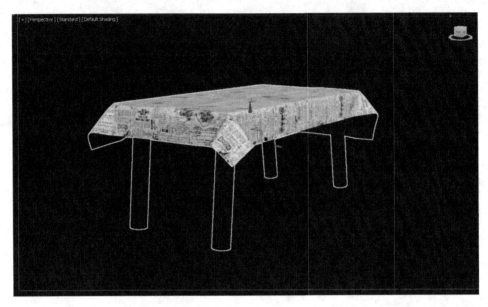

- Now in the cloth modifier click on object properties and select the objects (tabletop box and plane) (Natephra, W. et al. 2017).
- Now select box and change to check collision object column and select plane and click on cloth option select cotton in that. After that click on OK button, then click on simulate (if table cloth is aligning properly increase the width and height segments to 100 each in plane) (Wei Sun et al. 2002). Figure 23 shows the final cloth design with bitmap assign to it.

Add a material to the objects that to desire. Figure 24 shows the final design of the table

CARPET CREATION

Select a plane from standard primitives and material bitmap to the plane to give real time look (Yusuf Arayici, et al. 2005)(Hegazy, M. et al. 2022). Figure 25 shows the carpet design which is done using plane and material editor assign to it.

Figure 25. Carpet design.

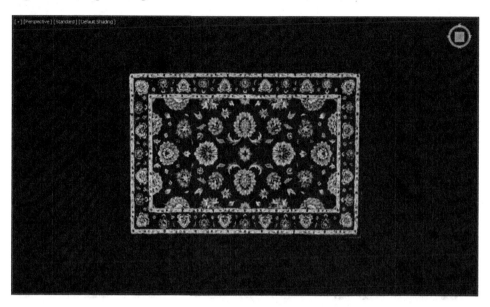

Figure 26. Tiles design.

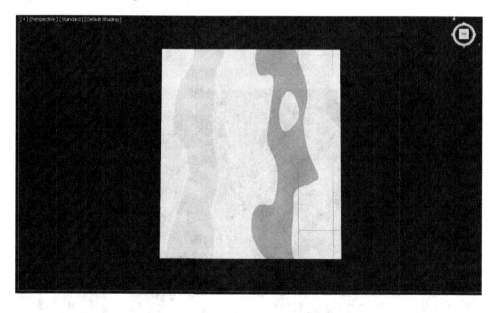

Figure 27. Cloning plane and placing carpet.

FLOOR TILES CREATION

Step 1: Select a plane from standard primitives and add tiles texture using material

Figure 28. Flower vase with plant.

Figure 29. Torus with increased values in y-axis.

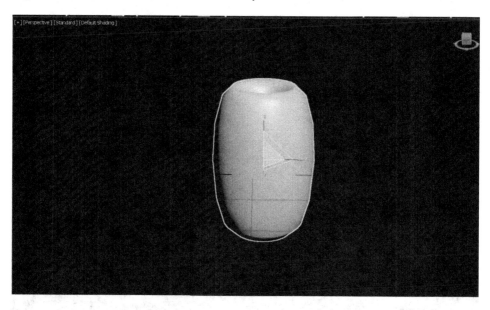

bitmap (Samanta, Debabrata et al. 2012). Figure 26 shows how design the tiles using plane and material editors.

Step2: Clone the planc to the all corner in the living room (Z. Pezeshki et al. 2017). Figure 27 shows the cloning of multiple tiles and placing the carpet on top of the tiles.

CREATION OF FLOWER VASE

Figure 28 shows the final design of the flower vase.

Step1: Drag a torus from standard primitives and with help of scale tool increases the values in y so that it will be a flower (Lungershausen, U. et al. 2013). Figure 29 shows how torus is enlarged by increasing the values in y-axis.

Step 2: Select AEC Extended and in the click on Foliage, now select the tree which you desire and drag into the viewport, with help scale tool reduce the size of tree and place it on top of the vase that we made earlier (Samanta, Debabrata et al. 2012b).

Figure 30. Television.

TELEVISION CREATION

Step1: Drag a box from standard primitives and made like a tv outer frame.

Step2: Drag a plane and place it in the frame that we made with box and add some material editor bitmap so that it will real tv Look. Figure 30 show how plane is placed in front of the box (TV frame) .

WOOD DESIGNING

Step1: Drag a box from standard primitives and add material bitmap for wood texture.
Step2: Clone the box around the tv so that it will be base for the design.

Step 3:   With help of Pro-Boolean create hallow space in those boxes for placing some things in it like books, vase, clock etc. Figure 31 gives the clear picture about wood designing in the background using box with material editors.

Figure 31. Television background design.

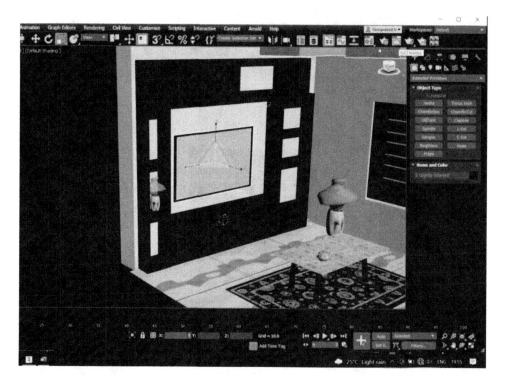

PHOTOMETRIC LIGHTS

Place a Photometric free light in most of the corners in living room. To give real life living room scene, and in the hallow spaces which is created in ceiling (Samanta, Debabrata et al. 2012d). Figure 32 gives the final scene of the living room.

CONCLUSION

3ds Max is a powerful computer program that is particularly designed to help 3D artists, designers in various need and in the implementation of their projects. Modelling a living room scene is complex task and for this reason, the most important step is to set up reference images from at least two views. Modelling process cannot be imagined without knowledge of working with polygons or editable poly. Adding the more details to the living room interior makes the final image to be more realistic. In this paper, in application of 3ds Max the following renders plugins: Scanline, Arnold is used for modelling and rendering the living room scene. It can be noticed

Figure 32. Final rendered view.

that the final result of rendering was best when Arnold is used, while weaker when scanline is applied.

REFERENCES

Arayici, Y., & Hamilton, A. (2005). Modeling 3D Scanned Data to Visualize the Built Environment. *Proceedings of the Ninth International Conference on Information Visualisation*, 509~514. 10.1109/IV.2005.82

Ardakani, H. K., Mousavinia, A., & Safaei, F. (2020). Four points: One-pass geometrical camera calibration algorithm. *The Visual Computer*, *36*(2), 413–424. doi:10.100700371-019-01632-7

Baskoro, A. S., & Haryanto, I. (2015). Development of travel speed detection method in welding simulator using augmented reality. *2015 International Conference on Advanced Computer Science and Information Systems (ICACSIS)*, 269-273. 10.1109/ICACSIS.2015.7415194

Castellani, U., Fusiello, A., Murino, V., Papaleo, L., Puppo, E., & Pittore, M. (2005). A complete system for on-line 3D modelling from acoustic images. *Signal Processing Image Communication, 20*(9-10), 832–852. doi:10.1016/j.image.2005.02.003

Choy, Lim, Wang, & Chan. (2012). Development CT-based three-dimensional complex skull model for Finite element analysis. *2012 IEEE Conference on Sustainable Utilization and Development in Engineering and Technology (STUDENT)*, 135-139. 10.1109/STUDENT.2012.6408383

Deryabin, N. B., Zhdanov, D. D., & Sokolov, V. G. (2017). Embedding the script language into optical simulation software. *Programming and Computer Software, 43*(1), 13–23. doi:10.1134/S0361768817010029

Esmaeili, H., Thwaites, H., & Woods, P. C. (2017). Workflows and Challenges Involved in Creation of Realistic Immersive Virtual Museum, Heritage, and Tourism Experiences: A Comprehensive Reference for 3D Asset Capturing. *2017 13th International Conference on Signal-Image Technology & Internet-Based Systems (SITIS)*, 465-472. 10.1109/SITIS.2017.82

Esmaeili, H., Woods, P. C., & Thwaites, H. (2014). Realisation of virtualised architectural heritage. *2014 International Conference on Virtual Systems & Multimedia (VSMM)*, 94-101. 10.1109/VSMM.2014.7136676

Filho, M. R., Negrão, N. M., & Damasceno, R. R. (2011). SwImax: A Web Tool Using Virtual Reality for Teaching the WiMAX Protocol. *2011 XIII Symposium on Virtual Reality*, 217-224. 10.1109/SVR.2011.27

Fritsch, D., & Klein, M. (2017). 3D and 4D modeling for AR and VR app developments. *2017 23rd International Conference on Virtual System & Multimedia (VSMM)*, 1-8. 10.1109/VSMM.2017.8346270

Günther-Diringer, D. (2016). Historisches 3D-Stadtmodell von Karlsruhe. *J. Cartogr. Geogr. Inf., 66*, 66–71. doi:10.1007/BF03545207

Hegazy, M., Yasufuku, K., & Abe, H. (2022). An interactive approach to investigate brightness perception of daylighting in Immersive Virtual Environments: Comparing subjective responses and quantitative metrics. *Building Simulation, 15*(1), 41–68. doi:10.100712273-021-0798-3

Khoroshko, L. L., Ukhov, P. A., & Keyno, P. P. (2018). *Development of a Laboratory Workshop for Open Online Courses Based on 3D Computer Graphics and Multimedia. In 2018 Learning With MOOCS.* LWMOOCS. doi:10.1109/LWMOOCS.2018.8534678

Kwon, Y. M., Lee, Y. A., & Kim, S. J. (2017). Case study on 3D printing education in fashion design coursework. *Fash Text, 4*(1), 26. doi:10.118640691-017-0111-3

Lungershausen, U., Heinrich, C., & Duttmann, R. (2013). Turning Human-nature Interaction into 3D Landscape Scenes: An Approach to Communicate Geoarchaeological Research. *J. Cartogr. Geogr. Inf., 63*, 269–275. doi:10.1007/BF03546142

Manson, A., Poyade, M., & Rea, P. (2015). A recommended workflow methodology in the creation of an educational and training application incorporating a digital reconstruction of the cerebral ventricular system and cerebrospinal fluid circulation to aid anatomical understanding. *BMC Medical Imaging, 15*(1), 44. doi:10.118612880-015-0088-6 PMID:26482126

Nadeem, A., Wong, A. K. D., & Wong, F. K. W. (2015). Bill of Quantities with 3D Views Using Building Information Modeling. *Arabian Journal for Science and Engineering, 40*(9), 2465–2477. doi:10.100713369-015-1657-2

Natephra, W., Motamedi, A., Fukuda, T., & Yabuki, N. (2017). Integrating building information modeling and virtual reality development engines for building indoor lighting design. *Vis. in Eng., 5*(1), 19. doi:10.118640327-017-0058-x

Park, S.-Y., & Subbarao, M. (2005). A multiview 3D modeling system based on stereo vision techniques. *Machine Vision and Applications, 16*(3), 148–156. doi:10.100700138-004-0165-2

Paul, M., & Sanyal, G. (2011). Segmentation technique of SAR imagery using entropy. *International Journal of Computer Technology and Applications, 2*(5).

Pezeshki, Z., Soleimani, A., & Darabi, A. (2017). 3Ds MAX to FEM for building thermal distribution: A case study. *2017 3rd Iranian Conference on Intelligent Systems and Signal Processing (ICSPIS),* 110-115. 10.1109/ICSPIS.2017.8311599

Samanta, D., & Paul, M. (2011). A Novel Approach of Entropy based Adaptive Thresholding Technique for Video Edge Detection. *Threshold (x, y), 1*, 1.

Samanta, D. (2011). A novel statistical approach for segmentation of SAR Images. *Journal of Global Research in Computer Science, 2*(10), 9–13.

Samanta, D., & Sanyal, G. (2011a). Automated Classification of SAR Images Using Moment. *International Journal of Computer Science Issues, 8*(6), 135.

Samanta, D., & Sanyal, G. (2011b). *Development of Adaptive Thresholding Technique for Classification of Synthetic Aperture Radar Images*. Academic Press.

Samanta, D., & Sanyal, G. (2011c). Development of edge detection technique for images using adaptive thresholding. *International Conference on Information Processing*, 671–676. 10.1007/978-3-642-22786-8_85

Samanta, D., & Sanyal, G. (2011d). SAR image segmentation using Color space clustering and Watersheds. *International Journal of Engineering Research and Applications*, *1*(3), 997–999.

Samanta, D., & Sanyal, G. (2012). Segmentation technique of SAR imagery based on fuzzy c-means clustering. *IEEE-International Conference On Advances In Engineering, Science And Management (ICAESM-2012)*, 610–612.

Samanta, D., & Ghosh, A. (2012). Automatic obstacle detection based on gaussian function in robocar. *J. Res. Eng. Appl. Sci*, *2*(2), 354–363.

Samanta, D., & Sanyal, G. (2012a). A novel approach of SAR image classification using color space clustering and watersheds. *2012 Fourth International Conference on Computational Intelligence and Communication Networks*, 237–240. 10.1109/CICN.2012.27

Samanta, D., & Sanyal, G. (2012c). An Approach of Segmentation Technique of SAR Images using Adaptive Thresholding Technique. *International Journal of Engineering Research & Technology (Ahmedabad)*, *1*(7).

Samanta, D., & Sanyal, G. (2012f). Novel Shannon's entropy based segmentation technique for SAR images. *International Conference on Information Processing*, 193–199. 10.1007/978-3-642-31686-9_22

Samanta, D., & Sanyal, G. (2012g). *SAR image classification using fuzzy CMeans*. Academic Press.

Samanta, D., & Sanyal, G. (2012h). Statistical approach for Classification of SAR Images. *International Journal of Soft Computing and Engineering (IJSCE)*, 2231–2307.

Samanta, D., & Sanyal, G. (2013). An Approach of Tabu Search for Unsupervised Classification for SAR Images. *Seven International Conference on Image and Signal Processing*.

Samanta, D., & Sanyal, G. (2012b). A novel approach of SAR image processing based on Hue, Saturation and Brightness (HSB). *Procedia Technology*, *4*, 584–588. doi:10.1016/j.protcy.2012.05.093

Samanta, D., & Sanyal, G. (2012d). Classification of SAR Images Based on Entropy. *Int. J. Inf. Technol. Comput. Sci*, *4*(12), 82–86. doi:10.5815/ijitcs.2012.12.09

Samanta, D., & Sanyal, G. (2012e). Novel approach of adaptive thresholding technique for edge detection in videos. *Procedia Engineering, 30*, 283–288. doi:10.1016/j. proeng.2012.01.862

Sun, W., & Lal, P. (2002). Pallavi Lal. Recent development on computer aided tissue engineering— A review. *Computer Methods and Programs in Biomedicine, 67*(2), 85–103. doi:10.1016/S0169-2607(01)00116-X PMID:11809316

Sun, W., Starly, B., Nam, J., & Darling, A. (2005). Bio-CAD modeling and its applications in computer-aided tissue engineering. *Computer Aided Design, 37*(11), 1097–1114. doi:10.1016/j.cad.2005.02.002

Tavares, J., Dutta, P., Dutta, S., & Samanta, D. (n.d.). *Cyber Intelligence and Information Retrieval.* Academic Press.

Toshihiro, A., Masayuki, K., & Naokazu, Y. (2005). 3D Modeling of Outdoor Environments by Integrating Omnidirectional Range and Color Images. *Proceedings of the Fifth International Conference on 3-D Digital Imaging and Modeling (3DIM'05).*

Tsipotas, D., & Spathopoulou, V. (2015). An assessment of research on 3D digital representation of ancient Greek furniture, using surviving archaelological artefacts. *Digital Heritage, 2015*, 325–328. doi:10.1109/DigitalHeritage.2015.7419515

Valdez, M. T., Ferreira, C. M., & Barbosa, F. P. M. (2016). 3D virtual laboratory for teaching circuit theory — A virtual learning environment (VLE). *2016 51st International Universities Power Engineering Conference (UPEC),* 1-4. 10.1109/ UPEC.2016.8114126

Van de Perre, G., De Beir, A., Cao, H. L., Esteban, P. G., Lefeber, D., & Vanderborght, B. (2019). Studying Design Aspects for Social Robots Using a Generic Gesture Method. *International Journal of Social Robotics, 11*(4), 651–663. doi:10.100712369-019-00518-x

Vu, S. (2018). Recreating Little Manila through a Virtual Reality Serious Game. *2018 3rd Digital Heritage International Congress (DigitalHERITAGE) held jointly with 2018 24th International Conference on Virtual Systems & Multimedia (VSMM 2018),* 1-4. 10.1109/DigitalHeritage.2018.8810082

Woop, S., Schmittler, J., & Slusallek, P. (2005). RPU: A Programmable Ray Processing Unit for Realtime Ray Tracing. *Siggraph 2005.*

Yang, Lee, Kim, & Kim. (2005). Adaptive Space Carving with Texture Mapping. *LNCS, 3482*, 1129-1138.

Yılmaz, Mülayim, & Atalay. (2002). Reconstruction of Three Dimensional Models from Real Images. *Proceedings of the First International Symposium on 3D Data Processing Visualization and Transmission (3DPVT.02).*

Chapter 9

Approach for 3D Modeling With Incandescent and Fluorescent Light in a Realistic View

Sean Leo Noronha
CHRIST University, India

ABSTRACT

Most fluorescent lights have been designed for commercial purposes to light up streets, houses, buildings, etc., and as such, these lights possess a light tube wherein light is generated via a thin filament like source. Most 3ds Max lights are point-source based, and therefore require us to transform the light objects available in the 3ds Max software, in order to prevent any unnecessary delays in rendering a scene or produce non-similar light effects. Though less energy efficient than fluorescent lights, incandescent lights still are manufactured in a variety of shapes and sizes; however, these lights are slowly but surely being replaced by better energy-efficient lights sources. Some other natural sources of incandescent lights are burning fireplace, bonfires, lava, burners on a stove, etc. As noted from the examples, most natural incandescent light sources don't require electricity to illuminate the surroundings but still produce light through chemical reaction or burning.

INTRODUCTION

There are many sources of illumination in real life, which allow living beings to better appreciate the aesthetic and real effects of light (A. S. Baskoro et al. 2015).

DOI: 10.4018/978-1-6684-4139-8.ch009

Some of these sources of light which better help light the environment around us like sunlight, bioluminescence, moon light, fire to artificial sources of lights like streetlights, bulbs, glow lights, and many more, help humans perceive the environment around them. Recreating such lighting effects available in real life in a virtual environment or game adds to the richness and appearance of such environments. There are various forms of lighting, one such lighting where in light is generated from an object due to it being heated is called Incandescent light. Such lights can be seen in real life as a burning fireplace, bonfires, even Lava (L. L. Khoroshko et al. 2018)(Samanta, Debabrata, et al. 2011a). There are many real-world processes which produce incandescent light such Glass making, etc. These sources of light result due to a phosphor glow due to particle bombardment or electrical excitement. Lights like a TV's glow, electric lamps. You might have already noticed that such lights are results of chemical reactions, and commercially available all over the world (Soon-Yong Park et al. 2005)(Samanta, Debabrata, et al., 2012g).

IMPORTANCE OF LIGHT

It is a known fact that most humans are able to analyse and gain about 85% information regarding their environment and surroundings through their sight (D. Fritsch et al. 2017). Hence, lighting their environments can help humans better perceive their environment as compared to that of a darkened environment devoid of any sort of light or illumination (Samanta, Debabrata, et al. (2011))(Samanta, Debabrata, et al. (2012d)).However, simply adding lights to any virtual environment or 3DS viewport without understanding the dynamics of the light source and the scene or environment created may lead to causing more harm than appeal.Better quality control or management of settings can highly impact a scene thus enabling us to producea professional 3D render which is appealing to clients, viewers, etc (H. Esmaeili et al. 2017).

COMPARATIVE STUDY ON INCANDESCENT LIGHT AND FLUORESCENT LIGHT

Both light sources mentioned above, are mostly used with respect to a real-world application inside a house or residential building, etc. These lights as mentioned previously are manufactured for commercial purposes and are used worldwide as artificial sources of light. However, there are specific differences and similarities that lie between both Incandescent and Fluorescent light.

Table 1. Comparison table

Property	Incandescent Light	Fluorescent light
Intensity	Variable	Medium to low
Colour	Warm spectrum (Possible to alter)	Cool spectrum (Possible to alter)
Direction	Any	Any
Diffuseness	Usually, low	High to medium
Shadow	Very hard to soft	Usually, soft
Shape	Any	Usually none
Contrast	High to medium	Usually medium to low
Movement	Any	Usually none
Size	Any	Usually medium to small

ADVANTAGES OF INCANDESCENT LIGHTS AND FLUOROSCENT LIGHT

Incandescent Light

As such lights provide an economic and performance improvement over fluorescent lights,these commercially used, incandescent lights are used in many households or buildings tolight up small areas (Tavares, J. et al.). These lights don't flicker so animators don't need to worry aboutfocusing on animating the flickering light (Samanta, Debabrata, et al. (2012h)).

FLUOROSCENT LIGHT

Fluorescent lamps are bigger light sources than incandescent lamps. Furthermore, mostfluorescent bulbs or tubes readily diffuse light that results in better distribution ofillumination within a particular area (Lungershausen, U. et al. 2013). In contrast, incandescent lamps are smaller lightsources, and they produce undiffuse light as evident from glares and uneven illumination (Hegazy, M. et al. 2022).

WORKING PROCEDURE

After studying the properties and possible applications of such lights, it is only fair to apply the above concepts towards creating and rendering the above lights i.e., Incandescent and Fluorescent lights in 3D software to better appreciate the aesthetics

Figure 1. 3DS max user interface

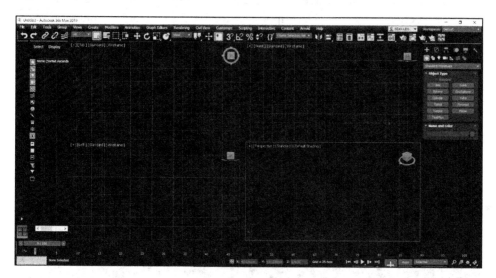

and application of these lights (Deryabin, N.B. et al. 2017). For demonstration purposes, the 3DS Max 2019 software will be used to recreate the required lights in a scene to illuminate the rendered environment (Natephra, W. et al. 2017)(Samanta, Deababrata, et al. (2012)). You may follow the given instructions or procedures to recreate Incandescent and Fluorescent lights in your own 3DS Max software.Figure 1 shows 3DS Max User Interface.

- Figure 1 depicts the 3DS Max software user interface which will be used to construct and illuminate the incandescent and fluorescent lights. The viewports along with the tools available at the common panel and additional menu options at the top of the window will be required for our purposes (Günther-Diringer et al. 2016).
- The four viewports namely the Top, Front, Left and Perspective viewports can be used to draw any object in 3DS Max.
- Since incandescent light bulbs and fluorescent light bulbs have differing designs, we will be constructing two separate bulbs in the 3DS Max viewports (Ardakani, H.K. et al. 2020).
- Firstly, we will construct the Fluorescent Light Bulb.

FLUOROSCENT LIGHT CREATION:

- In order to construct the fluorescentbulb's base, select the 'Cylinder' option from the Common Panel's 'Geometry' option and draw and scale the radius and height of the 'cylinder' inside any one of the viewports, preferably the Perspective Viewport (D. Tsipotas et al. 2015)(Samanta, Debabrata, et al. (2013)).

- By default, the newly added cylinder would be given a default name 'Cylinder001'. We can rename the cylinder to 'Base' as required for identification purposes as shown below in Figure 2, however this is completely optional (M. T. Valdez et al. 2016)(Manson, A. et al. 2015).

Figure 2. Renaming an object

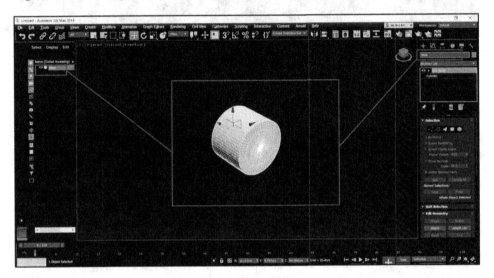

- Making sure that the 'Base' is selected, under the 'modify' option, select the drop menu of the modifiers and select the 'Edit Mesh' modifier in order to reshape the 'Base' and make it appear more life-like (Samanta, Debabrata, et al. (2011d)). You will notice that 'Edit Mesh' appears above the object's name indicating that the modifier is acting on the object. Now click the very same 'Edit Mesh' appearing above Cylinder as highlighted in Figure 3 to display the modifier's settings. Under the 'Selection' ribbon, select 'Edge' (H. Esmaeili et al. 2014)(Samanta, Debabrata, et al. (2011c)). With this option, we can change the position, scale and orientation of the selected edges visible on the 'Base' with the help of the select tools shown below.

Figure 3. Edit mesh modifier

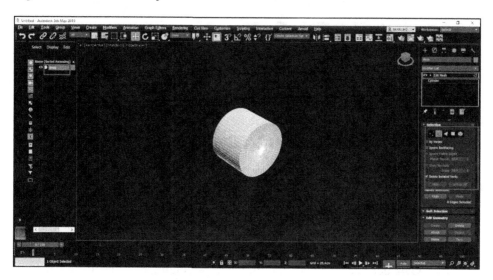

- In the 'Left viewport', a side view of the object is visible as wireframes. Select an approximate number of edges as shown below in Figure 4 and using the highlighted 'Select and Uniform Scale' tool, rescale the base to get a similar output as shown in Figure 5.

Figure 4. Selecting a group of vertices for reshaping object

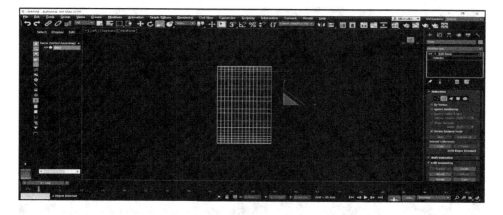

- Select another range of edges, extend the base by using the 'Select and Move' tool to reproduce the results as shown in Figure 5.

Figure 5. Select and move tool

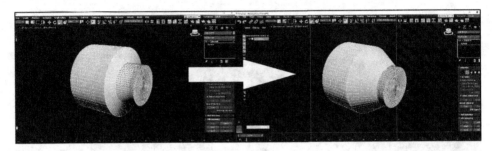

- Click the very same 'Edit Mesh' appearing above Cylinder as mentioned before, to stop making any more modifications to the 'Base' object (Samanta, Debabrata, et al. (2012b)).
- Add another 'Cylinder' to create the Glass tube of the bulb, ensuring that the 'Cylinder' has a small radiusand long height. Rename it as per your requirement.I have renamed it to 'GlassTube' (Samanta, Debabrata, et al. (2012)). Making sure that the GlassTube' is selected, under the 'modify' option, select the drop menu of the modifiers and select the 'Bend' modifier (Samanta, Debabrata, et al. (2012f)). Make sure the 'Bend' modifier settings match the same values as shown in Figure 6.

Figure 6. Bend modifier

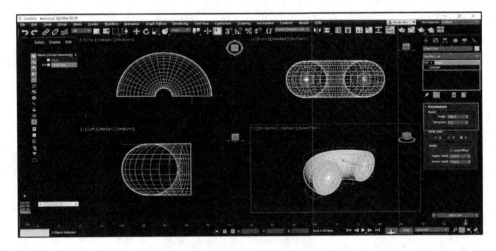

- Add another modifier, 'Edit Mesh' to the same 'GlassTube' object. Under the 'Selection' ribbon, select 'Edge' option. Select an approximate number of edges as shown below in Figure 7. Using the 'Select and Move' tool to reproduce the results as shown in Figure 7, by dragging the gizmo along the 'Y' axis (Toshihiro ASAI et al. 2005).

Figure 7. Extending shape of object through select and move tool

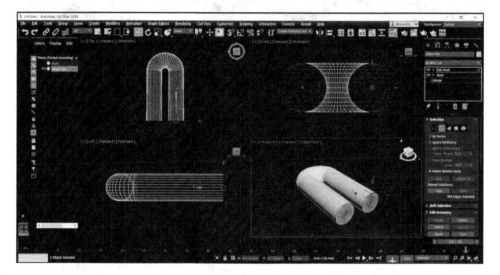

- Click the very same 'Edit Mesh' appearing above Cylinder as mentioned before, to stop making any more modifications to the 'GlassTube' object (Kwon, Y.M. et al. 2017) (Samanta, Debabrata, et al. (2011b)).
- Ensure that the 'GlassTube' object is selected, make a clone of the 'GlassTube' object by either right clicking the object and selecting the 'Clone' option or drag the 'Select and Move' tool gizmo in any direction while holding down the 'Shift' key on your keyboard to create a clone (Samanta, Debabrata. (2011)). A 'Clone Options' window will appear under which select the 'copy' option and number of clones as '2'. You should get a similar output as Figure 8.

- Reposition the newly created clones of 'GlassTube' as shown in Figure 9 using the 'Select and Move' tool and the 'Select and Rotate' tool. The objects now resemble a bulb.

- We must now add textures to the object to make it more life-like. In order to do so, open the 'Compact Material Editor' window by selecting it from the

Figure 8. Cloning an object.

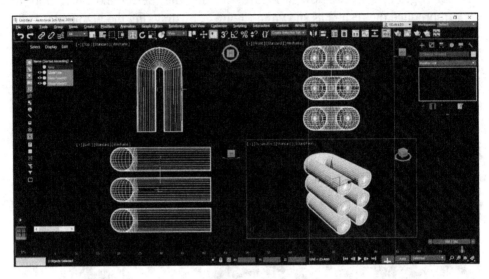

'Material Editor' option from the 'Rendering' menu (Samanta, Debabrata, et al. (2012e)).

- Select one of the Sample Slots as shown in Figure 10, and under 'Blinn Basic Properties' sub-menu, select the 'Ambient' and set the preferred choice of ambient color for the 'Base' object and click 'ok' when done. Once you've ensured that the 'Base' object is highlighted, select the 'Assign Material to

Figure 9. Select and rotate tool

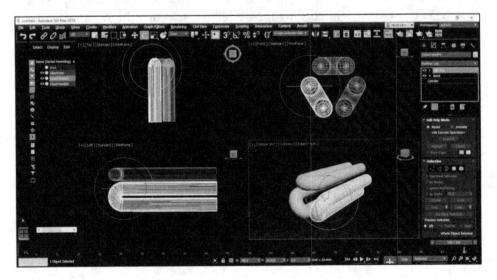

Selection' icon on the 'Compact Material Editor' window to add the material to the 'Base' object.

Figure 10. Sample slots in compact material editor.

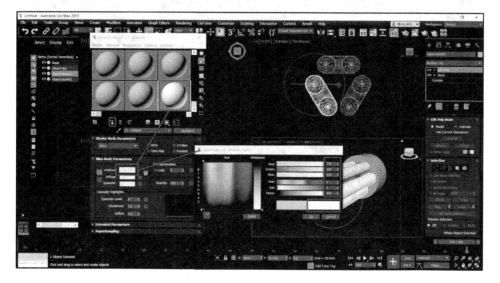

- A similar approach can be applied to set the materials for the 'Glass Tube' and its clones. Make sure you select a different Sample Slot and add a 'white' ambient color. Additionally, you set the 'Color' option under 'Self-Illumination' to 100 to get a brighter result and select the 'Assign Material to Selection' icon on the 'Compact Material Editor' window to add the material to the 'GlassTube' object and its clones (Samanta, Debabrata, et al. (2011)). You will get a similar result as shown in Figure 11.

- Before closing the 'Material Editor' window, we need to assign a material ID to the sample slot which was created for our glass tubes. Select and hold down the left mouse button on the 'Material ID Channel' and simultaneously navigate your mouse cursor over your preference of the ID to be given from the default available IDs (M. R. Filho et al. 2011)(Samanta, Debabrata, et al. (2012c)). Figure 12 is a reference for adding the material ID. This will be required at a later point.

Figure 11. Setting self illumination.

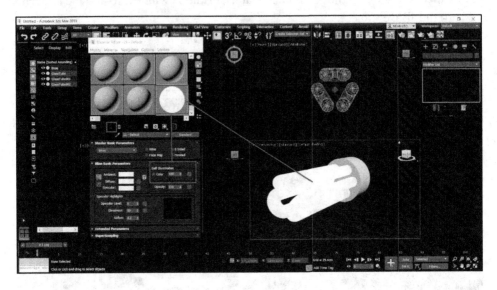

Figure 12. Setting material ID.

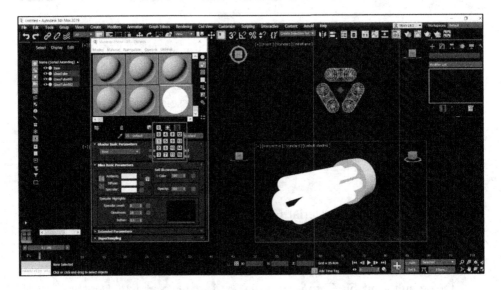

- Now when the scene is rendered, we can see a similar result as given in Figure 13.

Figure 13. Fluorescent bulb (first look).

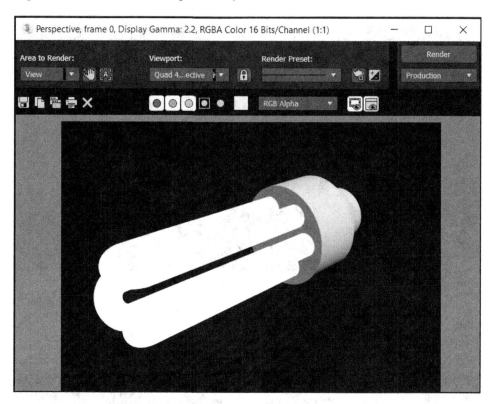

- We now only need to add an effect which will make the 'GlassTube' object glow.
- Under the 'Rendering' menu, select the 'Effects' options to bring up the 'Environment and Effects' window (Samanta, Debabrata, et al. (2012a)).
- Under the 'Effects' tab, select the 'Add' button, and add 'Lens Effects'. This will subsequently add the 'Lens Effects Parameters' section to this window, under which we must select the 'Glow' effect. We can adjust the 'Lens Effects Globals' as per our requirements as per the specifications visible in Figure 14.

- A 'Glow Element' section is also available, under which select 'Options' and add Material ID number similar to the Material ID specified earlier (S. Vu et al. 2018). This will add the Glow effect to the Sample Slot which is assigned to the earlier specified Material ID. Once done, return to the 'Parameters' ribbon and change the 'Radial Color' to white by using the colour selector window as shown in Figure 15.

Figure 14. Adding lens effects–glow.

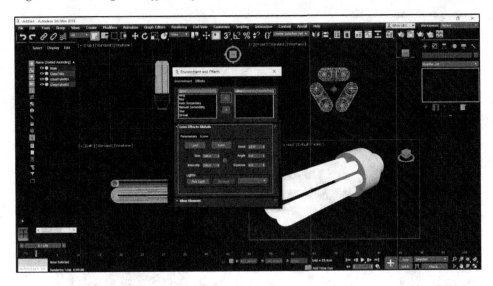

Figure 15. Setting glow properties.

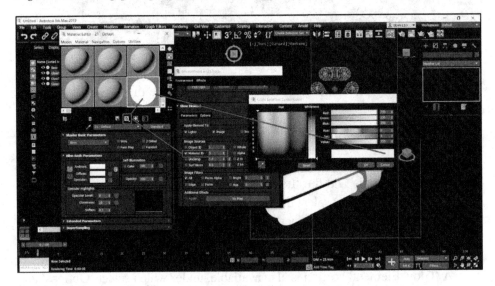

- Once all above configuration parameters are done, render the scene by selecting the 'Render' option under the 'Rendering' menu. Your final output should be similar to Figure 16.

Figure 16. Fluorescent bulb (final render).

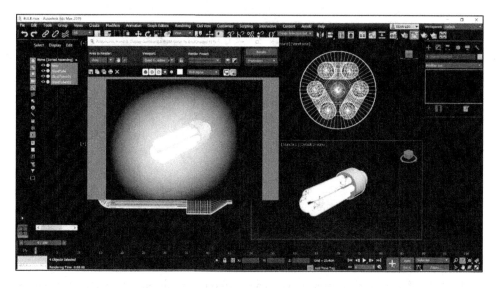

INCANDESCENT LIGHT CREATION:

- The construction of an Incandescent Light Bulb to construct the Base, Glass bulb, Tungsten filament, Glass support, two contact wires, and two support wires (Nadeem, A. et al. 2015).
- In order to construct the bulb's base, select the 'Cylinder' option from the Common Panel's 'Geometry' option and draw and scale the radius and height of the 'cylinder' inside any one of the viewports, preferably the Perspective Viewport (U. Castellani et al. 2005). It should be similar to Figure 17.

- By default, the newly added cylinder would be given a default name 'Cylinder001'. We can rename the cylinder to 'Base' as required for identification purposes, however this is completely optional (UlaşYılmaz et al. 2002).
- Making sure that the 'Base' is selected, under the 'modify' option, select the drop menu of the modifiers and select the 'Edit Mesh' modifier in order to reshape the 'Base' and make it appear more life-like (Van de Perre et al. 2019). You will notice that 'Edit Mesh' appears above the object's name indicating that the modifier is acting on the object. Now click the very same 'Edit Mesh' appearing above Cylinder as highlighted in Figure 18 to display the modifier's settings. Under the 'Selection' ribbon, select 'Edge' (W. Sun et

Figure 17. Adding bulb base

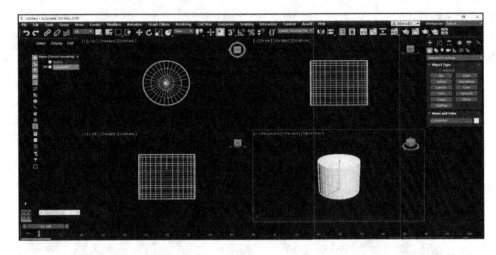

al. 2005). With this option, we can change the position, scale and orientation of the selected edges visible on the 'Base' with the help of the select tools shown below.

Figure 18. Base reposition and edit mesh modifier.

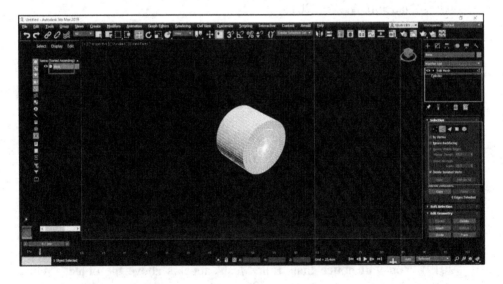

- In the 'Left viewport', a side view of the object is visible as wireframes. Select an approximate number of edges and using the 'Select and Uniform

Scale' tool, rescale the base and extend the base by using the 'Select and Move' tool to reproduce the results as shown in Figure 19.

Figure 19. Select and uniform and select and move tools.

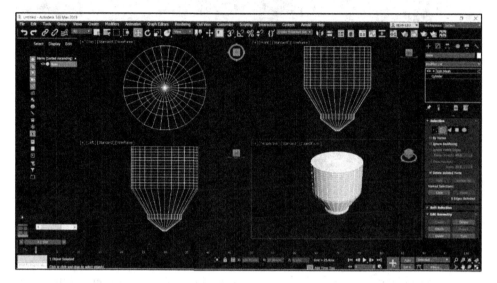

- Click the very same 'Edit Mesh' appearing above Cylinder as mentioned before, to stop making any more modifications to the 'Base' object (Wei Sun et al. 2002).
- Add a 'Sphere' to create the Glass Bulb, ensuring that the 'Sphere' has an appropriate radius. Rename it as per your requirement.I have renamed it to 'GlassBulb'. Making sure that the 'GlassBulb' is selected, under the 'modify' option, select the drop menu of the modifiers and select the 'TurboSmooth' modifier. A similar shape shall appear as shown in Figure 20.

- Add another modifier, 'Edit Poly' to the same 'GlassBulb' object. Under the 'Selection' ribbon, select 'Edge' option. Select an approximate number of edges and using the 'Select and Move' tool to reproduce the results as shown in Figure 21, by dragging the gizmo along the 'Z' axis.

- Click the very same 'Edit Poly' appearing above Sphere as mentioned before, to stop making any more modifications to the 'GlassBulb' object.

Figure 20. Sphere with TurboSmooth modifier.

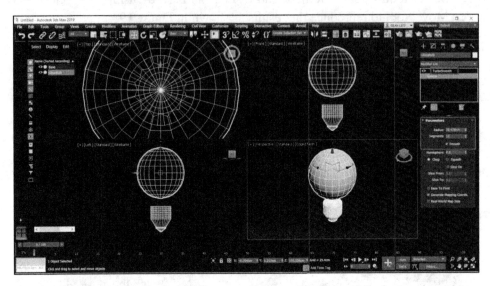

- To create the Glass Support, add a Cylinder to the viewport, with an appropriate radius and height, rename it to 'GlassSupp' or any other name as required (Woop, Sven et al. 2005). Add an 'Edit Mesh' modifier to this object by navigating the drop menu of the modifiers under the 'modify' option. Select an approximate number of edges and using the 'Select and Move' tool

Figure 21. Edit poly modifier and selection tools.

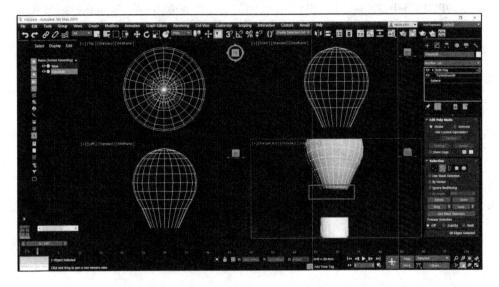

Figure 22. Helix shape and BendModifier.

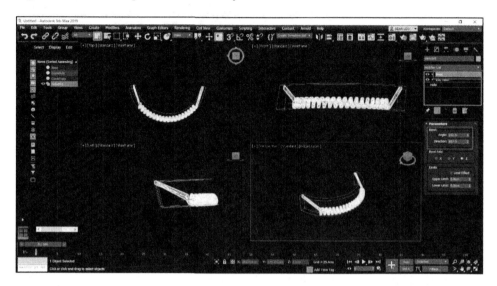

to reproduce the results as shown in Figure 22, by dragging the gizmo in the required axes.

- Construct the Contact Wire by using the 'Line' shape and draw the shape of the wire as shown in Figure 24. You may navigate to the modify pane and reposition the vertices of the Line by using the vertex option of the 'Selection' pane.

- Ensure that the 'Enable in Viewport' option is selected and thickness of the line is appropriately set.
- Make a clone of the 'Line' and reposition it to get a similar output as shown in Figure 25.

- We must now add textures to the object to make it more life-like. In order to do so, open the 'Compact Material Editor' window by selecting it from the 'Material Editor' (Z. Pezeshki et al. 2017) option from the 'Rendering' menu as shown in Figure 26.

Figure 23. Line shape for constructing contact wire.

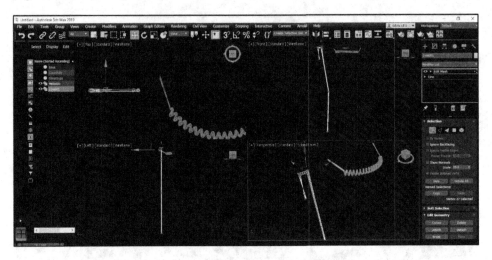

- Select one of the Sample Slots as shown in Figure 27, and under 'Blinn Basic Properties' sub-menu, select the 'Ambient' and set the preferred choice of ambient color for the 'Base' object and click 'ok' when done. Once you've ensured that the 'Base' object is highlighted, select the 'Assign Material to Selection' icon on the 'Compact Material Editor' window to add the material to the 'Base' object.

Figure 24. Cloning and mirroring contact wire.

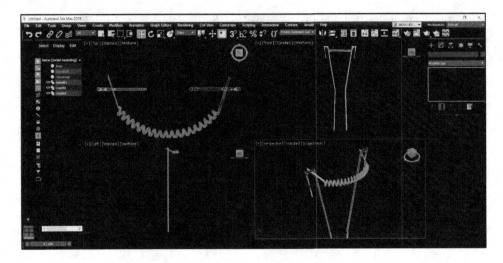

Figure 25. Opening the compact material editor.

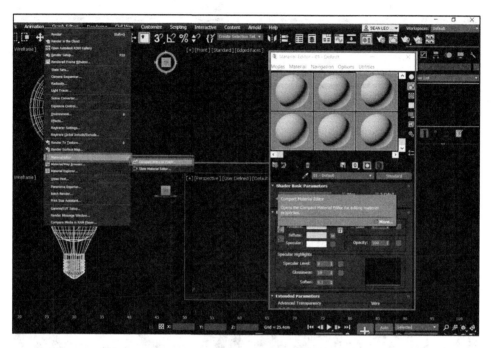

- A similar approach can be applied to set the materials for the ''GlassBulb' object. Make sure you select a different Sample Slot and set opacity to '10'. Select the 'Assign Material to Selection' icon on the 'Compact Material Editor' window to add the material to the 'GlassBulb' object. You will get a similar result as shown in Figure 28.

- You can follow similar steps to add textures to the Helix and lines by selecting an empty sample slot and choosing the 'Diffuse' and adding a bitmap image as a texture and assigning it accordingly.
- Add a sphere to the scene, rename it to 'illumination' and position it above the 'GlassBulb' object and in the compact material editor assign an empty sample slot to it whose opacity property is set to Zero (YeeWa Choy et al. 2012).
- Before closing the 'Material Editor' window, we need to assign a material ID to the sample slot which was created for our 'illumination' object. Select and hold down the left mouse button on the 'Material ID Channel' and simultaneously navigate your mouse cursor over your preference of the ID to

Figure 26. Sample slots in compact material editor.

Figure 27. Glass bulb material properties.

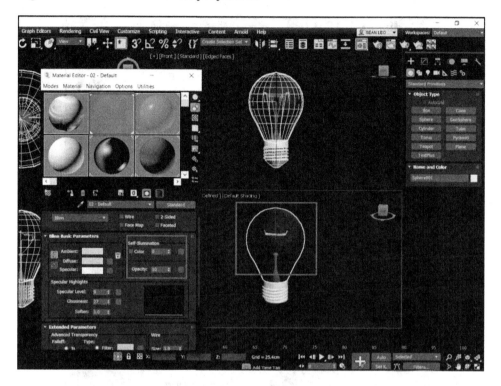

be given from the default available IDs (Yusuf Arayici et al. 2005,). Figure 29 is a reference for adding the material ID. This will be required at a later point.

- Now when the scene is rendered, we can see a similar result as given in Figure 30.

- We now only need to add an effect which will make the 'Illumination' object glow.
- Under the 'Rendering' menu, select the 'Effects' options to bring up the 'Environment and Effects' window.
- Under the 'Effects' tab, select the 'Add' button, and add 'Lens Effects'. This will subsequently add the 'Lens Effects Parameters' section to this window, under which we must select the 'Glow' effect. We can adjust the 'Lens Effects Global' as per our requirements as per the specifications visible in Figure 31.

Figure 28. Setting material ID for glow effect.

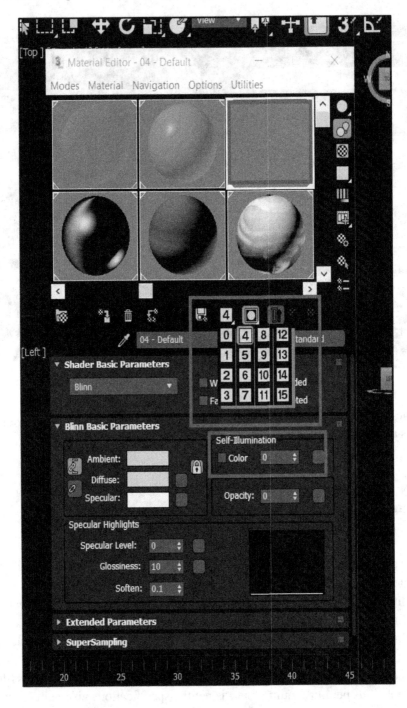

Figure 29. Incandescent bulb (first look).

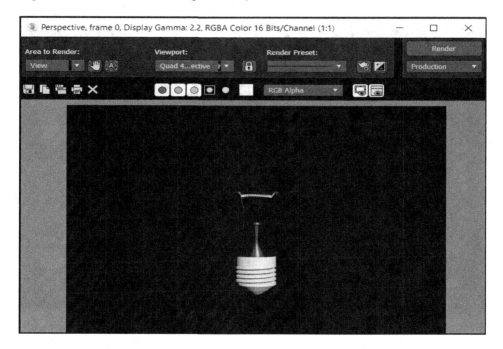

- A 'Glow Element' section is also available, under which select 'Options' and add Material ID number similar to the Material ID specified earlier. This will add the Glow effect to the Sample Slot which is assigned to the earlier specified Material ID (Yoo-Kil Yang et al. 2005). Once done, return to the 'Parameters' ribbon and change the 'Radial Color' to Yellow by using the colour selector window as shown in Figure 32.

- Once all above configuration parameters are done, render the scene by selecting the 'Render' option under the 'Rendering' menu. Your final output should be similar to Figure 33.

CONCLUSION

Observing both bulbs and light sources, along with their properties provides us a better appreciation of light sources in a scene or virtual environment because such light sources can set the atmosphere for a scene, for example, dim lights often

Figure 30. Setting lens effect – glow.

flickering can provide an eerie environment similar to a horror scene, while bright lights provide a sense of higher visibility, etc. Thus, analysing the lighting requirement for a scene can truly impact the hard work put in to create a scene.

Figure 31. Setting the glow properties.

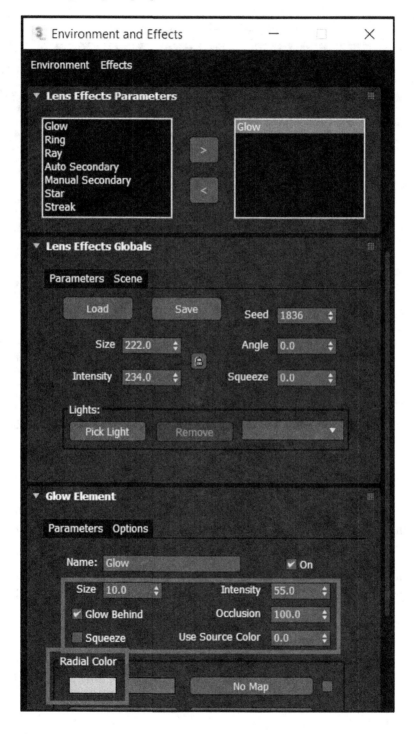

Figure 32. Incandescent bulb (final render).

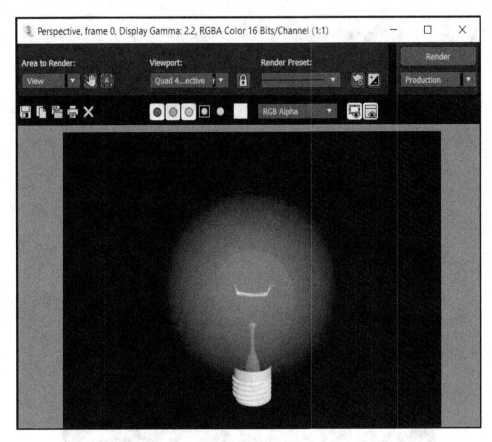

REFERENCES

Arayici, Y., & Hamilton, A. (2005). Modeling 3D Scanned Data to Visualize the Built Environment. *Proceedings of the Ninth International Conference on Information Visualisation*, 509-514. 10.1109/IV.2005.82

Ardakani, H. K., Mousavinia, A., & Safaei, F. (2020). Four points: One-pass geometrical camera calibration algorithm. *The Visual Computer*, *36*(2), 413–424. doi:10.100700371-019-01632-7

Baskoro, A. S., & Haryanto, I. (2015). Development of travel speed detection method in welding simulator using augmented reality. *2015 International Conference on Advanced Computer Science and Information Systems (ICACSIS)*, 269-273. 10.1109/ICACSIS.2015.7415194

Castellani, U., Fusiello, A., Murino, V., Papaleo, L., Puppo, E., & Pittore, M. (2005). A complete system for on-line 3D modelling from acoustic images. *Signal Processing Image Communication, 20*(9-10), 832–852. doi:10.1016/j.image.2005.02.003

Choy, Lim, Wang, & Chan. (2012). Development CT-based three-dimensional complex skull model for Finite element analysis. *2012 IEEE Conference on Sustainable Utilization and Development in Engineering and Technology (STUDENT)*, 135-139. 10.1109/STUDENT.2012.6408383

Deryabin, N. B., Zhdanov, D. D., & Sokolov, V. G. (2017). Embedding the script language into optical simulation software. *Programming and Computer Software, 43*(1), 13–23. doi:10.1134/S0361768817010029

Esmaeili, H., Thwaites, H., & Woods, P. C. (2017). Workflows and Challenges Involved in Creation of Realistic Immersive Virtual Museum, Heritage, and Tourism Experiences: A Comprehensive Reference for 3D Asset Capturing. *2017 13th International Conference on Signal-Image Technology & Internet-Based Systems (SITIS)*, 465-472. 10.1109/SITIS.2017.82

Esmaeili, H., Woods, P. C., & Thwaites, H. (2014). Realisation of virtualised architectural heritage. *2014 International Conference on Virtual Systems & Multimedia (VSMM)*, 94-101. 10.1109/VSMM.2014.7136676

Filho, M. R., Negrão, N. M., & Damasceno, R. R. (2011). SwImax: A Web Tool Using Virtual Reality for Teaching the WiMAX Protocol. *2011 XIII Symposium on Virtual Reality*, 217-224. 10.1109/SVR.2011.27

Fritsch, D., & Klein, M. (2017). 3D and 4D modeling for AR and VR app developments. *2017 23rd International Conference on Virtual System & Multimedia (VSMM)*, 1-8. 10.1109/VSMM.2017.8346270

Günther-Diringer, D. (2016). Historisches 3D-Stadtmodell von Karlsruhe. *J. Cartogr. Geogr. Inf., 66*, 66–71. doi:10.1007/BF03545207

Hegazy, M., Yasufuku, K., & Abe, H. (2022). An interactive approach to investigate brightness perception of daylighting in Immersive Virtual Environments: Comparing subjective responses and quantitative metrics. *Building Simulation, 15*(1), 41–68. doi:10.100712273-021-0798-3

Khoroshko, L. L., Ukhov, P. A., & Keyno, P. P. (2018). *Development of a Laboratory Workshop for Open Online Courses Based on 3D Computer Graphics and Multimedia. In 2018 Learning With MOOCS. LWMOOCS.* doi:10.1109/LWMOOCS.2018.8534678

Kwon, Y. M., Lee, Y. A., & Kim, S. J. (2017). Case study on 3D printing education in fashion design coursework. *Fash Text*, 4(1), 26. doi:10.118640691-017-0111-3

Lungershausen, U., Heinrich, C., & Duttmann, R. (2013). Turning Human-nature Interaction into 3D Landscape Scenes: An Approach to Communicate Geoarchaeological Research. *J. Cartogr. Geogr. Inf.*, 63, 269–275. doi:10.1007/BF03546142

Manson, A., Poyade, M., & Rea, P. (2015). A recommended workflow methodology in the creation of an educational and training application incorporating a digital reconstruction of the cerebral ventricular system and cerebrospinal fluid circulation to aid anatomical understanding. *BMC Medical Imaging*, 15(1), 44. doi:10.118612880-015-0088-6 PMID:26482126

Nadeem, A., Wong, A. K. D., & Wong, F. K. W. (2015). Bill of Quantities with 3D Views Using Building Information Modeling. *Arabian Journal for Science and Engineering*, 40(9), 2465–2477. doi:10.100713369-015-1657-2

Natephra, W., Motamedi, A., Fukuda, T., & Yabuki, N. (2017). Integrating building information modeling and virtual reality development engines for building indoor lighting design. *Vis. in Eng.*, 5(1), 19. doi:10.118640327-017-0058-x

Park, S.-Y., & Subbarao, M. (2005). A multiview 3D modeling system based on stereo vision techniques. *Machine Vision and Applications*, 16(3), 148–156. doi:10.100700138-004-0165-2

Paul, M., & Sanyal, G. (2011). Segmentation technique of SAR imagery using entropy. *International Journal of Computer Technology and Applications*, 2(5).

Pezeshki, Z., Soleimani, A., & Darabi, A. (2017). 3Ds MAX to FEM for building thermal distribution: A case study. *2017 3rd Iranian Conference on Intelligent Systems and Signal Processing (ICSPIS)*, 110-115. 10.1109/ICSPIS.2017.8311599

Samanta, D., & Paul, M. (2011). A Novel Approach of Entropy based Adaptive Thresholding Technique for Video Edge Detection. *Threshold (x, y)*, 1, 1.

Samanta, D. (2011). A novel statistical approach for segmentation of SAR Images. *Journal of Global Research in Computer Science*, 2(10), 9–13.

Samanta, D., & Sanyal, G. (2011a). Automated Classification of SAR Images Using Moment. *International Journal of Computer Science Issues*, 8(6), 135.

Samanta, D., & Sanyal, G. (2011b). *Development of Adaptive Thresholding Technique for Classification of Synthetic Aperture Radar Images*. Academic Press.

Samanta, D., & Sanyal, G. (2011c). Development of edge detection technique for images using adaptive thresholding. *International Conference on Information Processing*, 671–676. 10.1007/978-3-642-22786-8_85

Samanta, D., & Sanyal, G. (2011d). SAR image segmentation using Color space clustering and Watersheds. *International Journal of Engineering Research and Applications*, *1*(3), 997–999.

Samanta, D., & Sanyal, G. (2012). Segmentation technique of SAR imagery based on fuzzy c-means clustering. *IEEE-International Conference On Advances In Engineering, Science And Management (ICAESM-2012)*, 610–612.

Samanta, D., & Ghosh, A. (2012). Automatic obstacle detection based on gaussian function in robocar. *J. Res. Eng. Appl. Sci*, *2*(2), 354–363.

Samanta, D., & Sanyal, G. (2012a). A novel approach of SAR image classification using color space clustering and watersheds. *2012 Fourth International Conference on Computational Intelligence and Communication Networks*, 237–240. 10.1109/CICN.2012.27

Samanta, D., & Sanyal, G. (2012c). An Approach of Segmentation Technique of SAR Images using Adaptive Thresholding Technique. *International Journal of Engineering Research & Technology (Ahmedabad)*, *1*(7).

Samanta, D., & Sanyal, G. (2012f). Novel Shannon's entropy based segmentation technique for SAR images. *International Conference on Information Processing*, 193–199. 10.1007/978-3-642-31686-9_22

Samanta, D., & Sanyal, G. (2012g). *SAR image classification using fuzzy CMeans*. Academic Press.

Samanta, D., & Sanyal, G. (2012h). Statistical approach for Classification of SAR Images. *International Journal of Soft Computing and Engineering (IJSCE)*, 2231–2307.

Samanta, D., & Sanyal, G. (2013). An Approach of Tabu Search for Unsupervised Classification for SAR Images. *Seven International Conference on Image and Signal Processing*.

Samanta, D., & Sanyal, G. (2012b). A novel approach of SAR image processing based on Hue, Saturation and Brightness (HSB). *Procedia Technology*, *4*, 584–588. doi:10.1016/j.protcy.2012.05.093

Samanta, D., & Sanyal, G. (2012d). Classification of SAR Images Based on Entropy. *Int. J. Inf. Technol. Comput. Sci*, *4*(12), 82–86. doi:10.5815/ijitcs.2012.12.09

Samanta, D., & Sanyal, G. (2012e). Novel approach of adaptive thresholding technique for edge detection in videos. *Procedia Engineering, 30*, 283–288. doi:10.1016/j. proeng.2012.01.862

Sun, W., & Lal, P. (2002). Pallavi Lal. Recent development on computer aided tissue engineering— A review. *Computer Methods and Programs in Biomedicine, 67*(2), 85–103. doi:10.1016/S0169-2607(01)00116-X PMID:11809316

Sun, W., Starly, B., Nam, J., & Darling, A. (2005). Bio-CAD modeling and its applications in computer-aided tissue engineering. *Computer Aided Design, 37*(11), 1097–1114. doi:10.1016/j.cad.2005.02.002

Tavares, J., Dutta, P., Dutta, S., & Samanta, D. (n.d.). *Cyber Intelligence and Information Retrieval*. Academic Press.

Toshihiro, A., Masayuki, K., & Naokazu, Y. (2005). 3D Modeling of Outdoor Environments by Integrating Omnidirectional Range and Color Images. *Proceedings of the Fifth International Conference on 3-D Digital Imaging and Modeling (3DIM'05)*.

Tsipotas, D., & Spathopoulou, V. (2015). An assessment of research on 3D digital representation of ancient Greek furniture, using surviving archaelological artefacts. *Digital Heritage, 2015*, 325–328. doi:10.1109/DigitalHeritage.2015.7419515

Valdez, M. T., Ferreira, C. M., & Barbosa, F. P. M. (2016). 3D virtual laboratory for teaching circuit theory — A virtual learning environment (VLE). *2016 51st International Universities Power Engineering Conference (UPEC)*, 1-4. 10.1109/ UPEC.2016.8114126

Van de Perre, G., De Beir, A., Cao, H. L., Esteban, P. G., Lefeber, D., & Vanderborght, B. (2019). Studying Design Aspects for Social Robots Using a Generic Gesture Method. *International Journal of Social Robotics, 11*(4), 651–663. doi:10.100712369-019-00518-x

Vu, S. (2018). Recreating Little Manila through a Virtual Reality Serious Game. *2018 3rd Digital Heritage International Congress (DigitalHERITAGE) held jointly with 2018 24th International Conference on Virtual Systems & Multimedia (VSMM 2018)*, 1-4. 10.1109/DigitalHeritage.2018.8810082

Woop, S., Schmittler, J., & Slusallek, P. (2005). RPU: A Programmable Ray Processing Unit for Realtime Ray Tracing. *Siggraph 2005*.

Yang, Lee, Kim, & Kim. (2005). Adaptive Space Carving with Texture Mapping. *LNCS, 3482*, 1129-1138.

Yılmaz, Mülayim, & Atalay. (2002). Reconstruction of Three Dimensional Models from Real Images. *Proceedings of the First International Symposium on 3D Data Processing Visualization and Transmission (3DPVT.02).*

Chapter 10
Unseen Objects to Cast Shadows Using Clones to Cast Shadows With Sunlight and Skylight

Raghav Sham Kamat
CHRIST University, India

Ritwika Das Gupta
CHRIST University, India

ABSTRACT

3D modelling software has its importance and requirement priority in various fields, mostly in design sectors. Visualization, creating 3D models, representing scenes, and adding animation to objects can have their complications, but with 3ds Max software results can be expected with the large availability of modifiers, cameras, and lights made available for the modelers to create something with their creative perspective. By going through this chapter, readers can have an insight into topics like lights, camera paths, modifiers, Boolean, pro-Boolean, viewport, mesh, AEC extend by which modelers can have their desired output as a result. It also gives a glimpse of how material editors can be useful in giving a realistic look to any object or scene being created. Usage of various lights is also included with the importance of cloning objects. Cloning objects is an important aspect when modeling is considered. Casting shadows to clone objects can be interesting and complex. This chapter makes it easy by giving a clear perspective of its usage and importance.

DOI: 10.4018/978-1-6684-4139-8.ch010

Figure 1. Diagrammatic representation of shadow casted by target spot light

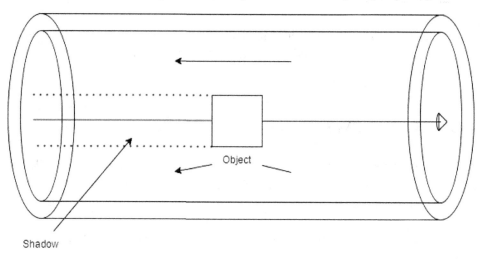

INTRODUCTION

A spot light is used when there is a requirement of a direct source of light. Being emitted by a cone, it allows us to easily have control over properties like width i.e. the area light should cover. Any object closer to a spotlight gets bright enough and harder (A. S. Baskoro et al. 2015). Target spot lights are very much useful in casting shadows as the light directly falls on the object. Shadow can be casted by enabling shadow property in the modifier list of the respected light, by clicking the shadow checkbox. A free spotlight has no targeted area. It has no specific focus. It is mostly used to create a glow effect depending on the scenario. A free direct light produces a parallel light ray over any object in a single straight direction same as the natural phenomena where sunlightfalls on the earth's surface (I. Haryanto et al. 2015). The most common usage of a free direct light would be using it to generate sunlight in any specific environment. The colour can easily be changed and the position as well can be adjusted easily in the given 3d space. Figure 1 show shadow created by target spotlight.

The above-mentioned lights are the most commonly used sources to produce the required light effect over any object so as to enhance it when rendered.

CREATING CLONES

One of the major advantages in 3ds Max is cloning .This is very much helpful when similar objects are to be created with the slightest change in properties. (Ardakani et al. 2020).

OBJECT SHADOWS

On creation of objects or any scene/environment, placing lights would be a task that has to be done with considering the position and accuracy. Adjusting the saturation and brightness with intensity has to be done to get the right amount of focus on the object or a scene.

Enable shadows in General Parameters and activate shadows by clicking the check box available under shadows. Fig 2 shows the changes made in light properties.(D. Fritsch et al. 2017)

USAGE

Lights are mostly used in simulating real light effects in different environment like office scene or any household lamps, lights are very much essential in film works for example creating light effects on a virtual stage and sometimes emitting sunlight. Lights are of great use when any architectural scene has to be represented in a lighted environment.(D. Tsipotas et al. 2015).

Advertising industries use various cameras with different lights placed at different position. With the presence of lights, representing an object or a scene using cameras becomes more attractive and convincing.

COMPARATIVE STUDY ON COPIES AND INSTANCE OF LIGHTS:

Keeping rendering as a main factor, render time when instances are used is much less compared to copies. Copies generally require more space compared to instance as it allows to work on an object with its properties same as the original objects as in reference. When copies are made, it becomes an individual object with its own properties which eventually takes up some memory space and also much more time whilst rendering. (Deryabin et al. 2017)

Figure 2. Modifying light properties

When different modifiers applied on any specific object and rendered, the presence of lights would enhance the detailing of the object to get absolute clarity and accuracy. Whilst creating any closed environment like a restaurant or an indoor stadium, the objects placed inside wouldn't appear on default lighting, here is when lights come in its best usage, especially when a light source is placed outside a particular context scene, buy enabling shadows the light rays can easily be produced over the objects placed inside.

PLACING CAMERAS

After the completion of positioning lights over any scene or an object, cameras are placed at an accurate position to have a clear perspective of the focused element so as to justify it completely.

Casting shadows using lights would also be of an advantage when keyframe animations are introduced.

The sunlight and daylight help in following the proper geographical Location of the sun and its movement. It allows us to choose Location, date, time, and compass orientation. This is suitable for studying the shadow of the sun at its various locations. We can also provide animation orientation, Location, direction, and orbital scale. (Günther-Diringer et al. 2016)

We can find the sunlight or daylight button in the following way:

- under create panel -> under systems->under object type rollout-> under the sunlight button or the daylight button.

Both sunlight and daylight have similar interface.

- Sunlight uses directional light while daylight, on the other hand, combines both of them.
- Both IES and Standard sunlight are possible.
- Both IES and normal skylight are possible
- Both Standard and skylights are not photometric. If the scene uses standard light, then these lights are more appropriate to be used.(H. Esmaeili et al. 2017)

WORKING PROCEDURE:

The interface of the daylight containing sunlight and skylight is: Fig 3 shows the position changes.

- To simulate the sun,the IES Sun object is used.
- In the case of Standard, to simulate the sun, direct target light is used.
- No light is simulated in case of No light.

Active:
It is used to turn on and off the sunlight in the viewport.
For skylight following options can be chosen:

Figure 3. Changes made in light position

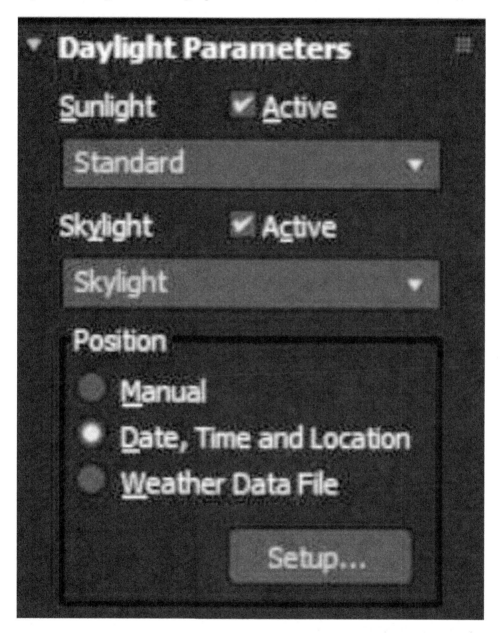

- IES Sky Uses- for simulating IES skylight.
- Skylight Uses – which uses skylight for simulating the sky.
- No skylight is simulated if no skylight option is selected.(Hegazy et al. 2022)

The Working of IES Sunlight is:

- To create the sunlight- under create panel -> under systems-> under create a Daylight system in your scene. -> under modify panel ->under daylight parameters rollout -> underSunlight -> choose IES Sun.
- After which the following interface can be seen:

Figure 4 shows the changes made in sunlight parameters.

- To turn the sunlight on and off in the viewport,the on parameter is used.
- Only when IES sun is applied directly targeted is used. When switched on,the light is targeted,and it can be changed by moving the target.
- The intensity of the sunlight can also be set.
  - When switched on, it indicates that the sun will cast a shadow.
  - The shadow methods contain which type of shadow is used- ray traced, advanced ray-traced, etc.Figure 5 shows the top view of scene.(Kwon et al.2017)

The Working of IES Skylight is:

- The IES Skylight can be accessed by- under create panel ->under systems ->under create a daylight system in your scene. ->under modify panel ->under daylight parameters rollout ->under skylight -> IES sky
- The following interface can be seen:Figure 6: Rendering light properties.

- Through On, the skylight can be switched on.
- The skylight's intensity can be adjusted through Multiplier.
- The colour swatch allows you to pick the colour of the sky. Even mapping of texture can be used through environment under rendering in the sky. This is done below.

Advantages of Sunlight:

- The sunlight helps us to understand the movement of the sun according to the geographic angle, Location, date, time, compass orientation concerning the earth.
- It helps us to animate the date and time along with the sun.

Figure 4. Making changes in sunlight parameters

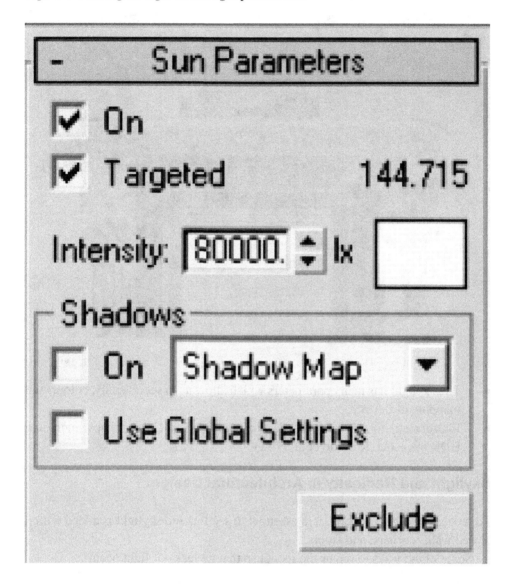

- The North Direction, Orbital Scale, latitude, andlongitude, can be animated.
- It gives the sun effect on the sky.(Lungershausen et al. 2013)

Advantages of Skylight:

- The skylight helps us to give the effect of the sky to the scene.
- The skylight is majorly used in architectural designs.

Figure 5. Top view of the scenery

- The skylight has many parameters which allow us to set intensity, colour, and mapping of the sky.
- Illumination for all renderers is provided by Sky Colour maps, including HDR maps.(M. R. Filho et al. 2011)

Skylight and Radiosity in Architectural Design:

To process skylight properly, it is essential to see that the skylight is added within closed walls, corners, and floors.

Some of the ways to repair the model so that no leaks of light occur:

- The floors and ceiling should have thickness.
- Wall command should be used to create walls.
- Ensure that floor and ceiling extend beyond walls.(M. T. Valdez et al. 2016)

Even sunlight is used for the exterior render of an architectural design. Along with the architectural design,games, and movies also use sunlight and skylight for exterior and interior renders

Figure 6. Making changes in sunlight parameters

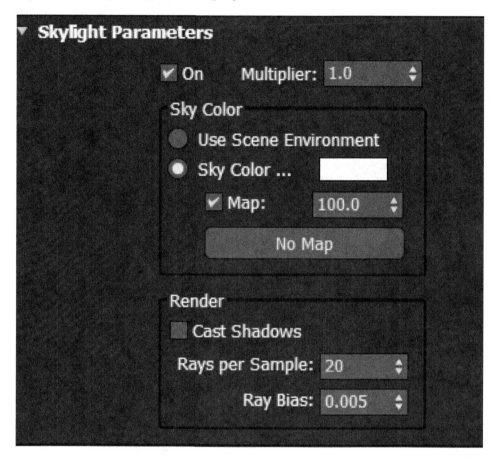

Comparative Study:

The sun positioner and physical sky are like most daylight and sunlight systems. This system is more suitable for studying shadows. The major advantage to thePhysical Sky and Sun Positioner over the sunlight and daylight systems is the efficiency and intuitiveness in the workflow. The sun positioner allows us to place the sun in the scene. Various other features such as Location, date, time can also be set.

Along with the sun positioner, the environment map controls are also available by default. The Material Editor's Physical Sun and sky rollout contain all parameters related to shading. This allows us to reduce inconsistency and simplifies the workflow. (Manson et al. 2015)

The Physical Sky and Sun Positioner are renderers. It is according to the renderer to understand whether it needs to internally support this feature using multiple light

Figure 7. Perspective view of the scene.(L. L. Khoroshko et al. 2018)

sources, like Scanline, or as a simple Environment map, like ART. It does implement the Scanline shading functions, so it is fully functional with the Scanline renderer as an Environment map but not for illumination. Thus, the sun positioner and physical sky are easier to use compared to the sunlight and daylight systems.

Project on Sunlight vs. skylight:

A small project is created in Autodesk 3ds Max to demonstrate the difference between sunlight and skylight. Each steps of creating this project is shown below:

Step 1: Open the Autodesk 3ds max window and set it to perspective view. shown in Fig7 below.

Step2: Import a building model from previous project and add required material to the building. Shown in Fig 8 below

Step3: Draw a plane below the building as grass plain. Assign grass material to the plane. Shown in Fig9 below. (Nadeem et al. 2015)

Step4: Use hair and fur modifier to create grass on the plane. Scale and reduce thickness of the grass as required. Change color of the grass from the modify panel. Shown in Fig 10 below. (Natephra et al. 2017)

Figure 8. The viewports.

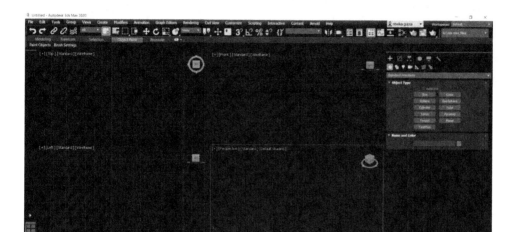

Step5: Make some trees on the plane using AEC extended under create panel. Shown in Fig 12 below.

Step 6: Return back to the default viewport. From the create panel, under lights, under standard select a skylight and place it using front and top view port.(marked in red circle) shown in Fig 13 below. (S. Vu et al. 2018)

Figure 9. The building model.

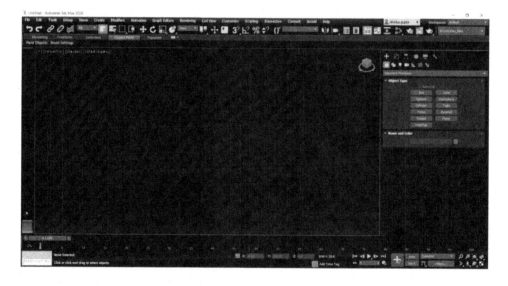

Figure 10. The plane for grasses.

Step 7: Select the sky light, under modify panel increase intensity, set the shadows on and change the required properties. Shown in Fig 14 below.

Step 8: The render image after assigning skylight is given in Fig 15 below.

Step9: To add a sun positioner, under create panel, under lights, under photometric select sun positioner. Now add the sun postioner using front and top view in proper

Figure 11. Grasses on the plane.

Figure 12. Trees models.

position.(marked in red circle). Shown in Fig 16 below. (Samanta Deababrata et al. 2012)

Step 10: The render view after adding sun positioners shown in Fig 17 below.

Step11: As shown in above figures the skylight gives color and to the sky and lights the sky up, where as the sun positioned acts as a sunlight.

When both sun postioner and skylight is added together the render view is shown in fig below. Shown in Figure 18 below. (Samanta Deababrata et al. 2011)

CONCLUSION

3D modelling software is essential and required in various fields, most notably in the design industry. Visualization, making 3d models, depicting sceneries, and adding motion to things can all be difficult. Still, with 3ds Max software, enamoring results can be expected thanks to the enormous number of modifiers, cameras, and lights available for modellers to use. By reading this chapter, readers will understand subjects such as lights, camera routes, modifiers, Boolean, Pro-Boolean, Viewport, Mesh, and AEC Extend, all of which can help modellers achieve their desired outcome. It also shows how material editors can effectively give any object or scene being made a realistic look. The necessity of cloning objects is also involved in the use of varied lights. When it comes to modelling, cloning objects is a crucial consideration. Casting shadows to clone objects can be exciting and challenging; nevertheless, this chapter simplifies the process by clearly understanding its application and importance.

Figure 13. Adding skylight to the scene.

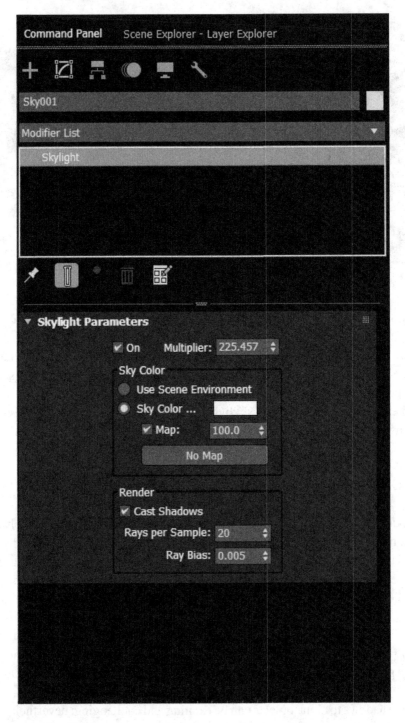

Figure 14. Skylight properties.

Figure 15. Skylight render view.

Figure 16. Adding sunlight to the scene.

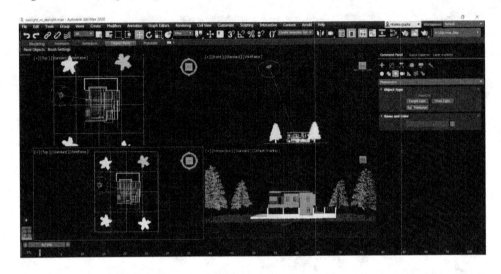

Figure 17. Sunlight render view.

Figure 18. Complete render using sunlight and skylight.

REFERENCES

Arayici, Y., & Hamilton, A. (2005). Modeling 3D Scanned Data to Visualize the Built Environment. *Proceedings of the Ninth International Conference on Information Visualisation*, 509-514. 10.1109/IV.2005.82

Ardakani, H. K., Mousavinia, A., & Safaei, F. (2020). Four points: One-pass geometrical camera calibration algorithm. *The Visual Computer*, *36*(2), 413–424. doi:10.100700371-019-01632-7

Baskoro, A. S., & Haryanto, I. (2015). Development of travel speed detection method in welding simulator using augmented reality. *2015 International Conference on Advanced Computer Science and Information Systems (ICACSIS)*, 269-273. 10.1109/ICACSIS.2015.7415194

Castellani, U., Fusiello, A., Murino, V., Papaleo, L., Puppo, E., & Pittore, M. (2005). A complete system for on-line 3D modelling from acoustic images. *Signal Processing Image Communication*, *20*(9-10), 832–852. doi:10.1016/j.image.2005.02.003

Choy, Lim, Wang, & Chan. (2012). Development CT-based three-dimensional complex skull model for Finite element analysis. *2012 IEEE Conference on Sustainable Utilization and Development in Engineering and Technology (STUDENT)*, 135-139. 10.1109/STUDENT.2012.6408383

Deryabin, N. B., Zhdanov, D. D., & Sokolov, V. G. (2017). Embedding the script language into optical simulation software. *Programming and Computer Software*, *43*(1), 13–23. doi:10.1134/S0361768817010029

Esmaeili, H., Thwaites, H., & Woods, P. C. (2017). Workflows and Challenges Involved in Creation of Realistic Immersive Virtual Museum, Heritage, and Tourism Experiences: A Comprehensive Reference for 3D Asset Capturing. *2017 13th International Conference on Signal-Image Technology & Internet-Based Systems (SITIS)*, 465-472. 10.1109/SITIS.2017.82

Esmaeili, H., Woods, P. C., & Thwaites, H. (2014). Realisation of virtualised architectural heritage. *2014 International Conference on Virtual Systems & Multimedia (VSMM)*, 94-101. 10.1109/VSMM.2014.7136676

Filho, M. R., Negrão, N. M., & Damasceno, R. R. (2011). SwImax: A Web Tool Using Virtual Reality for Teaching the WiMAX Protocol. *2011 XIII Symposium on Virtual Reality*, 217-224. 10.1109/SVR.2011.27

Fritsch, D., & Klein, M. (2017). 3D and 4D modeling for AR and VR app developments. *2017 23rd International Conference on Virtual System & Multimedia (VSMM)*, 1-8. 10.1109/VSMM.2017.8346270

Günther-Diringer, D. (2016). Historisches 3D-Stadtmodell von Karlsruhe. *J. Cartogr. Geogr. Inf.*, *66*, 66–71. doi:10.1007/BF03545207

Hegazy, M., Yasufuku, K., & Abe, H. (2022). An interactive approach to investigate brightness perception of daylighting in Immersive Virtual Environments: Comparing subjective responses and quantitative metrics. *Building Simulation*, *15*(1), 41–68. doi:10.100712273-021-0798-3

Khoroshko, L. L., Ukhov, P. A., & Keyno, P. P. (2018). *Development of a Laboratory Workshop for Open Online Courses Based on 3D Computer Graphics and Multimedia. In 2018 Learning With MOOCS*. LWMOOCS. doi:10.1109/LWMOOCS.2018.8534678

Kwon, Y. M., Lee, Y. A., & Kim, S. J. (2017). Case study on 3D printing education in fashion design coursework. *Fash Text*, *4*(1), 26. doi:10.118640691-017-0111-3

Lungershausen, U., Heinrich, C., & Duttmann, R. (2013). Turning Human-nature Interaction into 3D Landscape Scenes: An Approach to Communicate Geoarchaeological Research. *J. Cartogr. Geogr. Inf.*, *63*, 269–275. doi:10.1007/BF03546142

Manson, A., Poyade, M., & Rea, P. (2015). A recommended workflow methodology in the creation of an educational and training application incorporating a digital reconstruction of the cerebral ventricular system and cerebrospinal fluid circulation to aid anatomical understanding. *BMC Medical Imaging*, *15*(1), 44. doi:10.118612880-015-0088-6 PMID:26482126

Nadeem, A., Wong, A. K. D., & Wong, F. K. W. (2015). Bill of Quantities with 3D Views Using Building Information Modeling. *Arabian Journal for Science and Engineering*, *40*(9), 2465–2477. doi:10.100713369-015-1657-2

Natephra, W., Motamedi, A., Fukuda, T., & Yabuki, N. (2017). Integrating building information modeling and virtual reality development engines for building indoor lighting design. *Vis. in Eng.*, *5*(1), 19. doi:10.118640327-017-0058-x

Park, S.-Y., & Subbarao, M. (2005). A multiview 3D modeling system based on stereo vision techniques. *Machine Vision and Applications*, *16*(3), 148–156. doi:10.100700138-004-0165-2

Paul, M., & Sanyal, G. (2011). Segmentation technique of SAR imagery using entropy. *International Journal of Computer Technology and Applications*, *2*(5).

Pezeshki, Z., Soleimani, A., & Darabi, A. (2017). 3Ds MAX to FEM for building thermal distribution: A case study. *2017 3rd Iranian Conference on Intelligent Systems and Signal Processing (ICSPIS)*, 110-115. 10.1109/ICSPIS.2017.8311599

Samanta, D., & Paul, M. (2011). A Novel Approach of Entropy based Adaptive Thresholding Technique for Video Edge Detection. *Threshold (x, y)*, *1*, 1.

Samanta, D. (2011). A novel statistical approach for segmentation of SAR Images. *Journal of Global Research in Computer Science*, *2*(10), 9–13.

Samanta, D., & Sanyal, G. (2011a). Automated Classification of SAR Images Using Moment. *International Journal of Computer Science Issues*, *8*(6), 135.

Samanta, D., & Sanyal, G. (2011b). *Development of Adaptive Thresholding Technique for Classification of Synthetic Aperture Radar Images*. Academic Press.

Samanta, D., & Sanyal, G. (2011c). Development of edge detection technique for images using adaptive thresholding. *International Conference on Information Processing*, 671–676. 10.1007/978-3-642-22786-8_85

Samanta, D., & Sanyal, G. (2011d). SAR image segmentation using Color space clustering and Watersheds. *International Journal of Engineering Research and Applications, 1*(3), 997–999.

Samanta, D., & Sanyal, G. (2012). Segmentation technique of SAR imagery based on fuzzy c-means clustering. *IEEE-International Conference On Advances In Engineering, Science And Management (ICAESM-2012),* 610–612.

Samanta, D., & Ghosh, A. (2012). Automatic obstacle detection based on gaussian function in robocar. *J. Res. Eng. Appl. Sci, 2*(2), 354–363.

Samanta, D., & Sanyal, G. (2012a). A novel approach of SAR image classification using color space clustering and watersheds. *2012 Fourth International Conference on Computational Intelligence and Communication Networks,* 237–240. 10.1109/CICN.2012.27

Samanta, D., & Sanyal, G. (2012c). An Approach of Segmentation Technique of SAR Images using Adaptive Thresholding Technique. *International Journal of Engineering Research & Technology (Ahmedabad), 1*(7).

Samanta, D., & Sanyal, G. (2012f). Novel Shannon's entropy based segmentation technique for SAR images. *International Conference on Information Processing,* 193–199. 10.1007/978-3-642-31686-9_22

Samanta, D., & Sanyal, G. (2012g). *SAR image classification using fuzzy CMeans.* Academic Press.

Samanta, D., & Sanyal, G. (2012h). Statistical approach for Classification of SAR Images. *International Journal of Soft Computing and Engineering (IJSCE),* 2231–2307.

Samanta, D., & Sanyal, G. (2013). An Approach of Tabu Search for Unsupervised Classification for SAR Images. *Seven International Conference on Image and Signal Processing.*

Samanta, D., & Sanyal, G. (2012b). A novel approach of SAR image processing based on Hue, Saturation and Brightness (HSB). *Procedia Technology, 4,* 584–588. doi:10.1016/j.protcy.2012.05.093

Samanta, D., & Sanyal, G. (2012d). Classification of SAR Images Based on Entropy. *Int. J. Inf. Technol. Comput. Sci, 4*(12), 82–86. doi:10.5815/ijitcs.2012.12.09

Samanta, D., & Sanyal, G. (2012e). Novel approach of adaptive thresholding technique for edge detection in videos. *Procedia Engineering, 30,* 283–288. doi:10.1016/j.proeng.2012.01.862

Sun, W., & Lal, P. (2002). Pallavi Lal. Recent development on computer aided tissue engineering— A review. *Computer Methods and Programs in Biomedicine, 67*(2), 85–103. doi:10.1016/S0169-2607(01)00116-X PMID:11809316

Sun, W., Starly, B., Nam, J., & Darling, A. (2005). Bio-CAD modeling and its applications in computer-aided tissue engineering. *Computer Aided Design, 37*(11), 1097–1114. doi:10.1016/j.cad.2005.02.002

Tavares, J., Dutta, P., Dutta, S., & Samanta, D. (n.d.). *Cyber Intelligence and Information Retrieval.* Academic Press.

Toshihiro, A., Masayuki, K., & Naokazu, Y. (2005). 3D Modeling of Outdoor Environments by Integrating Omnidirectional Range and Color Images. *Proceedings of the Fifth International Conference on 3-D Digital Imaging and Modeling (3DIM'05).*

Tsipotas, D., & Spathopoulou, V. (2015). An assessment of research on 3D digital representation of ancient Greek furniture, using surviving archaelological artefacts. *Digital Heritage, 2015,* 325–328. doi:10.1109/DigitalHeritage.2015.7419515

Valdez, M. T., Ferreira, C. M., & Barbosa, F. P. M. (2016). 3D virtual laboratory for teaching circuit theory — A virtual learning environment (VLE). *2016 51st International Universities Power Engineering Conference (UPEC),* 1-4. 10.1109/UPEC.2016.8114126

Van de Perre, G., De Beir, A., Cao, H. L., Esteban, P. G., Lefeber, D., & Vanderborght, B. (2019). Studying Design Aspects for Social Robots Using a Generic Gesture Method. *International Journal of Social Robotics, 11*(4), 651–663. doi:10.100712369-019-00518-x

Vu, S. (2018). Recreating Little Manila through a Virtual Reality Serious Game. *2018 3rd Digital Heritage International Congress (DigitalHERITAGE) held jointly with 2018 24th International Conference on Virtual Systems & Multimedia (VSMM 2018),* 1-4. 10.1109/DigitalHeritage.2018.8810082

Woop, S., Schmittler, J., & Slusallek, P. (2005). RPU: A Programmable Ray Processing Unit for Realtime Ray Tracing. *Siggraph 2005.*

Yang, Lee, Kim, & Kim. (2005). Adaptive Space Carving with Texture Mapping. *LNCS, 3482,* 1129-1138.

Yılmaz, Mülayim, & Atalay. (2002). Reconstruction of Three Dimensional Models from Real Images. *Proceedings of the First International Symposium on 3D Data Processing Visualization and Transmission (3DPVT.02).*

Conclusion

3D Modelling software has its importance and requirement priority in various fields, mostly in design sectors. Visualization, creating 3d models, representing scenes, and adding animation to objects can have their complications, but with 3ds Max software, enamors results can be expected with the large availability of modifiers, cameras, and lights made available for the modelers to create something with their creative perspective. By going through this chapter readers can have an insight into topics like Lights, camera paths, Modifiers, Boolean, Pro- Boolean, Viewport, Mesh, AEC Extend by using which modelers can have their desired output as a result (U. Castellani., et al. 2005) (Y. Arayici et al. 2005). It also gives a glimpse of how material editors can be useful in giving a realistic look to any object or scene being created. Usage of various lights is also included with the importance of cloning objects. Cloning objects is an important aspect when modeling is considered. Casting shadows to clone objects can be interesting and complex, this chapter makes it easy by giving a clear perspective of its usage and importance. (V Kureethara et al. 2012)

The major application of 3DS Max is architectural visualization, movies, video games animation and even in advertisement industry. In architectural industry, 3ds max is used for critical compound modelling of various objects to create architectural visualization. Various lighting elements are used such as skylight, sun light for exterior visualization of architecture. Sunlight and skylight are a part of 3ds Max which makes environmental lighting very easy (V. Murino. et al. 2005). It is also used in gaming environments. The sunlight and daylight help in following the proper geographical Location of the sun and its movement. It allows us to choose Location, date, time, and compass orientation (Livio De Luca et al. 2006). This is suitable for studying the shadow of the sun at its various locations. We can also provide animation orientation, Location, direction, and orbital scale.

We can find the sunlight or daylight button in the following way:

· under create panel ->under systems->under object type rollout-> under the sunlight button or the daylight button.

Both sunlight and daylight have similar interface. (Anil Kumar et al. 2021)

· Sunlight uses directional light while daylight, on the other hand, combines both of them.
· Both IES and Standard sunlight are possible (Debabrata Samanta et al. 2011).
· Both IES and normal skylight are possible
· Both Standard and skylights are not photometric. If the scene uses standard light, then these lights are more appropriate to be used.

Sunlight:

· The sunlight helps us to understand the movement of the sun according to the geographic angle, Location, date, time, compass orientation concerning the earth.
· It helps us to animate the date and time along with the sun.
· The North Direction, Orbital Scale, latitude, and longitude, can be animated.
· It gives the sun effect on the sky.

Skylight:

· The skylight helps us to give the effect of the sky to the scene.
· The skylight is majorly used in architectural designs (C.H. Esteban et al. 2003).
· The skylight has many parameters which allow us to set intensity, color, and mapping of the sky.
· Illumination for all renderers is provided by Sky Color maps, including HDR maps.

(Anil Kumar et al. 2021)

To process skylight properly, it is essential to see that the skylight is added within closed walls, corners, and floors (Abhijit Guha et al. 2021).

Some of the ways to repair the model so that no leaks of light occur:

· The floors and ceiling should have thickness.
· Wall command should be used to create walls.
· Ensure that floor and ceiling extend beyond walls.

Even sunlight is used for the exterior render of an architectural design. Along with the architectural design, games, and movies also use sunlight and skylight for exterior and interior renders. (Anil Kumar et al. 2021)

The sun positioner and physical sky are like most daylight and sunlight systems. This system is more suitable for studying shadows. The major advantage to the Physical Sky and Sun Positioner over the sunlight and daylight systems is the efficiency and intuitiveness in the workflow. The sun positioner allows us to place the sun in the scene. Various other features such as Location, date, time can also be set (M. Maheswari et al. 2021).

Along with the sun positioner, the environment map controls are also available by default. The Material Editor's Physical Sun and sky rollout contain all parameters related to shading. This allows us to reduce inconsistency and simplifies the workflow. (Anil Kumar et al. 2021)

The Physical Sky and Sun Positioner are renderers. It is according to the renderer to understand whether it needs to internally support this feature using multiple light sources, like Scanline, or as a simple Environment map, like ART. It does implement the Scanline shading functions, so it is fully functional with the Scanline renderer as an Environment map but not for illumination. Thus, the sun positioner and physical sky are easier to use compared to the sunlight and daylight systems (Qin Lian et al. 2006).

Shadows are also important features for interior and exterior environment renders. There are several shadow features provided by Autodesk 3DS Max. A spot light is used when there is a requirement of a direct source of light. Being emitted by a cone, it allows us to easily have control over properties like width i.e., the area light should cover. Any object closer to a spotlight gets bright enough and harder. Target spot lights are very much useful in casting shadows as the light directly falls on the object. Shadow can be casted by enabling shadow property in the modifier list of the respected light, by clicking the shadow checkbox. A free spotlight has no targeted area. It has no specific focus (M. Sainz et al. 2004). It is mostly used to create a glow effect depending on the scenario. A free direct light produces a parallel light ray over any object in a single straight direction same as the natural phenomena where sunlight falls on the earth's surface. The most common usage of a free direct light would be using it to generate sunlight in any specific environment. The colour can easily be changed and the position as well can be adjusted easily in the given 3d space. The above-mentioned lights are the most commonly used sources to produce the required light effect over any object so as to enhance it when rendered. On creation of objects or any scene/environment, placing lights would be a task that has to be done with considering the position and accuracy. Adjusting the saturation and brightness with intensity has to be done to get the right amount of focus on the object or a scene (Debabrata Samanta et al. 2012). Lights are mostly used in simulating real light effects in different environment like office scene or any household lamps, lights are very much essential in film works for example creating light effects on a virtual stage and sometimes emitting sunlight. Lights are of great use when any architectural scene has to be represented in a lighted environment. (Binod Kumar et al. 2021)

Advertising industries use various cameras with different lights placed at different position. With the presence of lights, representing an object or a scene using cameras becomes more attractive and convincing. Clone or copies are also an integral part of 3d modelling in 3DS Max. Comparing Copies with instance of light. Keeping rendering as a main factor, render time when instances are used is much less compared to copies. Copies generally require more space compared to instance as it allows working on an object with its properties same as the original objects as in reference. When copies are made, it becomes an individual object with its own properties which eventually takes up some memory space and also much more time whilst rendering. (Binod Kumar et al. 2021)

When different modifiers applied on any specific object and rendered, the presence of lights would enhance the detailing of the object to get absolute clarity and accuracy. Whilst creating any closed environment like a restaurant or an indoor stadium, the objects placed inside wouldn't appear on default lighting, here is when lights come in its best usage, especially when a light source is placed outside a particular context scene, buy enabling shadows the light rays can easily be produced over the objects placed inside. (Manu M K et al. 2018)

The other important application of using 3ds Max is Cameras. 3ds Max provides aneasy-to-use camera feature. After the completion of positioning lights over any scene or an object, cameras are placed at an accurate position to have a clear perspective of the focused element so as to justify it completely.

Casting shadows using lights would also be of an advantage when keyframe animations are introduced.

SCOPE OF 3DS MAX

In future 3ds Max software will be in skilful use due to its easy to learn features. It will help various designers and developer to build great deal of designs faster and with basic knowledge. In visualizations, 3d printing as well as in advanced development of 3d industry 3ds max is in skilful use. As we know 3d Modelling is used as: (Soon-Yong Park et al. 2005)

- 3d architectural representation (interior or exterior)
- 3d automobile design implementation
- Games and movies
- 3d printing
- Product design and many more.

3d modelling can be integrated with many other technologies for making projects better. Apart from that major part of education related to digital image processing (learning about image techniques including holographic 3d images) use 3d model concepts. Different websites using 3d product customization also use 3d modelling concept. Each company in today's time require a designer to attract users which helps in their development. This software will also guide creative students to follow their passion and reach the destined goal. (W. Sun et al. 2005)

The major job roles as a 3d modeler would be:

- Video game designer
- 3D printing technician
- Graphic designer
- 3D animator
- 3D designer
- Architectural designer
- Professor
- Art director
- Web developer

CONCLUSION

If comparative study is made it is found rise of 3d industry is massive in India and abroad, it's just that experience and skills are what which is seen at the end of the day. Thus, the scope of 3d industry is rising across the globe and lifting the designers in its own way.

Ritwika Das Gupta
CHRIST University, India

REFERENCES

Arayici, Y., & Hamilton, A. (2005). Modeling 3D scanned data to visualize the built environment. *Ninth International Conference on Information Visualisation (IV'05)*, 509-514.

Biswal, A. K., Singh, D., Pattanayak, B. K., Samanta, D., & Yang, M.-H. (2021). IoT-Based Smart Alert System for Drowsy Driver Detection. Wireless Communications and Mobile Computing. doi:10.1155/2021/6627217

Castellani, U., Fusiello, A., Murino, V., Papaleo, L., Puppo, E., & Pittore, M. (2005, October). A complete system for on-line 3D modelling from acoustic images. *Signal Processing Image Communication*, *20*(9-10), 832–852. doi:10.1016/j. image.2005.02.003

De Luca, L., Veron, P., & Florenzano, M. (2006, April). Reverse engineering of architectural buildings based on a hybrid modeling approach. *Computers & Graphics*, *30*(2), 160–176. doi:10.1016/j.cag.2006.01.020

Esteban, C. H., & Schmitt, F. (2003). Silhouette and stereo fusion for 3D object modeling. *Fourth International Conference on 3-D Digital Imaging and Modeling, 2003. 3DIM 2003. Proceedings*, 46-53.

Guha, A., Samanta, D., Banerjee, A., & Agarwal, D. (2021). A Deep Learning Model for Information Loss Prevention From Multi-Page Digital Documents. *IEEE Access: Practical Innovations, Open Solutions*, *9*, 80451–80465. doi:10.1109/ ACCESS.2021.3084841

Kureethara, V., Biswas, J., & Debabrata Samanta, N. G. (n.d.). Balanced Constrained Partitioning of Distinct Objects. *International Journal of Innovative Technology and Exploring Engineering*. doi:10.35940/ijitee.K1023.09811S19

Lian, Q., Li, D.-C., Tang, Y.-P., & Zhang, Y.-R. (2006, May). Computer modeling approach for a novel internal architecture of artificial bone. *Computer Aided Design*, *38*(5), 507–514. doi:10.1016/j.cad.2005.12.001

Maheswari, M., Geetha, S., & Selva Kumar, S. (2021). PEVRM: Probabilistic Evolution Based Version Recommendation Model for Mobile Applications. *IEEE Access: Practical Innovations, Open Solutions*, *9*, 20819–20827. doi:10.1109/ ACCESS.2021.3053583

Manu, Roy, & Samanta. (2018). Effects of Liver Cancer Drugs on Cellular Energy Metabolism in Hepatocellular Carcinoma Cells. *International Journal of Pharmaceutical Research, 10*(3). . doi:10.31838/ijpr/2018.10.03.079

Park & Subbarao. (2005). A multiview 3D modeling system based on stereo vision techniques. *Machine Vision and Applications, 16*(3), 148-156.

Sainz, Pajarola, Mercade, & Susin. (2004). A simple approach for point-based object capturing and rendering. *IEEE Computer Graphics and Applications, 24*(4), 24-33.

Samanta & Sanyal. (2012a). Segmentation technique of sar imagery based on fuzzy c-means clustering. Academic Press.

Samanta & Sanyal. (2012b). A novel approach of sar image classification using color space clustering and watersheds. Academic Press.

Sanyal & Samanta. (2011). Segmentation technique of sar imagery using entropy. *International Journal of Computer Technology and Applications*, 2, 1548–1551.

Sun, W., Starly, B., Nam, J., & Darling, A. (2005, September). Bio-CAD modeling and its applications in computer-aided tissue engineering. *Computer Aided Design*, *37*(11), 1097–1114. doi:10.1016/j.cad.2005.02.002

Compilation of References

Althar, R. R., Samanta, D., Konar, D., & Bhattacharyya, S. (2021). *Software Source Code: Statistical Modeling.* Walter de Gruyter GmbH & Co KG. doi:10.1515/9783110703399

Arayici, Y., & Hamilton, A. (2005). Modeling 3D scanned data to visualize the built environment. *Ninth International Conference on Information Visualisation (IV'05),* 509-514.

Arayici, Y., & Hamilton, A. (2005). Modeling 3D Scanned Data to Visualize the Built Environment. *Proceedings of the Ninth International Conference on Information Visualisation,* 509-514. 10.1109/IV.2005.82

Ardakani, H. K., Mousavinia, A., & Safaei, F. (2020). Four points: One-pass geometrical camera calibration algorithm. *The Visual Computer, 36*(2), 413–424. doi:10.100700371-019-01632-7

Baskoro, A. S., & Haryanto, I. (2015). Development of travel speed detection method in welding simulator using augmented reality. *2015 International Conference on Advanced Computer Science and Information Systems (ICACSIS),* 269-273. 10.1109/ICACSIS.2015.7415194

Bhattacharya, A., Ghosh, G., Mandal, R., Ghatak, S., Samanta, D., Shukla, V. K., ... Mandal, A. (2022). Predictive Analysis of the Recovery Rate from Coronavirus (COVID-19). In *Cyber Intelligence and Information Retrieval.* Springer. doi:10.1007/978-981-16-4284-5_27

Biswal, A. K., Singh, D., Pattanayak, B. K., Samanta, D., & Yang, M.-H. (2021). IoT-Based Smart Alert System for Drowsy Driver Detection. Wireless Communications and Mobile Computing. doi:10.1155/2021/6627217

Biswal, A. K., Singh, D., Pattanayak, B. K., Samanta, D., Chaudhry, S. A., & Irshad, A. (2021). Adaptive Fault-Tolerant System and Optimal Power Allocation for Smart Vehicles in Smart Cities Using Controller Area Network. *Security and Communication Networks, 2021,* 2021. doi:10.1155/2021/2147958

Brand, M., Kang, K., & Cooper, D. B. (2004). Algebraic solution for the visual hull. *Proceedings of the 2004 IEEE Computer Society Conference on Computer Vision and Pattern Recognition,* I33-I35. 10.1109/CVPR.2004.1315010

Castellani, U., Fusiello, A., Murino, V., Papaleo, L., Puppo, E., & Pittore, M. (2005). A complete system for on-line 3D modelling from acoustic images. *Signal Processing Image Communication*, *20*(9-10), 832–852. doi:10.1016/j.image.2005.02.003

Chatterjee, R., Roy, S., Islam, S. H., & Samanta, D. (2021). An AI Approach to Pose-based Sports Activity Classification. *2021 8th International Conference on Signal Processing and Integrated Networks (SPIN)*, 156–161.

Choy, Lim, Wang, & Chan. (2012). Development CT-based three-dimensional complex skull model for Finite element analysis. *2012 IEEE Conference on Sustainable Utilization and Development in Engineering and Technology (STUDENT)*, 135-139. 10.1109/STUDENT.2012.6408383

De Luca, L., Veron, P., & Florenzano, M. (2006). Reverse engineering of architectural buildings based on a hybrid modeling approach. *Computers & Graphics*, *30*(2), 160–176. doi:10.1016/j.cag.2006.01.020

Deryabin, N. B., Zhdanov, D. D., & Sokolov, V. G. (2017). Embedding the script language into optical simulation software. *Programming and Computer Software*, *43*(1), 13–23. doi:10.1134/S0361768817010029

Dhenain, M., Ruffins, S. W., & Jacobs, R. E. (2001). Three-dimensional digital mouse atlas using high resolution MRI. *Developmental Biology*, *232*(2), 458–470. doi:10.1006/dbio.2001.0189 PMID:11401405

Eapen, N. G., Rao, A. R., Samanta, D., Robert, N. R., Krishnamoorthy, R., & Lokesh, G. H. (2022). Security Aspects for Mutation Testing in Mobile Applications. In *Cyber Intelligence and Information Retrieval*. Springer. doi:10.1007/978-981-16-4284-5_2

Esmaeili, H., Thwaites, H., & Woods, P. C. (2017). Workflows and Challenges Involved in Creation of Realistic Immersive Virtual Museum, Heritage, and Tourism Experiences: A Comprehensive Reference for 3D Asset Capturing. *2017 13th International Conference on Signal-Image Technology & Internet-Based Systems (SITIS)*, 465-472. 10.1109/SITIS.2017.82

Esmaeili, H., Woods, P. C., & Thwaites, H. (2014). Realisation of virtualised architectural heritage. *2014 International Conference on Virtual Systems & Multimedia (VSMM)*, 94-101. 10.1109/VSMM.2014.7136676

Esteban, C. H., & Schmitt, F. (2003). Silhouette and stereo fusion for 3D object modeling. *Fourth International Conference on 3-D Digital Imaging and Modeling, 2003. 3DIM 2003. Proceedings*, 46-53.

Esteban, C. H., & Schmitt, F. (2014). *Silhouette and stereo fusion for 3D object modeling. 3ds Max Projects: A Detailed Guide to Modeling, Texturing, Rigging, Animation and Lighting.*

Eyetronics. (2004). http://www.eyetronics.com

Filho, M. R., Negrão, N. M., & Damasceno, R. R. (2011). SwImax: A Web Tool Using Virtual Reality for Teaching the WiMAX Protocol. *2011 XIII Symposium on Virtual Reality*, 217-224. 10.1109/SVR.2011.27

Fritsch, D., & Klein, M. (2017). 3D and 4D modeling for AR and VR app developments. *2017 23rd International Conference on Virtual System & Multimedia (VSMM)*, 1-8. 10.1109/VSMM.2017.8346270

Gang, L., & Wang, Z. (2004). Peng Quensheng. Generating Visual Hulls From Freely Moving Camera. *Journal of Computer-Aided Design & Computer Graphics*, 16(11), 1501–1505.

Gang, L., Wang, Z., & Quensheng, P. (2004). Generating Visual Hulls From Freely Moving Camera. *Journal of Computer-Aided Design & Computer Graphics*, 16(11), 1501–1505.

Guha, A., Samanta, D., Pramanik, S., & Dutta, S. (2021). Concept of Indexing and Concepts associated with Journal Publishing. In *Interdisciplinary Research in Technology and Management: Proceedings of the International Conference on Interdisciplinary Research in Technology and Management (IRTM, 2021)*. CRC Press. 10.1201/9781003202240-3

Guha, A., Samanta, D., Banerjee, A., & Agarwal, D. (2021). A Deep Learning Model for Information Loss Prevention From Multi-Page Digital Documents. *IEEE Access: Practical Innovations, Open Solutions*, 9, 80451–80465. doi:10.1109/ACCESS.2021.3084841

Günther-Diringer, D. (2016). Historisches 3D-Stadtmodell von Karlsruhe. *J. Cartogr. Geogr. Inf.*, 66, 66–71. doi:10.1007/BF03545207

Gurunath, R., Samanta, D., Dutta, S., & Kureethara, J. V. (2021). Essentials of Abstracting and Indexing for Research Paper Writing. In *Interdisciplinary Research in Technology and Management*. CRC Press.

Gurunath, R., Alahmadi, A. H., Samanta, D., Khan, M. Z., & Alahmadi, A. (2021). A Novel Approach for Linguistic Steganography Evaluation Based on Artificial Neural Networks. *IEEE Access: Practical Innovations, Open Solutions*, 9, 120869–120879. doi:10.1109/ACCESS.2021.3108183

Halim, S., & Mohd Sharuddin, I. (2004). *Close Range Measurement and 3D Modeling*. Presented at the 1st International Symposium on Engineering Surveys for Construction Works and Structural Engineering.

Halim, S., & MohdSharuddin, I. (2004). Close Range Measurement and 3D Modeling. *1st International Symposium on Engineering Surveys for Construction Works and Structural Engineering*.

Halim, S., & MohdSharuddin, I. (2004). *Close Range Measurement and 3D Modeling*. Presented at the 1st International Symposium on Engineering Surveys for Construction Works and Structural Engineering.

Hegazy, M., Yasufuku, K., & Abe, H. (2022). An interactive approach to investigate brightness perception of daylighting in Immersive Virtual Environments: Comparing subjective responses and quantitative metrics. *Building Simulation*, 15(1), 41–68. doi:10.100712273-021-0798-3

Hegde, D. S., Samanta, D., & Dutta, S. (2022). Classification Framework for Fraud Detection Using Hidden Markov Model. In *Cyber Intelligence and Information Retrieval*. Springer. doi:10.1007/978-981-16-4284-5_3

Hu, J. Y. (2004). The Application of Computer Software—3D Studio Max, Lightscape and V-Ray in the Environmental Artistic Expression. *Image Understanding, 96*, 367–392.

Hu, J. Y. (2004). The Application of Computer Software—3D Studio Max, Lightscape and V-Ray in the Environmental Artistic Expression. *Image Understanding, 96*, 367–392.

Kajiya, J. T. (1986). *The rendering equation.* Academic Press.

Khoroshko, L. L., Ukhov, P. A., & Keyno, P. P. (2018). *Development of a Laboratory Workshop for Open Online Courses Based on 3D Computer Graphics and Multimedia. In 2018 Learning With MOOCS.* LWMOOCS. doi:10.1109/LWMOOCS.2018.8534678

Kriete, A., Breithecker, A., & Rau, W. (2001). 3D imaging of lung tissue by confocal microscopy and micro-CT. *Proceedings of SPIE - The International Society for Optical Engineering, 469*-476. 10.1117/12.434736

Kureethara, V., Biswas, J., & Debabrata Samanta, N. G. (n.d.). Balanced Constrained Partitioning of Distinct Objects. *International Journal of Innovative Technology and Exploring Engineering.* doi:10.35940/ijitee.K1023.09811S19

Kwon, Y. M., Lee, Y. A., & Kim, S. J. (2017). Case study on 3D printing education in fashion design coursework. *Fash Text, 4*(1), 26. doi:10.118640691-017-0111-3

Levoy, M., Pulli, K., Curless, B., Rusinkiewicz, S., Koller, D., Pereira, L., Ginzton, M., Anderson, S., Davis, J., Ginsberg, J., Shade, J., & Fulk, D. (2000). The digital Michelangelo Project: 3D scanning of large statues. Siggraph 2000, 131-144.

Lian, Q., Li, D.-C., Tang, Y.-P., & Zhang, Y.-R. (2006). Computer modeling approach for a novel internal architecture of artificial bone. *CAD Computer Aided Design, 38*(5), 507–514. doi:10.1016/j.cad.2005.12.001

Lin, T. H., Lan, C. C., Wang, C. H., & Chen, C. H. (2014). Study on realistic texture mapping for 3D models. *International Conference on Information Science, Electronics and Electrical Engineering (ISEEE), 3*, 1567-1571. 10.1109/InfoSEEE.2014.6946184

Lungershausen, U., Heinrich, C., & Duttmann, R. (2013). Turning Human-nature Interaction into 3D Landscape Scenes: An Approach to Communicate Geoarchaeological Research. *J. Cartogr. Geogr. Inf., 63*, 269–275. doi:10.1007/BF03546142

Maheswari, M., Geetha, S., & Selva Kumar, S. (2021). PEVRM: Probabilistic Evolution Based Version Recommendation Model for Mobile Applications. *IEEE Access: Practical Innovations, Open Solutions, 9*, 20819–20827. doi:10.1109/ACCESS.2021.3053583

Manson, A., Poyade, M., & Rea, P. (2015). A recommended workflow methodology in the creation of an educational and training application incorporating a digital reconstruction of the cerebral ventricular system and cerebrospinal fluid circulation to aid anatomical understanding. *BMC Medical Imaging, 15*(1), 44. doi:10.118612880-015-0088-6 PMID:26482126

Manu, Roy, & Samanta. (2018). Effects of Liver Cancer Drugs on Cellular Energy Metabolism in Hepatocellular Carcinoma Cells. *International Journal of Pharmaceutical Research, 10*(3). . doi:10.31838/ijpr/2018.10.03.079

Montenegro, A. A., Carvalho, P. C. P., Velho, L., & Gattass, M. (2004). Space carving with a hand-held camera. *Proceedings of the XVII Brazilian Symposium on Computer Graphics and Image Processing (SIBGRAPI'04)*, 396-403. 10.1109/SIBGRA.2004.1352986

Mueller, Vereenooghe, Vergauwen, Van Gool, & Waelkens. (n.d.). Photo-realistic and detailed 3D modeling: the Antonine nymphaeum at Sagalassos (Turkey). *Computer Applications and Quantitative Methods in Archaeology (CAA): Beyond the artifact - Digital interpretation of the past.* http://www.vision.ee.ethz.ch/~pmueller/documents/caa04_pmueller.pdf

Murdock. (2014). *Autodesk 3ds Max 2014 Bible.* Academic Press.

Nadeem, A., Wong, A. K. D., & Wong, F. K. W. (2015). Bill of Quantities with 3D Views Using Building Information Modeling. *Arabian Journal for Science and Engineering, 40*(9), 2465–2477. doi:10.100713369-015-1657-2

Natephra, W., Motamedi, A., Fukuda, T., & Yabuki, N. (2017). Integrating building information modeling and virtual reality development engines for building indoor lighting design. *Vis. in Eng., 5*(1), 19. doi:10.118640327-017-0058-x

Park & Subbarao. (2005). A multiview 3D modeling system based on stereo vision techniques. *Machine Vision and Applications, 16*(3), 148-156.

Park, S.-Y., & Subbarao, M. (2005). A multiview 3D modeling system based on stereo vision techniques. *Machine Vision and Applications, 16*(3), 148–156. doi:10.100700138-004-0165-2

Paul, M., & Sanyal, G. (2011). Segmentation technique of SAR imagery using entropy. *International Journal of Computer Technology and Applications, 2*(5).

Paul, Samanta, & Sanyal. (2011). Dynamic job Scheduling in Cloud Computing based on horizontal load balancing. *International Journal of Computer Technology and Applications, 2*(5), 1552-1556.

Paul, M., Samanta, D., & Sanyal, G. (2011). Dynamic job scheduling in cloud computing based on horizontal load balancing. *International Journal of Computer Technology and Applications, 2*(5), 1552–1556.

Pezeshki, Z., Soleimani, A., & Darabi, A. (2017). 3Ds MAX to FEM for building thermal distribution: A case study. *2017 3rd Iranian Conference on Intelligent Systems and Signal Processing (ICSPIS),* 110-115. 10.1109/ICSPIS.2017.8311599

Podder, S. K., & Samanta, D. (2022). Green Computing Practice in ICT-Based Methods: Innovation in Web-Based Learning and Teaching Technologies. *International Journal of Web-Based Learning and Teaching Technologies, 17*(4), 1–18. doi:10.4018/IJWLTT.285568

Raghavendra Rao, A., & Samanta, D. (2022). A Real-Time Approach with Deep Learning for Pandemic Management. In *Healthcare Informatics for Fighting COVID-19 and Future Epidemics*. Springer. doi:10.1007/978-3-030-72752-9_6

Sainz, Pajarola, Mercade, & Susin. (2004). A simple approach for point-based object capturing and rendering. *IEEE Computer Graphics and Applications, 24*(4), 24-33.

Sainz, M., Pajarola, R., Mercade, A., & Susin, A. (2004, July/August). A Simple Approach for Point-Based Object Capturing and Rendering. *IEEE Computer Graphics and Applications, 24*(4), 33. doi:10.1109/MCG.2004.1 PMID:15628083

Samanta & Sanyal. (2012a). Segmentation technique of sar imagery based on fuzzy c-means clustering. Academic Press.

Samanta & Sanyal. (2012b). A novel approach of sar image classification using color space clustering and watersheds. Academic Press.

Samanta, D., & Paul, M. (2011). A Novel Approach of Entropy based Adaptive Thresholding Technique for Video Edge Detection. *Threshold (x, y), 1*, 1.

Samanta, D., & Sanyal, G. (2011b). *Development of Adaptive Thresholding Technique for Classification of Synthetic Aperture Radar Images*. Academic Press.

Samanta, D., & Sanyal, G. (2011c). Development of edge detection technique for images using adaptive thresholding. *International Conference on Information Processing*, 671–676. 10.1007/978-3-642-22786-8_85

Samanta, D., & Sanyal, G. (2012). Segmentation technique of SAR imagery based on fuzzy c-means clustering. *IEEE-International Conference On Advances In Engineering, Science And Management (ICAESM-2012)*, 610–612.

Samanta, D., & Sanyal, G. (2012a). A novel approach of SAR image classification using color space clustering and watersheds. *2012 Fourth International Conference on Computational Intelligence and Communication Networks*, 237–240. 10.1109/CICN.2012.27

Samanta, D., & Sanyal, G. (2012f). Novel Shannon's entropy based segmentation technique for SAR images. *International Conference on Information Processing*, 193–199. 10.1007/978-3-642-31686-9_22

Samanta, D., & Sanyal, G. (2012g). *SAR image classification using fuzzy CMeans*. Academic Press.

Samanta, D., & Sanyal, G. (2012h). Statistical approach for Classification of SAR Images. *International Journal of Soft Computing and Engineering (IJSCE)*, 2231–2307.

Samanta, D., & Sanyal, G. (2013). An Approach of Tabu Search for Unsupervised Classification for SAR Images. *Seven International Conference on Image and Signal Processing*.

Compilation of References

Samanta, D., Karthikeyan, M. P., Agarwal, D., Biswas, A., Acharyya, A., & Banerjee, A. (2022). Trends in Terahertz Biomedical Applications. *Generation, Detection and Processing of Terahertz Signals*, 285–299.

Samanta, D. (2011). A novel statistical approach for segmentation of SAR Images. *Journal of Global Research in Computer Science*, 2(10), 9–13.

Samanta, D., & Ghosh, A. (2012). Automatic obstacle detection based on gaussian function in robocar. *J. Res. Eng. Appl. Sci, 2*(2), 354–363.

Samanta, D., & Sanyal, G. (2011a). Automated Classification of SAR Images Using Moment. *International Journal of Computer Science Issues*, 8(6), 135.

Samanta, D., & Sanyal, G. (2011d). SAR image segmentation using Color space clustering and Watersheds. *International Journal of Engineering Research and Applications*, 1(3), 997–999.

Samanta, D., & Sanyal, G. (2012c). An Approach of Segmentation Technique of SAR Images using Adaptive Thresholding Technique. *International Journal of Engineering Research & Technology (Ahmedabad)*, 1(7).

Samanta, D., Alahmadi, A. H., Karthikeyan, M. P., Khan, M. Z., Banerjee, A., Dalapati, G. K., & Ramakrishna, S. (2021). Cipher Block Chaining Support Vector Machine for Secured Decentralized Cloud Enabled Intelligent IoT Architecture. *IEEE Access: Practical Innovations, Open Solutions*, 9, 98013–98025. doi:10.1109/ACCESS.2021.3095297

Samanta, D., Dutta, S., Galety, M. G., & Pramanik, S. (2022). A Novel Approach for Web Mining Taxonomy for High-Performance Computing. In *Cyber Intelligence and Information Retrieval*. Springer. doi:10.1007/978-981-16-4284-5_37

Samanta, D., & Sanyal, G. (2012b). A novel approach of SAR image processing based on Hue, Saturation and Brightness (HSB). *Procedia Technology*, 4, 584–588. doi:10.1016/j.protcy.2012.05.093

Samanta, D., & Sanyal, G. (2012d). Classification of SAR Images Based on Entropy. *Int. J. Inf. Technol. Comput. Sci, 4*(12), 82–86. doi:10.5815/ijitcs.2012.12.09

Samanta, D., & Sanyal, G. (2012e). Novel approach of adaptive thresholding technique for edge detection in videos. *Procedia Engineering*, 30, 283–288. doi:10.1016/j.proeng.2012.01.862

Sanyal & Samanta. (2011). Segmentation technique of sar imagery using entropy. *International Journal of Computer Technology and Applications*, 2, 1548–1551.

Sarti, S. (2002). Tubaro. Image based multiresolution implicit object modeling. *EURASIP Journal on Applied Signal Processing*, 10, 1053–1066.

Sarti, S. T. (2002). Image based multiresolution implicit object modeling. *EURASIP Journal on Applied Signal Processing*, 10, 1053–1066.

Sun, W., & Lal, P. (2002). Recent development on computer aided tissue engineering— A review. *Computer Methods and Programs in Biomedicine, 67*(2), 85–103. doi:10.1016/S0169-2607(01)00116-X PMID:11809316

Sun, W., Starly, B., Nam, J., & Darling, A. (2005). Bio-CAD modeling and its applications in computer-aided tissue engineering. *Computer Aided Design, 37*(11), 1097–1114. doi:10.1016/j.cad.2005.02.002

Tavares, J. M. R. S., Dutta, P., Dutta, S., & Samanta, D. (2021). Cyber Intelligence and Information Retrieval. *Proceedings of CIIR 2021.*

Tavares, J., Dutta, P., Dutta, S., & Samanta, D. (n.d.). *Cyber Intelligence and Information Retrieval.* Academic Press.

Toshihiro, A., Masayuki, K., & Naokazu, Y. (2005). 3D Modeling of Outdoor Environments by Integrating Omnidirectional Range and Color Images. *Proceedings of the Fifth International Conference on 3-D Digital Imaging and Modeling (3DIM'05).*

Tsipotas, D., & Spathopoulou, V. (2015). An assessment of research on 3D digital representation of ancient Greek furniture, using surviving archaelological artefacts. *Digital Heritage, 2015,* 325–328. doi:10.1109/DigitalHeritage.2015.7419515

Valdez, M. T., Ferreira, C. M., & Barbosa, F. P. M. (2016). 3D virtual laboratory for teaching circuit theory — A virtual learning environment (VLE). *2016 51st International Universities Power Engineering Conference (UPEC),* 1-4. 10.1109/UPEC.2016.8114126

Van de Perre, G., De Beir, A., Cao, H. L., Esteban, P. G., Lefeber, D., & Vanderborght, B. (2019). Studying Design Aspects for Social Robots Using a Generic Gesture Method. *International Journal of Social Robotics, 11*(4), 651–663. doi:10.100712369-019-00518-x

Vu, S. (2018). Recreating Little Manila through a Virtual Reality Serious Game. *2018 3rd Digital Heritage International Congress (DigitalHERITAGE) held jointly with 2018 24th International Conference on Virtual Systems & Multimedia (VSMM 2018),* 1-4. 10.1109/DigitalHeritage.2018.8810082

Woop, S., Schmittler, J., & Slusallek, P. (2005). RPU: A Programmable Ray Processing Unit for Realtime Ray Tracing. *Siggraph 2005.*

Woop, S., Schmittler, J., & Slusallek, P. (2005). RPU: A Programmable Ray Processing Unit for Realtime Ray Tracing. *SIGGRAPH 2005.*

Yang, Lee, Kim, & Kim. (2005). Adaptive Space Carving with Texture Mapping. *LNCS, 3482,* 1129-1138.

Yılmaz, Mülayim, & Atalay. (2002). Reconstruction of Three Dimensional Models from Real Images. *Proceedings of the First International Symposium on 3D Data Processing Visualization and Transmission (3DPVT.02).*

Yılmaz, U., Mülayim, A., & Atalay, V. (2002). Reconstruction of Three Dimensional Models from Real Images. *Proceedings of the First International Symposium on 3D Data Processing Visualization and Transmission (3DPVT.02)*. 10.1109/TDPVT.2002.1024117

About the Contributors

Debabrata Samanta is presently working as Assistant Professor, Department of Computer Science, CHRIST (Deemed to be University), Bangalore, India. He obtained his Bachelors in Physics (Honors), from Calcutta University; Kolkata, India. He obtained his MCA, from the Academy of Technology, under WBUT, West Bengal. He obtained his PhD in Computer Science and Engg. from National Institute of Technology, Durgapur, India, in the area of SAR Image Processing. He is keenly interested in Interdisciplinary Research & Development and has experience spanning fields of SAR Image Analysis, Video surveillance, Heuristic algorithm for Image Classification, Deep Learning Framework for Detection and Classification, Blockchain, Statistical Modelling, Wireless Adhoc Network, Natural Language Processing, V2I Communication. He has successfully completed six Consultancy Projects. He has received funding 8,110 USD under Open Access, Publication fund. He has received funding under International Travel Support Scheme in 2019 for attending conference in Thailand. He has received Travel Grant for speaker in Conference, Seminar etc for two years from July, 2019. He is the owner of 21 Patents (3 Design Indian Patent and 2 Australian patent Granted, 16 Indian Patents published) and 2 copyright. He has authored and coauthored over 195 research papers in international journal (SCI/SCIE/ESCI/Scopus) and conferences including IEEE, Springer and Elsevier Conference proceeding. He has received "Scholastic Award" at 2nd International conference on Computer Science and IT application, CSIT-2011, Delhi, India. He is a co-author of 13 books and the co-editor of 11 books, available for sale on Amazon and Flipkart. He has presented various papers at International conferences and received Best Paper awards. He has author and co-authored of 08 Book Chapters. He also serves as acquisition editor for Springer, Wiley, CRC, Scrivener Publishing LLC, Beverly, USA. and Elsevier. He is a Professional IEEE Member, an Associate Life Member of Computer Society Of India (CSI) and a Life Member of Indian Society for Technical Education (ISTE). He is a Convener, Keynote speaker, Session chair, Co-chair, Publicity chair, Publication chair, Advisory Board, Technical Program Committee members in many prestigious International and National conferences. He was invited speaker at several Institutions.

* * *

Ritwika Das Gupta is a final year student of BCA, Christ (Deemed to be University) Bangalore, India.

Muskaan Jain is a final year student of BCA, Christ University, Bengaluru, India.

Raghav Sham Kamat is a final year student of Bachelor of Computer Applications, Christ (Deemed To Be University) India. His research area is Graphics, Machine Learning, Information technology and Artificial Intelligence.

Guruprasad N. is a final year student of the Department of Computer Science, CHRIST Deemed to be University, India.

Sean Leo Noronha is a final year student of the Department of Computer Science, CHRIST Deemed to be University, India.

Tamanna Pramanik is a final year student of BCA, CHRIST (Deemed to be University).

Dinesh Sharma is currently working as an L1 Technical Support Engineer at DXC Technology, Bangalore, India.

Index

M

material editor 2, 23, 25, 32-33, 37, 39, 48-49, 52-55, 57-60, 67-68, 70, 75, 110-111, 115, 119, 123, 137, 171-172, 175, 182-183, 185, 197-198, 200-201, 203-206, 210, 225-227, 235-238, 259

Material ID Channel 227, 237

mesh 3-4, 8-25, 36, 48-51, 53-60, 105-106, 111, 115, 122, 136-137, 142-145, 167, 172-173, 182-183, 192-193, 195, 222-225, 231-234, 250, 263

multiplechamfer boxes 191, 197

P

Photometric 71-72, 74, 77-83, 86, 183-184, 191-192, 197, 211, 254, 262

photometric light 72, 191, 197

polygons 4-5, 49, 109-110, 137, 140, 211

primitives 2, 4, 31-34, 37, 68, 105-108, 110-111, 115, 122-123, 167-171, 173-175, 179, 181, 183-184, 192, 194-195, 197-199, 201-206, 208-210

Pro Boolean 107-108, 110, 113, 115, 167, 171, 174, 182-184

Pro-Boolean 108, 170, 175-176, 194-198, 200, 210, 250, 263

ProBoolen 105, 107

ProCutter 66, 68

R

rendering 1-2, 25, 27-28, 31-33, 37, 42, 48-49, 63-64, 66, 73-74, 76-77, 79, 81-82, 86, 105, 110-111, 118-121, 123, 126-127, 129-130, 133-134, 166-168, 182, 185, 201, 211-212, 218, 220, 226, 229-230, 235, 239, 241, 252, 256

Rigging 1, 26, 62, 129, 133

S

ShapeMerge 66, 68

shapes 2-3, 6, 48, 68, 106-107, 109, 115, 134, 137-138, 161, 167, 172, 179, 181-183, 192, 202, 218

shell modifier 1, 7, 21, 49, 52, 55-58, 160-161

spline 2-3, 6-7, 9, 48, 111, 134, 137-138, 192-194, 201-202

splines 1-3, 31-33, 35-36, 148, 192, 201

standard primitives 2, 4, 31-34, 37, 68, 105-108, 110-111, 115, 122-123, 169-171, 173-175, 179, 181, 183-184, 194-195, 197-199, 201-203, 205-206, 208-210

sun positioner 72, 74, 82-83, 259-260, 262

Symmetry modifier 1

T

target light 32, 72-73, 78-79, 183, 254

Turbo smooth 1, 7-11, 13-14, 16-17, 21, 49-50, 53-54, 58, 61, 109, 173-174, 183

U

UVM Map 32, 39

V

viewport 3, 107, 109-110, 120-121, 125, 137, 144, 148, 172, 182-185, 192, 194-195, 201, 209, 219, 222-223, 231-232, 234-235, 250, 254, 256, 261, 263

Visualization 30, 32, 47, 65, 104, 120, 132-133, 168, 190-191, 217, 249-250, 263, 271

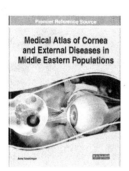
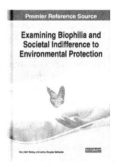
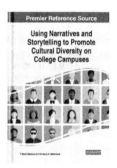

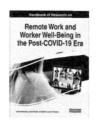

Printed in the United States
by Baker & Taylor Publisher Services